Strategic Investment for Health System Resilience

HUMAN DEVELOPMENT PERSPECTIVES

Strategic Investment for Health System Resilience

A Three-Layer Framework

Feng Zhao, Rialda Kovacevic, David Bishai, and Jeff Weintraub, *Editors*

 **WORLD BANK GROUP**

ISBN (paper): 978-1-4648-2116-5
ISBN (electronic): 978-1-4648-2117-2
DOI: 10.1596/978-1-4648-2116-5

Cover and interior design: Bill Pragluski, Critical Stages, Inc.

Library of Congress Control Number: 2024910801

Human Development Perspectives

The books in this series address main and emerging development issues of a global/regional nature through original research and findings in the areas of education, gender, health, nutrition, population, and social protection and jobs. The series is aimed at policy makers and area experts and is overseen by the Human Development Practice Group Chief Economist.

Previous titles in this series

Magdalena Bendini and Amanda E. Devercelli (eds.), *Quality Early Learning: Nurturing Children's Potential* (2022).

Margaret Grosh, Phillippe Leite, Matthew Wai-Poi, and Emil Tesliuc (eds.), *Revisiting Targeting in Social Assistance: A New Look at Old Dilemmas* (2022).

Feng Zhao, Clemens Benedikt, and David Wilson (eds.), *Tackling the World's Fastest-Growing HIV Epidemic: More Efficient HIV Responses in Eastern Europe and Central Asia* (2020).

Meera Shekar and Barry Popkin (eds.), *Obesity: Health and Economic Consequences of an Impending Global Challenge* (2020).

Truman Packard, Ugo Gentilini, Margaret Grosh, Philip O'Keefe, Robert Palacios, David Robalino, and Indhira Santos, *Protecting All: Risk Sharing for a Diverse and Diversifying World of Work* (2019).

Damien de Walque (ed.), *Risking Your Health: Causes, Consequences, and Interventions to Prevent Risky Behaviors* (2014).

Rita Almeida, Jere Behrman, and David Robalino (eds.), *The Right Skills for the Job? Rethinking Training Policies for Workers* (2012).

Barbara Bruns, Deon Filmer, and Harry Anthony Patrinos, *Making Schools Work: New Evidence on Accountability Reforms* (2011).

Harold Alderman (ed.), *No Small Matter: The Impact of Poverty, Shocks, and Human Capital Investments in Early Childhood Development* (2011).

All books in the Human Development Perspectives series are available at
https://openknowledge.worldbank.org/handle/10986/2161.

Contents

Foreword   *xiii*
Acknowledgments   *xv*
About the Contributors   *xvii*
Context for the Book   *xxi*
Executive Summary   *xxiii*
Abbreviations   *xxvii*

**Part 1: What Is the Three-Layer Framework, and How Are
Countries Aligning Resources toward It?**   **1**

**Chapter 1   Three Layers in Health Systems:
Protecting Population Health Every Day
and during Disease Outbreaks**   **3**

Rialda Kovacevic, Jeff Weintraub, Feng Zhao, and Sulzhan Bali

In Summary   3
Introduction   4
A Closer Look at the Three-Layer Framework   7
Cross-Cutting Elements of All Three Layers   22
Conclusion   26
Notes   27
References   27

**Chapter 2   An Implementation Pathway to Build
Resilience in Health System Layers**   **33**

David Bishai and Karima Saleh

In Summary   33
Introduction   34
Defining Resilience   35

Building Resilience Requires Investment in
  Core Capabilities   35
Achieving Resilience by Measuring Essential
  Public Health Functions   38
Implementing a Pathway for Resilience   40
Challenges and Options for the Way Forward   47
Annex 2A: Tools for Assessing Essential Public
  Health Functions   48
References   49

**Chapter 3   Minding What We Spend on Resilience:
               Global Data, Local Examples   51**

*David Bishai, Katelyn Jison Yoo, Karima Saleh,
and HuiHui Wang*

In Summary   51
Introduction   52
Methods to Track Spending on the Three Layers   54
Mapping Health Accounts Data to the
  Three-Layer Framework   56
Data Availability   56
Results: Levels and Trends in the Three Layers of the
  Health System   61
Discussion: Layered Spending Priorities in the
  Health System   65
Investment Stewardship   66
Setting an Agenda for the Future   69
Setting an Agenda for Effective Country Engagement   70
Note   70
References   70

Part 2: Country Case Studies   73

**Chapter 4   Financial Analysis of Local Public Health
               Activity in Urban Pakistan   75**

Cynthia Wang, David Bishai, Ammarah Ali, and Shehla Zaidi

In Summary   75
Introduction   75
Methods   77
Data Source   78
Analysis   79
Results   79
District Health Office Spending by
  Public Health Capability   81
Discussion   82

Conclusion	83
Note	84
References	85

Chapter 5   Three-Layer Health Sector Investment: Digital Health Interventions for Pandemic Preparedness in Low- and Middle-Income Countries   87

Siobhan Lazenby, Caitlyn Mason, Rachel Stuhldreher, Meredith Kimball, and Rebecca Bartlein

In Summary	87
Layer 1: Risk Reduction—Promoting Prevention and Community Preparedness	89
Layer 2: Focus on Detection, Containment, and Mitigation Capabilities	94
Layer 3: Advanced Case Management and Surge Response	100
Notes	103
References	103

Chapter 6   From MERS to COVID-19: Building a Resilient Health System in the Republic of Korea   105

Huihui Wang, Patricio V. Marquez, and Inuk Hwang

In Summary	105
Country Context: Demographic Profile and Health Risks	106
Health System Structure and Features	106
Three Layers of Health System Pandemic Preparedness in Korea	109
Lessons Learned	117
Notes	118
References	118

Chapter 7   Three-Layer Health Sector Investment in Thailand   121

Piya Hanvoravongchai, Paul Li Jen Cheh, Ham Suenghaitaiphorn, Wasin Laohavinij, Aungsumalee Pholpark, Natchaya Ritthisirikul, Melanie Coates, Moytrayee Guha, Arielle Cohen Tanugi-Carresse, Lucia Mullen, Sara Bennett, Jennifer Nuzzo, William Wang, Siobhan Lazenby, and Anne Liu

In Summary	121
Country Context	122
Health System Structure and Features	123

Lessons Learned		130
Notes		131
References		131

Chapter 8   Three-Layer Health Sector Investment in the Dominican Republic   133

Magdalena Rathe, Laura Rathe, Ian Paulino, Moytrayee Guha, Arielle Cohen Tanugi-Carresse, Lucia Mullen, Sara Bennett, Jennifer Nuzzo, Jacqueline Maloney, Siobhan Lazenby, and Anne Liu

In Summary		133
Country Context		134
Health System Structure and Features		134
Lessons Learned		140
Challenges		141
Notes		142
References		142

Chapter 9   Three-Layer Health Sector Investment in Costa Rica   143

Andrea Prado, Andy Pearson, Claudio Mora, Moytrayee Guha, Arielle Cohen Tanugi-Carresse, Lucia Mullen, Sara Bennett, Jennifer Nuzzo, Jacqueline Maloney, Siobhan Lazenby, and Anne Liu

In Summary		143
Country Context		143
Health System Structure and Features		144
Lessons Learned		152
Challenges		152
References		153

Chapter 10   Three-Layer Health Sector Investment in Uganda   155

Alice Namale, Steven N. Kabwama, Fred Monje, Rawlance Ndejjo, Susan Kizito, Suzanne N. Kiwanuka, Rhoda K. Wanyenze, Siobhan Lazenby, William Wang, Jacqueline Maloney, Rowan Hussein, and Anne Liu

In Summary		155
Country Context		156
Health System Structure and Features		157
Lessons Learned		165
Notes		166
References		166

Boxes

1.1   Community Health Worker Network in Liberia   12
1.2   Community-Based Surveillance in Somalia   14
1.3   Early and Effective Response to COVID-19 in Senegal   17
1.4   Information Systems and Strengthening Human
       Resources to Deliver Health Care   18
1.5   Early Detection and Response: Prior Crisis Experience
       Did Not Go to Waste in Singapore and Viet Nam   18
1.6   A Strong Layer 2 Response to COVID-19 in the Republic of Korea   19
1.7   Getting Ahead of COVID-19 Misinformation   26
2.1   Capabilities Assessment of District and Regional
       Health Authorities: A Case from Ghana   37
2.2   Using Tools to Build Capacity of Layer 1 at District
       Health Departments in Angola, Botswana, and
       Mozambique   43
2.3   Comparing Top-Down and Bottom-Up Measurement   46
3.1   Tracking Primary Health Care Spending in Nigeria   60
3.2   Financial Needs and a Package of Universal Health Coverage
       Health Benefits in Select Countries of Sub-Saharan Africa   63
3.3   Findings from an Experiment on Social Recognition to Improve
       Recordkeeping in Public Health Care Clinics in Select States
       in Nigeria   68

Figures

1.1   The Three-Layer Framework for Strengthening
       Health Systems   8
3.1   Sources of Health Financing in Low-Income Countries and
       Globally, 1995–2022   53
3.2   The SHA 2011 Framework and Its Three Classifications   55
3.3   Incompleteness of NHA Data Sets Based on
       Reporting up to 2017   58
3.4   Proportion of Countries That Reported Spending on
       Prevention, by Country Income Level, 2017   59
3.5   Per Capita Spending on Health, by Country Income Level
       and Layer of the Health System, 2002–17   62
4.1   Government Health Expenditures in Pakistan, by Source of
       Financing, 2017–18   77
4.2   Average Self-Assessed Capacity Scores of Provincial
       and District Public Health Personnel in Sindh Province,
       Pakistan, 2014   78
4.3   Share of Total Spending on District Full-Time Equivalent
       Staff in Karachi, Pakistan, by Public Health Activity, 2022   81
4.4   Allocation of the District Health Budget in Karachi,
       Pakistan, by Public Health Capability, 2022   82

5.1   Timeline of Key Events for the Development and
       Scale-Up of CommCare in Burkina Faso   91
5.2   Data Flow and Integration of CommCare with the Levels
       of Burkina Faso's Health System   92
5.3   Multisectoral Approach to Use of the DHIS2 COVID-19
       Response Package in Sri Lanka   96
5.4   How SORMAS Operates in Nigeria   98
5.5   Key Design Principles of the Unified COVID-19 Data
       Platform in Uttar Pradesh, India   101
6.1   Number of COVID-19 Vaccine Doses Administered per 100
       Population in Select Countries, as of November 20, 2022   116
7.1   Contact-Tracing Efforts by Surveillance and Rapid Response
       Teams and Village Health Volunteers in Thailand   124
8.1   Health System Financing in the Dominican Republic   135
8.2   Total Occupancy of Intensive Care Units in the
       Dominican Republic, 2020–22   138
9.1   The Costa Rican National Health System   145
9.2   The Costa Rican Social Security Fund's Integrated System
       of Health Care   146
9.3   Contingency Fund Spending on COVID-19 Needs
       in Costa Rica, 2020   151
10.1   Prepandemic Demographic Indicators for Uganda   156

Map

5.1   Deployment of the CommCare App in Primary Health
       Care Facilities across Health Districts of Burkino Faso,
       June 2020–December 2021   93

Tables

2.1   Comparison of Essential Public Health Functions and
       the Resilience Index   39
2A.1   Tools for Assessing Essential Public Health Functions   48
3.1   Linking the Three-Layer Framework and the
       SHA 2011 Framework   57
3.2   Number of Countries Reporting Any NHA Data,
       by Health Care Function, 2016 and 2017   59
3.3   Average Primary Health Care Spending per Capita,
       by Layer and Country Income Level, 2017   61
4.1   Government Health Expenditures in Pakistan,
       by Function, 2017–18   76
4.2   Descriptive Data on District Health Personnel in Karachi,
       Pakistan, by Basic Pay Scale and Median Income, 2022   79

Foreword

For all of the heartbreaking and vast devastation left in its wake, the COVID-19 pandemic was also a valuable learning experience. It demonstrated that the world was underprepared to fend off a global disease outbreak and that countries, with the support of international institutions, must take steps to harden their health security defenses against future outbreaks.

This important publication, *Strategic Investment for Health System Resilience: A Three-Layer Framework*, is essential reading for country leaders and members of the global health community as they prepare for future pandemics. Readers will find in-depth policy analysis and illustrative country case studies that illuminate many of the pandemic's most profound lessons.

The authors stress the importance of investments in public health interventions that can detect and prevent emerging infectious diseases from spreading in the first place and, in the event that a dangerous pathogen arises, defuse an outbreak before it grows to epidemic or even pandemic proportions.

The publication makes a powerful case for interventions before an outbreak as a first layer of protection. Layer 1 and 2 investments strengthen existing primary health care systems and improve the staffing and performance of health workers who deliver essential routine care during normal times; they also head off potentially dangerous disease outbreaks to prevent and control a crisis. Other priorities for layer 1 and 2 investments are early-warning and surveillance systems, health promotion and education, and multisectoral interventions, such as clean water, sanitation, and hygiene and One Health practices.

The authors also point out that the costs of investing in precrisis interventions are, like an insurance premium, far more affordable than the costs of dealing with a full-blown crisis. COVID-19 collectively cost countries trillions of dollars in lost economic productivity and in cash outlays to support health providers and to manufacture equipment, treatments, and vaccines.

Perhaps the most important message offered in this publication is that we must break the cycle of panic and neglect that often accompanies major public health crises. It might be tempting, once the danger of an epidemic has lifted, to put off critical investments in hardening health security. Doing so would be a perilous misunderstanding of the trauma we lived through only a few short years ago. Failing to act now will risk severe losses in lives and economic well-being when the next health emergency arises.

Juan Pablo Uribe
Global Director, Health, Nutrition, and Population
World Bank Group

Acknowledgments

The analyses and country case studies presented in this book were supported by the Health, Nutrition, and Population Global Practice of the World Bank and the Exemplars in Global Health program. The publication was made possible by a large team of global health and development professionals working across diverse regions, disciplines, and organizations over the past two years. More than 40 authors collaborated on this publication; their affiliations and other details are listed in the "About the Contributors" section. Specific funding sources are detailed in respective chapters.

The report builds on a three-layer investment framework on health systems that was developed by the World Bank in 2020. The framework was published by *BMJ Global Health* (Zhao et al. 2021) and was central to the World Bank's flagship report on resilient health systems (World Bank 2022).

The book was peer-reviewed by Timothy Johnston, Shiyong Wang, and David Wilson and received additional technical comments from Rekha Menon and Clementine Fu (World Bank).

This work also benefited from the guidance of the Health, Nutrition, and Population Global Practice management: Juan Pablo Uribe, Monique Vledder, and David Wilson. Mamta Murthi and Alberto Rodriguez also provided guidance on the three-layer investment framework in the context of the 2022 flagship report on resilient health systems.

The following individuals from the World Bank are recognized for their editing, coordination, and administrative support: Adiam Berhane, Sabrina Haque, Jewel McFadden, and Stephen Pazdan.

References

World Bank. 2022. *Change Cannot Wait: Building Resilient Health Systems in the Shadow of COVID-19*. Washington, DC: World Bank. https://hdl.handle.net/10986/38233.

Zhao, Feng, Sulzhan Bali, Rialda Kovacevic, and Jeff Weintraub. 2021. "A Three-Layer System to Win the War against COVID-19 and Invest in Health Systems of the Future." *BMJ Global Health* 6 (12): e007365.

About the Contributors

Editors

David Bishai is a clinical professor in public health and director of the School of Public Health, University of Hong Kong. Prior to joining the University of Hong Kong, he was a professor at the Johns Hopkins Bloomberg School of Public Health for 27 years and served in the Maryland Department of Health as a local health officer in 2021. He was president of the International Health Economics Association from 2017 to 2019 and maintains certification by both the American Board of Internal Medicine and the American Board of Pediatrics. He holds a BA in philosophy and physics from Harvard University; an MPH from the University of California, Los Angeles; an MD from the University of California, San Diego; and a PhD from Wharton Business School at the University of Pennsylvania.

Rialda Kovacevic has an extensive background in medicine, public health, and clinical as well as epidemiological research and data analysis and specializes in health systems strengthening. She has served as a consulting health specialist for the World Bank's Health, Nutrition, and Population (HNP) Global Practice and Africa East Region Practice since 2018, where she has worked on national, regional, and global technical agendas while supporting the executive leadership through the front office of the global director for HNP. She holds an MD from the American International Medical University and an MPH from the Johns Hopkins Bloomberg School of Public Health.

Jeff Weintraub has more than three-and-a-half decades of experience managing communications and advocacy for US and international nongovernmental organizations, US and foreign government entities, corporations, trade associations, and research institutions. In 2013, he formed Weintraub Communications following a 13-year tenure at the Washington, DC, office of FleishmanHillard International Communications. Previously, at the American Jewish Committee, he ran communications, intergroup relations, and advocacy programs on a broad spectrum of domestic and international public policy issues. He has an undergraduate degree from Northwestern University and a master's degree in urban planning and policy from the University of Illinois Chicago.

Feng Zhao brings 30 years of experience in public health, medicine, economics, and demography across the globe. Currently, he oversees World Bank health programs in South Asia. Previously, he was practice manager of the Health Global Engagement Program of the World Bank, where he led strategy development and flagship initiatives. He spearheaded the World Bank's COVID-19 response as head of the Emergency Operations Center and was a principal architect of the global COVID-19 Multiphase Program. He has held various positions at the World Bank, including program leader for human development in Belarus, Moldova, and Ukraine; task manager for several African nations; and chair of the Health Partner Group in Ethiopia. From 2011 to 2014, he was the health manager at the African Development Bank, overseeing operations in 54 countries. He holds a PhD in population and health economics from Johns Hopkins University; an MPH from the University of California, Berkeley; and a medical degree from China. He is a faculty member at several universities, including the Harvard Finance Minister Executive Leadership Program.

Authors

Ammarah Ali is with the Department of Community Health Sciences at Aga Khan University, Karachi, Pakistan.

Sulzhan Bali is a senior health specialist at the World Bank.

Rebecca Bartlein is with the Exemplars in Global Health program based at Gates Ventures.

Sara Bennett is with the Johns Hopkins Bloomberg School of Public Health.

Paul Li Jen Cheh is with the Thailand National Health Foundation.

Melanie Coates is with the Thailand National Health Foundation.

Moytrayee Guha is with the Brown University School of Public Health.

Piya Hanvoravongchai is with the Thailand National Health Foundation. He holds an MD and a PhD.

Rowan Hussein was formerly with the Exemplars in Global Health program based at Gates Ventures.

Inuk Hwang is an assistant professor at Seoul National University, Republic of Korea. He holds an MD and a PhD.

Steven N. Kabwama is with the Makerere University School of Public Health, Uganda.

Meredith Kimball is with the Exemplars in Global Health program based at Gates Ventures.

Suzanne N. Kiwanuka is with the Makerere University School of Public Health, Uganda.

Susan Kizito is with the Makerere University School of Public Health, Uganda.

Wasin Laohavinij is with the Thailand National Health Foundation.

Siobhan Lazenby is with the Exemplars in Global Health program based at Gates Ventures.

Anne Liu is with the Exemplars in Global Health program based at Gates Ventures.

Jacqueline Maloney was formerly with the Exemplars in Global Health program based at Gates Ventures.

Patricio V. Marquez is a former lead public health specialist for the World Bank.

Caitlyn Mason was formerly with the Exemplars in Global Health program based at Gates Ventures.

Fred Monje is with the Makerere University School of Public Health, Uganda.

Claudio Mora is with the Instituto Centroamericano de Administración de Empresas (INCAE).

Lucia Mullen is an associate scholar at the Johns Hopkins Center for Health Security and an associate at the Johns Hopkins Bloomberg School of Public Health.

Alice Namale is with the Makerere University School of Public Health, Uganda.

Rawlance Ndejjo is with the Makerere University School of Public Health, Uganda.

Jennifer Nuzzo is with the Brown University School of Public Health.

Ian Paulino is with Fundación Plenitud.

Andy Pearson is with the Instituto Centroamericano de Administración de Empresas (INCAE).

Aungsumalee Pholpark is with the Thailand National Health Foundation.

Andrea Prado is with the Instituto Centroamericano de Administración de Empresas (INCAE).

Laura Rathe is with Fundación Plenitud.

Magdalena Rathe is with Fundación Plenitud.

Natchaya Ritthisirikul is with the Thailand National Health Foundation.

Karima Saleh is a senior economist (health) in the World Bank's Health, Nutrition, and Population Global Practice. She holds a PhD.

Rachel Stuhldreher was formerly with the Exemplars in Global Health program based at Gates Ventures.

Ham Suenghaitaiphorn is with the Thailand National Health Foundation.

Arielle Cohen Tanugi-Carresse was formerly with the Brown University School of Public Health.

Cynthia Wang is in the Public Health Studies Program at Johns Hopkins University.

HuiHui Wang is a senior economist in the World Bank's Health, Nutrition, and Population Global Practice. She holds an MD and a PhD.

William Wang is with the Exemplars in Global Health program based at Gates Ventures.

Rhoda K. Wanyenze is with the Makerere University School of Public Health, Uganda.

Katelyn Jison Yoo is a health economist in the World Bank's Health, Nutrition, and Population Global Practice.

Shehla Zaidi is with the Department of Community Health Sciences at Aga Khan University, Karachi, Pakistan.

Context for the Book

The economic progress of any country is related closely to the health of its population and its investments in health. To achieve desired health outcomes, investments ought to be made systematically and strategically. Given the complexity of the health sector as well as the connection of health outcomes to other sectors, health system investments are best made in a phased and strategic approach. Prior disease outbreaks—and, more recently, the COVID-19 pandemic—have tested countries' ability to invest in such health system improvements.

A brief synopsis of the three-layer framework (Zhao et al. 2021) was the foundation for the World Bank's recent global flagship report on resilient health systems (World Bank 2022). That flagship report elaborates in detail on major enablers (governance and partnership, human resources, financing and innovation) and capacities (health intelligence, service delivery, risk communication, community engagement, supply chain) of health system resilience.

This book closely examines the three-layer investment framework and reveals the functional apparatus of a strong health system. It shows how those functions help to address a range of health problems, including pandemic preparedness; studies how countries have invested in the foundational layers of their health systems; and examines the extent to which they have identified opportunities for action. Such a framework integrates thinking about long-term systems and emergency response. It highlights the intersection of health systems and pandemic preparedness and response.

Uniquely, this book integrates the elements that cross over from health systems to pandemic preparedness and response. The approach is not prescriptive; indeed, investments should be made on a country-by-country basis. However, the analysis highlights what considerations countries should apply when investing in resilient health systems that can achieve population health objectives and simultaneously prevent, contain, and respond to disease outbreaks. The book explores how countries have been investing to date, the gaps in their investments, the consequences of the same, and the steps countries should consider prioritizing and why.

This book builds on "walking-the-talk" learnings based on the World Bank flagship report on primary health care (Barış et al. 2021). The three-layer investment framework uses primary health care as the foundation for building strong public health infrastructure. Simply put, failing to invest in these elements leads to unstable health systems and inadequate capacity to contain and respond to an infectious disease outbreak.

References

Barış, Enis, Rachel Silverman, Huihui Wang, Feng Zhao, and Muhammad Ali Pate. 2021. *Walking the Talk: Reimagining Primary Health Care after COVID-19.* Washington, DC: World Bank. https://hdl.handle.net/10986/35842.

World Bank. 2022. *Change Cannot Wait: Building Resilient Health Systems in the Shadow of COVID-19.* Washington, DC: World Bank. https://hdl.handle.net/10986/38233.

Zhao, Feng, Sulzhan Bali, Rialda Kovacevic, and Jeff Weintraub. 2021. "A Three-Layer System to Win the War against COVID-19 and Invest in Health Systems of the Future." *BMJ Global Health* 6 (12): e007365.

Executive Summary

A Three-Layer Approach to Health System Strengthening Can Harden Defenses against Health Threats

At the center of this publication is a recommendation that countries adopt a three-layer framework when considering how to invest in essential improvements to their defenses against future health threats. This framework prioritizes interventions that prevent a public health threat from developing in the first place (layer 1), limit its spread should one emerge (layer 2), and manage a widespread crisis that compromises the ability of health systems to deliver care sustainably (layer 3). The three layers include the following elements:

- *Layer 1: risk reduction—promoting prevention and community preparedness.* Layer 1 includes having well-functioning, widely distributed primary health care facilities, ensuring support for essential public health activities; utilizing early-warning systems and strong surveillance systems; having a public health and health care service delivery workforce; engaging in health promotion and education for behavior change; and undertaking strong coordination of multisectoral interventions, including the availability of clean water, sanitation, and hygiene, and One Health practices that address the interconnectedness of people, animals, and the environment.
- *Layer 2: detection, containment, and mitigation capabilities.* Layer 2 responds to a specific disease or public health threat and operates primarily through the identification and protection of at-risk populations. Once high-risk populations are identified, efforts can be intensified to protect them by altering the risk factors. In the case of an epidemic of infectious disease, layer 2 includes scaling up testing, isolating suspect cases, conducting

epidemic intelligence and contact tracing, and implementing nonpharmaceutical interventions, such as social distancing, masking, isolation, quarantine, and other measures that inhibit the transmission of infectious diseases at the local level.

- *Layer 3: advanced case management and surge response.* Layer 3 includes secondary and tertiary hospital interventions that require advanced case management and efforts to respond to a widespread health crisis.

Investments in Layers 1 and 2 Are Far More Cost-Effective Than Investments in Layer 3 Alone

This book offers a glimpse at the relatively low cost of investments in improving the operation of the weakest parts of the three layers. It analyzes spending data from national health accounts stratified by high-, middle-, and low-income country status and raises concerns that most low-income countries do not collect data about layer 1 expenditures.

This analysis shows that layer 1 functions (emergency-ready primary health care, public health, prevention, and community preparedness) cost between US$2 per capita in low-income countries and US$4 per capita in lower-middle-income countries. The share of spending on layer 1 functions is typically between 3 percent and 5 percent of total health spending. Efforts to track this spending more systematically would help countries to assess the quality of layer 1 functions and inform decisions about improving the value of these efforts.

The costs of investments in layers 1 and 2 are much lower and far more effective at managing disease outbreaks than the costs of hospitalization related to advanced treatment. Indeed, the deployment and function of layers 1 and 2 ideally can help to stave off the need for layer 3 interventions.

Building higher capacity at the third layer is the most costly of the three layers. A focus on the third layer may be unavoidable in places where the needs of sick individuals are already quite high, but neglecting layers 1 and 2 to finance layer 3 is bad for economies and bad for population health.

The Three-Layer Framework Applies Not Just to Pandemic Preparedness and Response but Also to the Well-Being of Health Systems at All Times

Shoring up the ability to detect and reduce threats to health has important benefits for health systems even in the absence of a pandemic. The framework applies equally to short-term epidemics of communicable diseases and to slow-moving trends in noncommunicable diseases.

Health threats vary in the pace of the needed response, but all threats require a system that is resilient across multiple layers of response. For example, should an infectious disease break through a first layer of defense and begin to spread rapidly and widely, countries must be prepared to commit resources and know-how immediately toward a third layer equipped to absorb a surge of infections that can overwhelm health systems, leave many sick or dead, and severely disrupt social and economic life. Across a longer horizon, systematically neglecting the primary prevention of smoking, obesity, and sedentary lifestyles leads to a large and costly population of patients with heart disease and diabetes. Their immediate needs require spending on costly surgeries and medications instead of on primary prevention.

There Is No Universal Blueprint for Every Setting, but It Behooves All Countries to Invest in the Three Layers in Ways That Fit Their Needs

Although the three-layer framework is conceptually simple, real-world complexities and expenses are required to operationalize and sustain it for the long term. However, as the world has learned from COVID-19, failure to attend to the systems that protect people from harm will lead to far more difficult and expensive outcomes.

Many countries are facing a future of aging populations with preventable chronic diseases, climate-induced threats to health, and the certainty of future outbreaks of infectious disease. As is often the case in health policy, setting up default systems that prevent disease is far less expensive and easier to implement than curing a full-blown malady.

Abbreviations

BPS	basic pay scale
CCSS	Caja Costarricense de Seguro Social (Costa Rican Social Security Fund)
CDC	Centers for Disease Control and Prevention
CDCU	Communicable Disease Control Unit
CDSCHQ	Central Disaster and Safety Countermeasures Headquarters
CEACO	Centro Especializado de Atención de Pacientes con COVID-19 (Specialized Center for Care of Patients with COVID-19)
CENARE	Centro Nacional de Rehabilitación (National Rehabilitation Center)
CHW	community health worker
COVID-19	coronavirus disease 2019
DAH	development assistance for health
DHIS2	District Health Information Software 2
EBAIS	equipo básico de atención integral en salud (basic health care team)
EGH	Exemplars in Global Health
EPHF	essential public health function
eRDS	electronic Results Dispatch System
eRHMIS	electronic Reproductive Health Management Information System
FETP	Field Epidemiology Training Program
FTE	full-time equivalent
GDP	gross domestic product
GHED	Global Health Expenditure Database
GIS	geographic information system
H1N1	swine flu
H5N1	avian flu
HC	spending for a health care function
HF	source of health financing
HISP	Health Information Systems Programme

HIV/AIDS	immunodeficiency virus/acquired immunodeficiency syndrome
HP	health provider
ICU	intensive care unit
IDSR	Integrated Disease Surveillance and Response
IeDA	Integrated e-Diagnostic Approach
IHME	Institute for Health Metrics and Evaluation
IMCI	integrated management of childhood illnesses
KDCA	Korea Disease Control and Prevention Agency
MERS	Middle East respiratory syndrome
MOH	Ministry of Health
MOHW	Ministry of Health and Welfare
MOPH	Ministry of Public Health
MSIT	Ministry of Science and Information and Communication Technology
NGO	nongovernmental organization
NHA	national health account
NHI	National Health Insurance
NIDSS	National Infectious Disease Surveillance System
OECD	Organisation for Economic Co-operation and Development
PCR	polymerase chain reaction
PETS	public expenditure tracking survey
PFM	public financial management
R&D	research and development
RDT	rapid diagnostic test
RT	reverse transcription
SARS	severe acute respiratory syndrome
SARS-CoV2	the virus that causes coronavirus disease (COVID-19)
SDG	Sustainable Development Goal
SHA	System of Health Accounts
SMS	short message service
SORMAS	Surveillance Outbreak Response Management and Analysis System
SRRT	surveillance and rapid response team
TB	tuberculosis
USAID	United States Agency for International Development
VHT	village health team
VHV	village health volunteer
WASH	water, sanitation, and hygiene
WHO	World Health Organization

PART 1

What Is the Three-Layer Framework, and How Are Countries Aligning Resources toward It?

The three-layer framework accounts for what it takes to build health system resilience: a strong foundation that promotes preventive measures through public health functions and the capacity to mitigate and contain an infectious disease outbreak, should one occur. Having well-functioning first layers of defense translates to nonevents or well-contained events, which leaves these preventive measures often neglected with regard to their implementation, leverage, tracking, and ultimately their financing. This book examines expenditure tracking for public health functions that finance these preventive actions across low-income, lower-middle-income, and high-income countries. It illustrates that many countries are inconsistent in monitoring and compiling their spending patterns. Further, it shows that spending on layer 1 and layer 2 is a fraction of what countries spend on layer 3 (advanced case management) and makes the case that all three layers, and not primarily layer 3, need investment to achieve health system resilience. Building resilience entails having strong high-level support and commitment, adopting a community and participatory approach, building and using resilience teams to measure the resilience efforts, leveraging the feedback loop of the measures of resilience, and having adequate financing. Finally, a case is made for considering and prioritizing investment in human resources for public health who are a key, yet underutilized, workforce of strong health systems.

1

Three Layers in Health Systems: Protecting Population Health Every Day and during Disease Outbreaks

Rialda Kovacevic, Jeff Weintraub, Feng Zhao, and Sulzhan Bali

IN SUMMARY

The COVID-19 pandemic alerted leaders around the world about the need to strengthen mechanisms to prevent and respond quickly to emerging infectious disease outbreaks.

- Countries would do well to fortify their earliest lines of defense against threats to human health.
- Countries seeking to build resilient health systems and institutions and to integrate their public health functions into their delivery networks could consider a three-layer framework of prevention and response. This three-layer framework identifies priority investments needed at multiple layers of the health system:
  - *Layer 1. Risk reduction: promoting prevention and community preparedness.* Layer 1 includes having well-functioning, widely distributed primary health care facilities that support essential public health activities, early-warning systems and strong surveillance systems, and strong coordination of multisectoral interventions, including the wide availability of clean water, sanitation, and hygiene and One Health practices, a strong public health and health care service delivery workforce, and health promotion and education for behavior change practices.
  - *Layer 2. Detection, containment, and mitigation capabilities.* Layer 2 operates primarily through the identification and protection of at-risk populations. Once high-risk populations are identified, efforts can be intensified to protect them by altering risk factors. In the event of an infectious epidemic, these efforts include scaling up testing, isolating suspect cases, conducting epidemic intelligence and contact tracing, and implementing nonpharmaceutical interventions at the primary and community levels.[a]
  - *Layer 3. Advanced case management and surge response.* Layer 3 includes secondary and tertiary hospital interventions for cases requiring advanced case management. At layer 3, patients receive medical treatments to preserve life and restore organ function.

(continued)

IN SUMMARY *(continued)*

- While all three layers are essential, investments in layers 1 and 2 are much lower and far more effective in managing disease outbreaks than the costs of hospitalization and advanced treatment. Indeed, the successful deployment and function of layers 1 and 2 can help to stave off the need for layer 3 interventions. COVID-19 forced communities and countries to rely mainly on layer 3, the most cost-intensive and least impactful of the three layers. Doing so is reasonable and may even be unavoidable when societies are in crisis mode. However, in the absence of robust precrisis tiers, the long-term impact will ultimately overtax the health system.

- The following are worthy goals for countries to consider: (a) engage nonhealth sector players and private sector providers as well as nongovernmental organizations and civil society organizations to strengthen trust and connection with the public; (b) build trust in public health systems by managing communications effectively and responding to misinformation; (c) optimize data collection and analysis as well as protection of patient confidentiality and rights; (d) embrace digital tools and telemedicine that can improve monitoring, treatment, efficiency, and reach of care; (e) address human resource planning, capacity building, and networking, both formal and informal, including the use of community health workers; (f) take a systems approach to top-down and bottom-up planning, financing, and coordination; (g) enhance financing and affordability for public health goods and primary health care; and (h) consider regulatory changes that can allow for all of the above.

a. The US Centers for Disease Control and Prevention defines nonpharmaceutical interventions—sometimes called community mitigation strategies—as "actions, apart from getting vaccinated and taking medicine, that people and communities can take to help slow the spread of illnesses like pandemic influenza (flu)." Refer to https://www.cdc.gov/places/measure-definitions/prevention/index.html#:~:text=Accessing%20preventive%20healthcare%20services%2C%20such,and%20mortality%20from%20chronic%20diseases.

Introduction

In every corner of the world, people will long remember the early stages of the COVID-19 pandemic: hospitals overflowing with patients teetering precariously between life and death, harrowing stories about lives lost and battered by the disease, the unprecedented shutdown of whole economies and daily life, the record-setting race for new vaccines to blunt the spread of the SARS-CoV-2 virus, and the monumental effort to administer those vaccines on an unprecedented scale.

Aside from the human trauma and societal disruptions, the COVID-19 pandemic offers profound reminders not only about how countries survived the pandemic but also about what they must do differently to prevent another global outbreak of devastating infectious disease. It is an evolutionary certainty that more outbreaks will emerge. Indeed, in a recent study, Marani et al. (2021) assert, "The yearly probability of occurrence of extreme epidemics can increase up to threefold in the coming decades." The only thing we can control is how we—communities, countries, and global health organizations—prepare for that challenge and harden our defenses against it.

Will We Again Ignore the Alarms?

It is impossible to know how differently COVID-19 might have arisen and evolved had countries around the world been more prepared to respond to it. But, long before the SARS-CoV-2 virus appeared in China in late 2019, there was sufficient understanding of the tools and practices that might have stopped or limited a relatively isolated outbreak from becoming a worldwide pandemic.

For years, many leaders and institutions, including the World Bank, had sounded the alarm about the perils of inaction. They urged governments to take proactive steps to arm themselves against tenacious new infectious diseases. Several severe disease outbreaks—most recently, the emergence of the deadly Ebola virus in West Africa between 2014 and 2016—should have shaken the world to take appropriate steps.

Ultimately, however, few governments—even those of wealthier and supposedly better-prepared countries—marshaled the resources and political will to heed those warnings. Nevertheless, case studies included in this volume demonstrate that some countries went to great lengths and expense to strengthen their defenses. If some countries can seize the moment, so can others.

At the heart of this publication is the hope that the shock of COVID-19 will motivate overdue reforms in the health system. By offering a framework, practical strategies, and case studies, it aims to motivate readers to take action. One of the biggest lessons is that countries need to fortify the earliest lines of defense to stop a small flame from igniting in the first place and, failing that, to act quickly and decisively to snuff it out before it spreads.

This book outlines a three-layer framework for post-COVID-19 investments that integrates public health system functions and primary health care. This framework integrates health security investments within the overall health system and identifies priority investments needed at the intersection of pandemic preparedness and health system strengthening before a crisis or epidemic spreads. Investments in preventive interventions or preparedness before an epidemic are critical because they can yield substantial immediate returns to the daily functioning of the health system (Burwell et al. 2020; World Bank 2017).

This publication, a collaboration of leading global health experts, offers insight into the why and how of the three-layer framework for strengthening health systems and pandemic preparedness. It examines the financing levels of these three layers in the past, surveys efforts in several countries to build strong pandemic defenses and employ cross-cutting tools and mechanisms before COVID-19 arrived, and describes how they responded when it did.

The Broader Context: Strong and Resilient Health Systems

Health systems around the world face similar challenges to stepping up the provision of essential health services that were deprioritized during the COVID-19 emergency: rising demand for health care services, aging populations, changing burden of disease, climate change, rapid scientific discoveries in diagnostics and therapeutics, and rising costs of care (World Bank 2022). More than ever, the interconnectedness of people, animals, and the environment highlights the need to adopt a One Health approach.[1] The ease of disruptions—whether from a social, health, political, or economic perspective—indicates the need to be flexible and ready for a variety of possible threats. The readiness to adapt to a wide variety of challenges requires coordination among people, communities, political systems, and scientific data (Global Innovation Hub for Improving Value in Health 2020).

Health systems are dynamic, complex, and adaptive social systems encompassing a wide variety of people, organizations, and networks, each with its own set of values and interests that must be aligned to achieve health and other health system goals. For this reason, health system strengthening is a multipronged and iterative learning process among many actors, structures, services, and subsystems (Swanson et al. 2015). This process is context-dependent and occurs across various levels, including the local community and subnational, national, regional, and global levels.

Most important, building strong health systems is a responsibility not just of the health sector, but of other sectors as well, including private enterprise, the environment, finance, agriculture, and transportation. Factors such as a country's water, sanitation, and hygiene (WASH) systems, educational structures and outcomes, social protection and justice mechanisms, and macrofiscal well-being also influence the strength of health systems. Stronger health systems move societies closer to the goal of universal health coverage and improve health outcomes for all (United Kingdom, FCDO 2021).

Spending to strengthen health systems is an investment that generates material, social, and health improvements. Globally, about US$8.3 trillion is spent annually on health care (WHO 2020a). Concentrating investments on improving health outcomes and lowering waste and unnecessary costs can create additional cost savings and allow health systems to allocate resources to precrisis activities.

Countries around the world recognize that they need to pay attention to and strengthen their core public health capacities, response and readiness, human resources, community engagement, supply chain operability, technology, and governance, including the need to provide more financing in these areas. In nearly every country, however, the fundamental problem is that they fail to measure how resources are being spent.

This shortcoming involves assessments of how core capacities are performing as well as how and how much countries spend on them. Such information provides a near-immediate return on investment. If a country wants to deliver a certain commodity, such as a COVID-19 vaccine or personal protective equipment, it must have the core capacities for this delivery to be efficient. Unfortunately, knowledge about capacities and efforts to improve them have been given low priority in policy making. Countries need to—and should—make informed decisions about what they spend and need to spend on the long-term resilience of their health systems. Resilience can be measured, and the work it takes to improve resilience can be costed and used to track expenditures on health system strengthening. The chapters that follow elaborate on the pathway of achieving health system resilience and provide past trends in health sector spending toward each of the three layers to reveal opportunities and gaps that must be corrected in the short, medium, and long terms.

A Practical Framework of a Three-Layer Defense System

One of the most perilous moments for any soccer team arises when an opposing player with the ball breaks through the team's defenses to face their goalkeeper one on one. At that point, even the most talented goalkeeper is in big trouble, especially if a second opponent is running alongside the one with the ball. With only a few, last-resort tools in her defensive repertoire, the goalkeeper must shoulder the entire burden of stopping a tenacious striker from scoring. More likely than not, she will fail, and the cost of the goal will be dear.

In public health, where the stakes are orders of magnitude higher than they are on the soccer pitch, the dynamic is similar. The layers of defense must be formidable enough, first, to identify and prevent the threat of an infectious disease and, second, to keep a few early cases from spiraling into a hard-to-control outbreak. Relying on the third layer of defense—critical care units and specialized health providers—makes the task of protecting everyone from the ravages of an infectious disease far more difficult.

The three-layer framework can fortify the ability of health systems to prevent and arrest the rise of epidemics and strengthen the efficient use of limited resources for high-impact precrisis systems. It integrates prevention, detection, and response capacities with service delivery. This strengthened foundational layer prevents escalation of crisis and a need for subsequent overtasking of the tertiary layer. While investments in all three layers enhance resilience, investments in foundational layers for risk reduction and community preparedness—as well as detection, containment, and mitigation—are especially critical to relieve pressure on the health system as a whole.

A Closer Look at the Three-Layer Framework

Figure 1.1 illustrates the three-layer framework and how it integrates health system strengthening with preparedness for a wide variety of health threats. At the base of the triangle, layer 1 operates at the front level, with people and populations who are at risk, but not yet affected by a health condition. It designates activities that build institutions and norms that affect the health of the population. Layer 2 designates activities that mitigate a breaking crisis by detecting cases and mobilizing responses and communications. Layer 3 designates activities to serve stricken people and populations and restore their health and well-being. This section examines each layer in more detail.

Figure 1.1   The Three-Layer Framework for Strengthening Health Systems

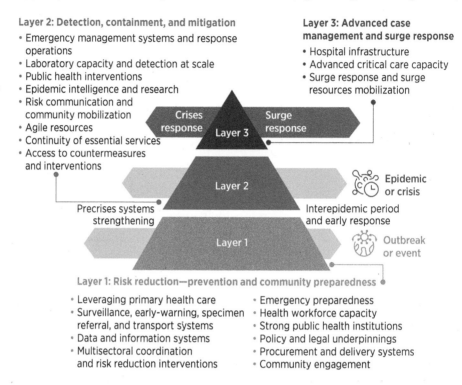

Layer 2: Detection, containment, and mitigation
- Emergency management systems and response operations
- Laboratory capacity and detection at scale
- Public health interventions
- Epidemic intelligence and research
- Risk communication and community mobilization
- Agile resources
- Continuity of essential services
- Access to countermeasures and interventions

Layer 3: Advanced case management and surge response
- Hospital infrastructure
- Advanced critical care capacity
- Surge response and surge resources mobilization

Layer 1: Risk reduction—prevention and community preparedness
- Leveraging primary health care
- Surveillance, early-warning, specimen referral, and transport systems
- Data and information systems
- Multisectoral coordination and risk reduction interventions
- Emergency preparedness
- Health workforce capacity
- Strong public health institutions
- Policy and legal underpinnings
- Procurement and delivery systems
- Community engagement

Sources: Based on the analysis set out in Zhao et al. 2021 and the country experiences and recommendations in Collins et al. 2020.

Layer 1: Risk Reduction—Promoting Prevention and Community Preparedness

The first layer is the foundation of the "precrisis" lines of pandemic defense before an outbreak of infectious disease materializes. Among its core elements are a well-functioning local, regional, and national public health system. This layer relies on widely distributed primary health care facilities and access to services, early-warning systems, and strong surveillance mechanisms that closely monitor and detect outbreaks of new diseases.

This layer should allow direct engagement with patients and the broader population to promote healthy behaviors and prevent and treat conditions that make them vulnerable to emerging infectious diseases. It also should include community, district (or subnational), and national planning (including health policies and regulations) for epidemic threats and health emergencies; strong public health institutions; well-trained health workers, including public health and health services workers; a broad reach of immunization services; strong multisectoral coordination for multisectoral interventions, including the private sector; strong and widely available clean water, sanitation, and hygiene; health promotion and education for behavior change; One Health practices that closely examine health connections among people, animals, plants, and their shared environment; financing and management of population health; and communication. In addition to strong primary health care services, a good portion of layer 1 includes strong essential public health services (United States, CDC 2020).

Layer 1 aims to prevent a breach of health security in the first place. If infiltration occurs, layer 1 supports the subsequent layers of defense to limit the breach and mitigate the impact. It is the foundation of an effective health security strategy, operating in relative quiet, long before a mounting crisis alerts the broader public to its importance. Expansion of this and other system layers greatly enhances a country's ability to detect and contain epidemic threats as well as to deliver critical services, including public health services that yield better individual and collective health outcomes, cost savings, and even broader economic and social advances. Investments in community engagement, primary health care, population health, and community preparedness are critical to ensure community trust in the health system, ensure adherence to public health measures and nonpharmaceutical interventions, and enable access to and demand for diagnostic, preventive, and therapeutic interventions during and between epidemics.

Like the hangar mechanic who is responsible for ensuring that planes take off and land without incident, success at this stage largely means nonevents—the absence of a threat or disaster. Layer 1 encompasses investments not only in the health sector but also in multisectoral efforts to reduce risks in health and other sectors—for example, leveraging collaboration with a country's education sector to promote behavior change and public health compliance; mainstreaming a One Health approach to mitigate epidemic risks at the intersection of animals, humans, and the environment; and ensuring coordination across relevant sectors at local, national, and regional levels.

Resilient health systems integrate essential public health functions with health services that address challenges such as aging populations, chronic comorbidities, and socioeconomic and gender inequalities as well as climate change.

Primary Health Care

Primary health care addresses the majority of a person's health needs, including physical, mental, and social well-being, throughout his or her lifetime. Primary health care focuses on people instead of diseases. It demands a whole-of-society approach that includes health promotion, disease prevention, treatment, rehabilitation, and palliative care.

Investments in the first layer are intended to improve the ability of primary health care and public health systems—for example, the ability to carry out immunization campaigns, ensure water safety and hygiene (or WASH) measures, and support good nutrition and food security. Primary health care helps people at the local level to engage in activities (such as screening, exercise, a healthy diet, and smoking cessation) that can prevent conditions that make them more vulnerable to disease. These investments improve access to preventive and promotive health care.

The strength of a country's primary health care depends on whether it integrates pandemic preparedness and response measures, shows adaptability during a health crisis, and ensures minimal disruption of essential health services. Investments in facility readiness, such as strong telemedicine capabilities and essential health service continuity plans, exemplify this approach.

In addition to disease prevention, this layer reflects strong community engagement and a robust community-level public health system. Experience with COVID-19 and recent epidemics suggests that widespread community buy-in can strengthen both the detection of outbreaks and the delivery of an effective response.

Effective primary health care is physically, financially, and culturally more accessible to local communities. Accessibility helps to address the burden of disease that disproportionately affects poor and vulnerable populations. With a focus on health promotion and disease prevention, primary health care and public health together can lower household expenditures for health as well as prevent health conditions from escalating into more complex diseases that require hospitalization (Sirleaf and Clark 2021).

According to the World Health Organization (WHO), primary health care is "an essential foundation for the global response to COVID-19," emphasizing the role of primary care in preventing cases from occurring, diagnosing and treating persons already infected, and mitigating long consequences in managing non-COVID conditions at the primary health care level and thus reducing the demand for hospital services during the health crisis (WHO 2020b). Whether in a time of health crisis or routine service provision, primary health care saves lives and financial resources, as it is the first step for most people encountering ill health.

COVID-19 exposed both underlying system weaknesses and the need for integrating public health and primary health care. Strong primary health care systems are critical to delivering essential health services efficiently. The pandemic also highlighted how, during a health emergency, both public health services and primary health care can play a critical role in testing, contact tracing, surveillance, immunization, treatment, and management of the overflow of critically ill patients at hospitals and other facilities. They play complementary roles in maintaining health system resilience. During a health crisis, primary health care is responsible for providing a prompt diagnosis and medical treatment for persons inflicted by the pathogen; together, the public health sector and primary health care sector provide preventive and essential health services, respectively, that, if ignored, strain the health system long after the outbreak has passed.

Both the 2018 Astana Declaration and the 1978 Alma-Ata Declaration emphasize the need for integrating primary health care with public health. Yet very few countries have successfully met this goal. The following reasons explain why. Public health and medical care are delivered by separate institutions with separate leadership, information, and reporting systems. These institutions have different workforces, different professional traditions, and separate funding systems. Overlapping operations—surveillance systems, for example—are not regularly coordinated. Finally, the health workforce of the service delivery sector and the public health sector have quite different roles and responsibilities, yet many health systems do not sufficiently recognize these differences or leverage them properly. Although both play an important role in promoting health, preventing disease, and controlling outbreaks, the public health workforce[2] is often overshadowed by the need for medical care and the activities of care providers. However, investing in the public health workforce is worthwhile, as shown later in this book.

Public Health Workforce

A strong and resilient health system can respond to, adapt to, and learn from a crisis. Essential public health functions are a path to achieving resilience in the health system, and public health workers are the chief stewards to foster resilience throughout the system.

Investing simply to expand all parts of the health care workforce will not improve resilience. For the public health workforce to fulfill its potential, an assessment of its current strengths and weaknesses is needed to identify priorities for improvement. An extensive set of tools is available to help the public health workforce to assess its ability to steward resilience. These tools are the checklists and interventions that support improving essential public health functions. Chapter 2 elaborates in more detail about strengthening the public health workforce and implementing essential public health functions as a pathway to achieving health system resilience.

Health Care Providers

Layer 1 depends on the availability and constitution of health care providers. Many countries lack enough health workers to meet their needs. In low- and middle-income countries, shortages of health workers are common; low-income countries have only 3 physicians and 11 nurses per 10,000 people, whereas high-income countries have 34 doctors and 81 nurses per 10,000 people.

The number of providers needs to expand to meet the growing burden of disease, including that of aging populations. More innovative and thoughtful use of providers at the primary care level can spare human resources, particularly in a time of crisis. The team-based model of care, also known as "task shifting" and "task sharing," leverages nurses, physicians, midwives, nursing assistants, and potentially other health workers such as community health workers (CHWs), which allows their efficient use for tasks appropriate to their skills and competencies. The COVID-19 pandemic identified some valuable lessons for addressing the challenges facing human resources for health. These lessons include assessing and mapping health workforce needs, developing a census of available health workers, developing an evidence-based strategy for human resources for health, and professionalizing CHWs.

CHWs play an immensely helpful role in preventing and responding to disease outbreaks. Their significance is even more visible in underserved communities, where they may be the only care providers. It is not uncommon for their work to be voluntary and temporary and their training only sporadic.

Recognizing their importance, many governments introduced measures to mobilize, support, and incentivize new and existing CHWs before and during the pandemic (box 1.1 describes efforts in Liberia). When CHWs are trained, paid, supervised, and supplied to bring primary health services to the doorsteps of people living far from care, they can improve health outcomes and save lives. They are foundational to resilient health systems and vital to achieving universal health coverage.

Public Health Services and Institutions and Essential Public Health Functions

Many aspects of layer 1 are defined through essential public health functions. Various reputable institutions have compiled operational checklists of these core capacities, and a recent WHO publication identifies a common list of public health functions using a crosswalk analysis of authoritative lists (WHO 2021).

Box 1.1

Community Health Worker Network in Liberia

Liberia launched its first community health worker (CHW) program in 2008. At the time, only 51 doctors served the country's population of roughly 4.3 million, more than 1 million of whom lived in remote areas. To improve access to basic health care, Liberia expanded its network of CHWs to more than 8,000 nationwide by 2013. Still, because of fragmented and parallel work by government and nongovernmental organizations and a lack of standardization and training protocols, many of these volunteers were unable to deliver quality services consistently.

The Ebola epidemic of 2014–16 exposed weaknesses in the volunteer system and constrained access to health care in profound and tangible ways: roughly 10 percent of Liberia's doctors and 8 percent of its nurses and midwives contracted Ebola and died; moreover, a lack of paid, well-supported CHWs fueled the spread of the epidemic from rural communities to cities, claiming thousands of lives. These challenges revealed the need for a more formal, integrated rural program.

In 2016 Liberia developed a new CHW program—the National Community Health Assistant Program—that aimed to reach the most vulnerable communities in rural areas by providing a higher quality of services that mirrored the local burden of disease. Government officials monitored and managed the program and integrated it into the formal health system. By paying and professionalizing CHWs, the Community Health Assistant Program became a core component of the public health system and was integrated into the continuum of care. In addition, community health assistants received supplies through the same supply chain as other health care facilities, and the data they collected were folded into the same health data system.

Today, 4,000 trained and deployed CHWs and 400 community health supervisors are working in 14 of Liberia's 15 counties. Liberia thus made a strong investment in layer 1.

Source: Summarized from "What Did Liberia Do?" Exemplars in Global Health website, https://www.exemplars.health/topics/community-health-workers/liberia/what-did-liberia-do.

All of these lists include monitoring and surveillance, governance and legislation, health promotion and protection including communication and community engagement, health workforce, emergency management, social protection, and research.

The essential public health functions facilitate assessments of the population's health and engage the community to facilitate responses to the identified health needs. They help to improve public health practices and build resilient health systems that enable countries to meet the goal of universal health coverage. As the WHO notes, essential public health functions are "the most cost-effective, comprehensive, and sustainable way to enhance the health of populations and individuals and to reduce the burden of disease," adding that they are "generally regarded as a fundamental and indispensable set of collective actions under the responsibility of the State which are needed to meet public health goals, including the attainment and maintenance of the highest level of population health possible within given resources" (WHO 2021, xi). The list of and the way of operationalizing them depend on societal and health contexts in a country or region; they are interconnected and interdependent.

Community Engagement

For public health to be responsive and effective, it must be anchored deeply at the local and community levels. Community engagement—an essential layer 1 ingredient—involves strengthening the core capacities of disease prevention, detection, and response readiness at the national and most local levels. Its role includes building trust, fostering dialogue, and promoting health through guided information and health education. The strength of a resilient health system is measured by its capacity for communicating risk and engaging communities (and community leaders) in decision-making structures.

Health systems start at a local community level and are an integral part of national health systems. Communities are active contributors to the structure of health systems and play an important role in their improvement. Communities can identify needs and priorities, implement programs, monitor health trends and emerging outbreaks of new diseases, conduct evaluations, improve the quality of care, and advocate for and enact essential public policy reforms. Leveraging local community assets creates an opportunity for building capacity and improving health outcomes.

Communities carry significant influence in responses to a potential health crisis. Moreover, with communities engaged, there is an opportunity to build well-functioning community-based surveillance; improve access to preventive, diagnostic, and treatment services; build the capabilities of the community and primary care health workers; and ensure preparedness training and access to appropriate personal protective equipment.

Outbreaks start at a local level. Particularly if an outbreak is occurring in remote areas, it can take a while for traditional surveillance systems to identify the outbreak. Community-based surveillance allows systematic, community-by-community, real-time detection and reporting of events significant for public health. Therefore, community-based surveillance can prevent outbreaks from turning into large-scale epidemics and pandemics. When paired with technology and real-time reporting, it helps to contain the spread, not just at the local level, but globally, too. Paired with training of CHWs while leveraging technology, community-based surveillance can be effective in addressing a local outbreak, as box 1.2 on surveillance in Somalia demonstrates.

Although community engagement plays a crucial role in the resilience of the health system, it is often neglected, particularly with regard to investment. The implementation of community-level activities needs to be given appropriate priority. For example, there is no substitute for the role that community engagement plays in communicating risk and changing social behavior. At the same time, community-based surveillance is most effective when implemented in hard-to-reach areas with limited access to routine surveillance. It is not a substitute for routine surveillance systems, where they are possible to implement.

Box 1.2

Community-Based Surveillance in Somalia

The Red Cross Red Crescent Movement—a network of 17 million active volunteers worldwide—makes tools available so that community volunteers can capture unusual events or health risks and report them in a timely fashion (Jung et al. 2024).

Somalia is part of this Red Cross Red Crescent surveillance network. Over the years, the country has experienced various disease outbreaks, including cholera, typhoid, pneumonia, measles, meningococcal meningitis, and, most recently, COVID-19. Somalia first implemented community-based surveillance in May 2018. Local volunteers in the initiative are trained to recognize the signs and symptoms of epidemic-prone diseases. Community focal points are given simple phones for reporting health risks through short, coded text messages.

The Nyss software platform—the data collection, management, and analysis system for the Red Cross Red Crescent Movement—receives the phone-message data, aggregates and analyzes the information, shares it with users of the platform, and sends automatic alerts in real time to Nyss's supervisors and health authorities.[a]

In Somalia, close to 500 trained volunteers have been reporting on various health risks like diarrheal disease, fever and rash, acute malnutrition, a cluster of unusual illnesses or deaths in people, and coughs and respiratory challenges. Since the implementation of this platform, 732 health risks have been reported with 105 alerts escalated. The first case of COVID-19 in Somalia was detected through community-based surveillance and reported through the Nyss platform.

a. Refer to Red Cross Red Crescent, "What Is Nyss?" https://cbs.ifrc.org/what-nyss#:~:text =Nyss%20is%20a%20custom%20software,%2Dbased%20surveillance%20(CBS).

Supply Chain

Layer 1 should aim to strengthen procurement and delivery systems. A supply chain is an important component of a strong health system. Strong and sustainable supply chains help governments to reduce costs, stock-outs, and waste.[3]

Supply chains need to be responsive and resilient—capable of adapting to shifting demands for routine products, while preparing for emergency situations. During the COVID-19 pandemic, supply chains were required to respond with unprecedented speed and agility to cope with the situation at hand. Complete, end-to-end inventory visibility was vital to understand when essential commodities such as therapeutics, diagnostics, or vaccines would be available for use (Kovacevic et al. 2021). Further, supply chains are protecting other essential elements of a health system, such as health workers, particularly those on the front lines, who, without personal protective equipment, cannot safely deliver services. For building and maintaining strong supply chains, focusing on enablers such as capacity building and training local staff ensures sustainability and proper coordination at local, national, and even regional levels so that all efforts are synergistic.

Collaboration

Layer 1 should also aim to promote multisectoral coordination and enact legislation and policies (such as public health acts and wildlife trade acts) that promote disease prevention, preparedness, and resilience to epidemic threats. Layer 1 exists to leverage regional, multisectoral (whole-of-government), and whole-of-society (including private sector) partnerships to create trust and build resilience within and beyond the health sector. This effort includes establishing One Health platforms for coordination, joint planning, and implementation of resilience-sensitive activities. A One Health approach to connect human, animal, and environmental health is essential to reducing risks of spillovers and enabling adaptation to climate change. Such multisectoral approaches are important not just in layer 1, but also in layer 2, which is discussed next.

Layer 2: Scaling Detection and Ensuring Containment and Mitigation

Layer 2 focuses on medical care for mild cases of illness. During noncrisis periods, it provides outpatient services. During crises, it identifies and protects at-risk populations, scales up testing, isolates suspect cases, performs epidemic intelligence and contact tracing, and implements nonpharmaceutical interventions at the primary care level.

While detection cuts across layers, timely detection is especially critical to contain an epidemic. It should be based on both a stronger first layer and well-functioning, existing laboratory capacities. It can help to flatten the infection curve and reduce the number of cases that require hospitalization.

This layer counts on further investments in integrated public health functions: mass testing; risk communications and social mobilization; infection prevention and control capabilities; the availability of competent medical professionals and, where they are in short supply, CHWs who can manage some of the demand; and access to sufficient stocks of personal protective equipment, diagnostics, therapeutics, and vaccines.

This layer also relies on surveillance systems that connect local, regional, national, international, and interministerial levels and on essential services to continue prevention, monitoring, and treatment of all other health conditions. Layer 2 builds on existing layer 1 activities and repurposes them to an extent. For example, when a health system has a well-trained health workforce, their services can be redirected to a specific activity (such as testing) during an initial outbreak.

Layer 2 rests on strong first-layer components. Once an outbreak occurs, the existing structures from layer 1 can enable layer 2 to activate an early response to contain the epidemic. Layer 2 also can leverage multisectoral partnerships and integrate inputs from public health and primary health care systems to allow for timely interventions. A strong first layer can reduce the frequency of outbreaks and, when an outbreak does occur, support layer 2 in rapid containment.

The COVID-19 pandemic highlighted the urgent need to invest in integrated disease surveillance and response, which includes scaling up contact tracing and testing, isolating suspect cases, and ensuring implementation of public health measures and interventions to generate compliance and demand and allow greater access and delivery.

Moreover, the pandemic highlighted the value of technology and innovation—including telemedicine and artificial intelligence—to ensure that health care can continue during a crisis and reduce the stress on health systems that are overly taxed. This layer helps to flatten the curve of rising infection and to reduce the number of cases that require hospitalization.

The COVID-19 pandemic strongly articulated the value of trust and its impact in a successful pandemic response. Nonpharmaceutical interventions play a critical role in the early response to an outbreak of infectious disease— before vaccines or treatment are available. Public communication is essential to their timely and effective implementation. Social distancing may be the earliest public health measure ever recorded. Isolation, quarantine, and other measures that are now called social distancing have been part of people's intuitive reactions to protect themselves from infectious diseases.

At the very beginning of an outbreak, when little is known about the infectious agent, nonpharmaceutical interventions are the first action to prevent an increase of new cases. Their implementation and practice are akin to, in medicine, moving quickly to ensure the viability of tissue ("time" equals "tissue"). In infections, this relationship translates into timely intervention that prevents transmission. During COVID-19, such interventions included the use of masks, isolation, prompt quarantine, restrictions on movement, handwashing, and so on.

Their implementation and compliance "buy time" for the development of pharmacological agents. Many studies have illustrated the effectiveness of a single type of intervention in reducing COVID-19 transmission, and a study published in the *International Journal of Infectious Diseases* found that the simultaneous implementation of two or more types of nonpharmaceutical interventions is effective for containing the spread of COVID-19 (Bo et al. 2021).

University of Michigan researchers examined the relationship between overall good pandemic response across 34 countries, including early implementation of nonpharmaceutical interventions, the role of public trust in public health measures, and a country's leadership. Countries such as Denmark, the Republic of Korea, New Zealand, and Viet Nam, generally considered to have well-established public trust, had very early implementation (and adoption by the public) of interventions such as wearing face masks. They also had robust early pandemic response, such as prompt testing and contact tracing. Box 1.3 describes the early response in Senegal. The situation was quite different in countries such as Brazil, the Russian Federation, and the United States, which lacked coherent public health policies. In all cases, the value of proper leadership was found to be far more relevant than the capacity to respond alone (Pires 2021).

Layer 2 and layer 3 rely on workers trained in medicine, nursing, pharmaceuticals, and allied health care areas. Given the global shortage of health

---

Box 1.3

Early and Effective Response to COVID-19 in Senegal

When COVID-19 arrived in Senegal among travelers returning from Europe, the country consciously and deliberately was prepared to respond (Resolve to Save Lives 2021). Senegal's Health Emergency Operations Center, which was set up in response to the 2014–16 West African Ebola outbreak, had been running simulations for years to prepare for such an outbreak. In January 2020, Senegal began assessing the country's preparedness, supporting improvements based on that assessment, and relying on its strong national laboratory system.

Senegal's emphasis on testing enabled it to detect early cases. In February 2020, the Institut Pasteur de Dakar was one of two labs in Africa able to test for SARS-CoV-2. A series of orders to close schools and workplaces, cancel religious festivals, and institute international and regional travel restrictions was followed by a declaration of a state of emergency, which imposed a nighttime curfew and a requirement to wear masks outside of the home. These efforts, supported by clear, comprehensive communications from the government, were credited with high levels of public support for the public health measures. The country's COVID-19 response was ranked second among 36 countries evaluated by *Foreign Policy* magazine.[a]

a. COVID-19 Global Response Index, https://globalresponseindex.foreignpolicy.com/.

workers, it is important to think differently about health teams. It is beneficial to develop a census of health workers ahead of time, because having it in time of an emergency helps to minimize shortages of human resources. It takes time to train a health workforce, and some countries have used technology to close the training gap. Countries should consider training more primary care doctors as opposed to specialists alone, shifting tasks from doctors to nurses, as well as relying on CHWs. Box 1.4 examines such approaches in Kenya, Uganda, and Sub-Saharan Africa generally. Box 1.5 describes efforts in Singapore and Viet Nam. Box 1.6 describes efforts in Korea.

Box 1.4

Information Systems and Strengthening Human Resources to Deliver Health Care

Uganda's human resources for health information system has enabled the country to tackle health workforce issues ranging from absenteeism to credential verification to geographic or training gaps. Kenya's use of iHRIS Suite, an open-source software tool, has supported the hiring, tracking, and managing of health workers in the country's northeast province (Dalberg 2021).

The Africa Centres for Disease Control and Prevention (Africa CDC) played a crucial role in mitigating the pandemic on the continent. At the start of COVID-19, the Africa CDC launched the Partnership to Accelerate COVID-19 Testing, among other measures. The key element of this initiative was to engage community health workers (CHWs) in risk communication and community engagement, conduct surveillance activities for early case identification, perform contact tracing, and facilitate referrals for testing and continuum of care (Africa CDC 2021). To date, more than 20,000 CHWs have been trained and deployed locally to 29 member states (Africa CDC 2022). Some of these lessons learned came from Liberia's leveraged experience with the Ebola outbreak, described in box 1.1.

Box 1.5

Early Detection and Response: Prior Crisis Experience Did Not Go to Waste in Singapore and Viet Nam

Singapore benefited from prior experience with epidemics—namely, the 2003 outbreak of the severe acute respiratory syndrome (SARS), which spread to four health care facilities and led to more than 238 cases and 33 deaths, making Singapore one of the worst-affected countries (Lee, Chiew, and Khong 2020). In 2020, aggressive contact tracing, testing, social distancing, and a multipronged surveillance strategy that drew on a network of primary care providers and primary health centers helped Singapore to slow the spread of COVID-19 (Lee, Chiew, and Khong 2020).

Further, Singapore used a network of more than 800 private-public health preparedness clinics to manage the need for high-volume testing and to train

(continued)

Box 1.5

Early Detection and Response: Prior Crisis Experience Did Not Go to Waste in Singapore and Viet Nam (*continued*)

primary care physicians in infection, prevention, and control and response and early case management. The engagement of private sector providers and the provision of free testing enabled triage and allowed the country to manage the volume of testing. However, increasing mobility, emergence of the Delta strain, and transmission of COVID-19 among migrant worker populations and hidden communities highlighted the importance of community preparedness and underscored the importance of community engagement and mobilization (Yip et al. 2021).

In Viet Nam, well-developed grassroots health systems, including primary health facilities and primary health providers, provided health education and preventive measures for COVID-19. At the same time, the country started preparing for isolation, surveillance, and management of COVID-19 well in advance of its index case (Resolve to Save Lives 2021).

Viet Nam drew on its learnings from previous epidemics to scale up contact tracing and surveillance, including 12,000 contact tracers, a national disease surveillance system, and a national public health operations center set up in 2016. Strong contact tracing and isolation coupled with swift implementation of nonpharmaceutical interventions and the use of digital media and mobile apps helped to mitigate the impact of COVID-19 in Viet Nam. A YouTube video created by the government for COVID-19 prevention went viral, with more than 32 million views (Ha et al. 2020).

On January 30, 2021, the country had fewer than 1,800 COVID-19 cases and 35 deaths. However, Viet Nam experienced several surges of COVID-19 cases, including one at the beginning of 2022. To date, the country has endured more than 11.4 million cases and more than 43,000 deaths, according to World Health Organization figures.[a] In the summer of 2021, the country had vaccinated less than 8 percent of its population, and it was one of the Southeast Asian countries with the lowest vaccination rates. However, Viet Nam promptly realized that, to address this pandemic successfully, vaccination was going to be a critical part of the response. In just four months, Viet Nam vaccinated more than 90 percent of the population (Le 2022). This experience underscores the value of having a strong surveillance system and delivering interventions such as vaccines quickly.

a. Refer to the World Health Organization COVID-19 dashboard for up-to-date figures, https://covid19.who.int/region/wpro/country/vn.

Box 1.6

A Strong Layer 2 Response to COVID-19 in the Republic of Korea

Korea is credited with having one of the world's best overall responses to COVID-19 (Dyer 2021). The country drew on lessons learned during the outbreak of the Middle East respiratory syndrome (MERS) in 2015. Despite experiencing several waves of COVID-19, Korea remains one of the greatest successes of the COVID-19 pandemic response.

(continued)

Box 1.6

A Strong Layer 2 Response to COVID-19 in the Republic of Korea (*continued*)

After identifying its first case, the country expanded the screening of incoming travelers, implemented restrictions on travel in areas with high infection rates, and imposed quarantines. The success of these containment efforts was due to expanded testing, quarantine of exposed individuals, and prompt treatment of the ill.

Korean officials initially dubbed their approach TRUST: Transparency, Robust screening and quarantine, Unique but universally applicable testing, Strict control, and Treatment (Oh 2020). Implementing TRUST required the government to focus on three fronts: testing, contact tracing, and a health-focused response with clear lines of communication and authority.

Authorities developed a smartphone app that informed users when they had been exposed to a confirmed case of COVID-19. Korea put public health authorities at the head of its COVID-19 response, which created clear lines of communication and authority in this health-focused response. Moreover, the emergency response system provided both clear lines of command and legal empowerment of local governments, melding a centralized and decentralized approach.

Korea's response was not without challenges, but the government's effort and delineation of institutional responsibilities were a marked improvement over its response to MERS in 2015. Korea's struggles with MERS led to numerous reforms that positioned it to deal with COVID-19 more effectively. By focusing on identifying and isolating individuals exposed to the COVID-19 virus, Korea was able to avoid the more draconian economic closures enacted elsewhere.

Layer 3: Advanced Case Management and Surge Response

The third layer of defense is made up of surge response and secondary and tertiary hospital interventions for cases requiring advanced case management. These interventions were on full display during the most acute stages of the COVID-19 crisis, when hospitals and other facilities became the focal points for the tremendous crush of patients severely stricken by the disease and were overwhelmed by heavy caseloads.

Even though layer 3 should be the last and, ideally, rarely needed line of defense, countries must also invest in advanced case management and surge response to ensure that there is a sufficient supply and distribution of secondary and specialized hospitals as well as critical care capacity, essential equipment and stockpiles, and surge financing to meet the extraordinary costs of a full-force epidemic. The third layer is thus a necessary and important part of the response. However, communities, countries, and the world cannot lean heavily on layer 3 to be the primary response to an outbreak.

The cost of strengthening preparedness and scaling testing is much lower than the cost of hospitalizations related to advanced treatment (Sousa-Pinto et al. 2020). One study estimated that in September 2021 the average billed charge for a complex COVID-19 hospitalization in the United States was US$317,810,[4] with state variances of between US$472,213 in Nevada to

US$131,965 in Maryland.[5] Another study examined the daily costs of inpatient care for COVID-19 in South Africa and found that "average daily costs per patient increased with the level of care" (Edoka et al. 2022, 1354). According to the study, the highest average daily cost was for care in an intensive care unit, and the lowest cost was for care in a general ward.

Investments in precrisis layers that focus on prevention and preparedness and strengthen service delivery are far smaller and ultimately more effective in preventing epidemics and their secondary impacts than investments in the final layer (building more hospital capacity and stockpiling ventilators and therapeutic drugs for COVID-19). For more on that distinction, part two of this publication examines investment—or, more accurately, underinvestment—in precrisis layers and illustrates the disproportionality of overinvesting in layer 3 in contrast to layers 1 and 2.

The response to COVID-19 forced communities and countries to rely mainly on the third layer, which, although important, is the most resource-intensive and the least effective (in terms of health outcomes) of the three layers. A focus on the third layer is reasonable and may even be unavoidable when societies are in crisis mode. However, in the absence of robust precrisis tiers, the long-term impact will ultimately overtax the health system (Waldman et al. 2020).

For an efficient post-COVID-19 response and recovery, it is crucial to focus investments on the high-impact, cost-efficient layers preceding hospitalization. Instead of reacting, especially at the more advanced stages of a health crisis, it is incumbent to act differently. Instead of reinventing, there is a need to modify existing health systems' infrastructures, create stronger linkages, and promote better collaboration and communication between and within components.

The third layer of defense includes investment in surge response and secondary and tertiary hospital interventions that require advanced case management. Early detection, containment, and treatment of cases through stronger precrisis tiers can serve a preemptive and gatekeeping function and avert congestion at secondary and tertiary facilities.

As the framework makes explicit, weak health systems with inadequate preplanning can stress health systems during epidemics and draw outsize levels of resources in the bottomless third layer. Without strong first and second layers, even health systems perceived to be stable will find themselves swamped with cases that overwhelm their capacity.

Globally, hospitals have been facing a surge in demand for critical care and a shortage of hospital beds, tests, medical equipment like ventilators, and personal protective equipment, resulting in difficult ethical choices for providers (Shortland 2020). As multiple analyses and real-time situations highlight, hospital systems worldwide were not prepared to cope with the astronomic surge in demand for critical care associated with COVID-19.

In the United States, for example, many hospitals reported experiencing financial instability because of increased expenses associated with responding to a pandemic and lower revenues from decreased use of other hospital services (United States, Department of Health and Human Services 2021). A reactive post-COVID-19 response suggests that increasing investments in the critical care capacity of hospitals, including intensive care beds, seems obvious. However, maintaining a full three-layer view helps planners to see the whole array of inherent systemic needs in a health system.

Hospitals are an important element of a well-functioning health system, and they deserve investment. However, proportionate investment is needed in layers that are used the most and that show the greatest efficiency and reach desired health outcomes.

As the threat of COVID-19 grew in many countries and regions, overwhelming hospitals, the tyranny of the urgent meant that much of COVID-19 and post-COVID-19 investments focused on providing secondary- or tertiary-level clinical care and strengthening critical care capacity. However, there is a need to shift from prioritizing costly curative services at the secondary and tertiary levels to prioritizing low-cost, high-impact approaches that emphasize prevention and early case detection and management and promoting efficient use of health services.

Cross-Cutting Elements of All Three Layers

The three layers need cross-cutting integration. They cannot operate independently. A critical cross-cutting function is surveillance and integrated health information systems, along with digital technologies. A related cross-cutting function is governance and leadership accountability. The three-layer framework emphasizes that information about health threats and responses needs to flow readily between the layers and that operatives must be accountable for cooperating across all layers and not just doing so to achieve a narrowly assigned task. Creating the incentives to work across other layers requires easy access to information across all layers.

Health Intelligence: Real-Time Surveillance and Information Systems, Strong National Laboratory Systems, and Digital Technologies

All three layers of the system should include stronger information systems and vital registration mechanisms to improve the capture and reporting of data. Having such systems and mechanisms would promote evidence-based decision-making and prioritization of resources for greater impact. A lack of early-warning systems and surveillance systems can delay the detection of outbreaks, ultimately increasing the cost of epidemics and exacerbating their severity (Bali et al. 2019; Kieny et al. 2014). These tools also assist with the identification of beneficiaries and the targeting of potentially vulnerable people.

Surveillance systems that integrate input from public health and primary health care are highly effective at detecting cases early at the community level, especially in fragile and conflict areas with limited health facilities.

Timely interventions can prevent small sparks from turning into megafires (Ratnayake et al. 2020). Surveillance and detection are cross-cutting functions across all layers. Rapid detection requires early-warning systems, community-based surveillance systems, sample collection, strong sample and patient referral, and networking among national, regional, and global laboratories in the first layer. It also depends on strong laboratories, laboratory capacity, and epidemic intelligence in the second layer.

The severity of health threats pivots on a population's vulnerability and gaps within the health system. Data and information systems can help to close those gaps. Integrating data from the public and private sectors increases the probability of detecting an emerging threat. There are many sources of data, including cell phones, electronic medical records, internet search data, satellite, and disease notification systems. Yet the greatest challenge is to share and leverage data simultaneously for stronger and more timely responses. Their integration will support the timely detection of a threat, even in settings where data systems may be slow or dysfunctional.

An estimated 30 percent of the world's data are related to health (Greene 2023), but little of that data goes to improving health, especially in low- and middle-income countries. The pandemic has shown countries how they can use digital and transformative technologies to reimagine service delivery for better human development outcomes, ranging from the rapid rollout of the COVID-19 vaccine, telemedicine services, remote learning, or virtual cash payouts for social safety nets. The COVID-19 crisis offers a compelling lesson about the need to scale up these technologies for widespread use in service delivery. Therefore, one of the key areas for countries to consider prioritizing is fortifying their digital technologies.

Although more and better-quality data are needed, data alone have no inherent value in the absence of appropriate infrastructure and a trained workforce to use it. Simply put, the infrastructure also needs to be considered so that the captured data have translational value for disease control.

Data generated during the COVID-19 pandemic suggest that containment strategies—such as reducing contact, shielding the elderly, and implementing social distancing—can drastically reduce the burden of disease, avert deaths and the need for critical care, and reduce pressure on hospitals (Branas et al. 2020).

Early crisis responses in many instances depended on how quickly systems detected a disease. COVID-19 offered a great opportunity to test the capacities of the national, regional, and global surveillance systems and whether countries had used prior outbreaks to improve their systems for the inevitable arrival of subsequent outbreaks. Some countries were able to respond quickly thanks to their well-functioning surveillance systems. Some countries learned from prior epidemics and were better prepared for the COVID-19 health crisis in terms of surveillance and mitigating measures. Others supported the health services by partnering with private sector providers. Technology was part of the pandemic's successful response in many countries. And countries that had the systems set up well before the pandemic fared better.

Having timely, complete, real-time, and accurate data at the local to global levels enables adequate prevention, detection, and response to outbreaks. Investments in these areas are no longer an option. Countries with a successful pandemic response gave priority to the efficient processing of new data. To stay abreast of the evolving situation, countries that could monitor the number of available tests, human resource needs, and amount of personal protective equipment or medications could redirect limited resources to places they were needed most.

For example, the Rwandan government relied heavily on digitization in its response to the crisis, including contact tracing, surveillance, and infection prevention and control. Rwanda's paperless Open Data Kit mobile device application was very beneficial in contact tracing. For COVID-19 surveillance, Rwandan health facilities' digital reporting surveillance systems, which regularly monitor influenza-like illnesses and severe acute respiratory infections in real time, provided an early warning of suspected COVID-19 cases.

In terms of preventing infection exposure of health care workers, Rwanda used robots for simple errands, like checking temperatures and monitoring patients. Finally, to assess the need for lockdown measures, monitoring at-risk populations, or providing focused interventions, Rwanda used a geographic information system (GIS) to monitor COVID-19 cases at the household level (IMF 2020).

Nairobi, Kenya's Silicon Savannah, used various technological solutions to stop the spread of the virus and to facilitate the spread of information on staying safe. The *Jitenge* system, named after the Swahili word for *self-isolate*, was developed to support government efforts to control the spread (Mukoa Wabuge 2021). The system supports registration at the beginning of the quarantine, be it at home or in a facility, either by the patient or a health professional. It engages the user with prompts such as reminders to report on health signs and symptoms or provide any other pertinent information. The system has been used effectively to manage home-based care, self-quarantine, conduct follow-up after isolation, and monitor the health of long-distance truck drivers.

Iceland, whose index case emerged on February 28, 2020, focused on early and extensive detection of cases by testing suspected and high-risk persons in the general population. It also used digital technology (Rakning C-19 app) to conduct contact tracing. In collaboration with the private sector (the biopharmaceutical company deCODE Genetics), Iceland continued to have one of the highest testing rates, as of June 2022.

Governance and Building Trust across All Layers

Health systems depend on the social, political, and cultural context of the countries in which they exist. The functions of all three layers are determined by the capacity for governance, expectations of people, and societal trust. One of COVID's lessons for leadership and governance is that countries need to support development of strong leadership with clearly defined roles and responsibilities, support their capacity building, support clear lines of communication, and invest in societal trust for the sustainability of a system's resilience. The relationship between governance, trust, and expectations was laid bare during the COVID-19 pandemic through the great variability in responses to the pandemic and the resulting health and economic impacts.

Many factors can explain this variation in impacts, including the age of the population (the elderly are considered high risk and have weaker immune response), the health of the population (reflected in the prevalence of risk factors and noncommunicable diseases), gross domestic product per capita, seasonality, altitude, and so on. However, these factors do not explain all of the variability of infection rates and responses to the pandemic.

Soft, intangible elements are present across countries and regions. A study published in *The Lancet* in 2022 examined SARS-CoV-2 infections and COVID-19 deaths in 177 countries (COVID-19 National Preparedness Collaborators 2022). It found that commonly used variables cannot explain 45 percent of cross-national variation in infection fatalities. Based on the data, the study suggests that if populations across the globe had had trust in their governments that was at least as high as in Denmark (which is in the 75th percentile), 13 percent fewer global infections would have occurred.

In Denmark, there is a relatively high level of trust that government policies benefit the nation and are in the interest of the public's well-being. In turn, the government trusts Danish citizens to support good relationships and societal cohesion. During the pandemic, Denmark remained united, and policies to contain the virus averted the politicization that plagued many other democracies (Bala, Behsudi, and Jaqueiry 2021). Even more astonishing, if countries had had stronger interpersonal trust, the effect would have been even larger: more than 40 percent fewer global infections would have occurred (COVID-19 National Preparedness Collaborators 2022).

As Thomas Bollyky, the lead author of the study remarked, "Trust is an area where governments can move the needle, and the fact that it outweighs traditional measures of health care capacity and pandemic preparedness should be a wakeup call for all of us as we face the ongoing pandemic and the threat of future disease outbreaks" (Thornton 2022).

Public health officials often earn and sustain trust at the local levels, even as they set national and subnational policies. Integration of "top-down" health policies with "bottom-up" engagement from communities and providers who engage directly with patients not only will enhance preventive behavior, surveillance, and risk communication but also will inform context-specific policies through collaboration.

Trust starts with a transparent exchange of information and clear communication. In a fast-moving environment where information needs are constantly evolving and basic facts are sometimes in dispute, clear communication and trust have no substitute. All countries were facing this challenge, especially as misconceptions and myths began to spread about the origins of the virus, the modes of transmission, and preventive measures. Some countries were more successful than others in communicating with their citizens, as discussed in box 1.7.

Box 1.7

Getting Ahead of COVID-19 Misinformation

"Info-demic" is a term that describes the proliferation of misinformation, and it has spared no country. Some countries, such as Kenya, were able to get ahead of it. When the first case of COVID-19 was documented in Kenya, digital media and news stations had already begun to broadcast messages to the public about how individuals could remain safe. The same platforms augmented communication on precautions that people should take.

The Kenyan Ministry of Health facilitated streamlining and harmonizing messages across the media, helping to unify the message. Communities also contributed to amplifying these efforts and creating awareness. Along with providing services, the health workforce was the key ingredient in combating misinformation and getting people back to clinics.

Conclusion

This three-layer framework has significant policy implications for future investments. While systematically filling the critical gaps in all three layers is essential, policy makers must resist the tendency to invest in crises only when they occur. As the COVID-19 pandemic has demonstrated, the first two layers of defense against disease outbreaks in many countries were found wanting during a crisis.

Further, the brunt of COVID-19 on some of the most "prepared" countries highlights a need to reduce fragmentation of health security and health care systems and to enable prioritization of foundational and integrated investments in risk reduction, preparedness, community resilience, and service delivery systems (Lal et al. 2020). Countries that have strong precrisis tiers can stop outbreaks from happening and, when they occur, can mitigate pressure on the third layer, before the crisis overwhelms the health system. While investment across all three layers is critical for resilience, investments in the first two layers and the cross-cutting issues of information, data, surveillance, and technology systems and governance are foundational and will benefit public health and health care systems during times of relative normalcy and times of crisis.

Investments in pandemic preparedness and health system resilience not only increase the chance of containing outbreaks but together enable stronger global research and response on emerging diseases and vaccine development. They also allow more targeted approaches for nonpharmaceutical interventions, which, in turn, could mitigate the social and economic consequences of lockdowns.

What remains to be worked out is how to invest. The first step is to build a vision of seamless integration of disease outbreak prevention and pandemic preparedness into an overall health system that has been built to be "emergency ready." Creating a siloed cadre of pandemic specialists in their own units is too costly and ineffective. Being prepared comes from having all three layers functioning well all the time, and this preparation happens when information is used to assess their functionality and hold them accountable for being informed and prepared all the time. Preparedness funding must be planned and built into national health systems, as it is recurrent and the needs are long term, not one-offs.

Subsequently, for efficient response and recovery, it is crucial to focus investments on the high-impact and cost-efficient precrisis layers (Burwell et al. 2020; GPMB 2021; Kieny et al. 2014; Sirleaf and Clark 2021; Sousa-Pinto et al. 2020; WHO 2018). The most impactful and cost-effective public investments are those that strengthen interventions upstream in a country's public health system—that is, enhancements in disease prevention, preparedness (especially community preparedness), early detection, and second-layer containment and mitigation capabilities.

These first two layers collectively can avert the congestion of secondary and tertiary facilities during epidemics. Investments in the precrisis tiers not only will ensure the efficiency and resilience of health systems but also will make it more likely that a post-COVID-19 world can address future health challenges effectively. Only by doing so is there a chance to break the "panic and neglect" cycle.

Notes

1. One Health refers to "a collaborative, multisectoral, and transdisciplinary approach—working at the local, regional, national, and global levels—with the goal of achieving optimal health outcomes recognizing the interconnection between people, animals, plants, and their shared environment." Refer to https://www.cdc.gov/onehealth/index.html.
2. Neglect of the cadre of public health workers is universal and to be expected for reasons rooted in human nature. When public health work succeeds, nothing visible happens. When nothing happens, resources look like they can be reallocated, and politicians will inevitably begin to propose cutting public health budgets.
3. Refer to "Strengthening Supply Chains: Delivering Life-Saving Care to Children in Need," UNICEF website, https://www.unicef.org/health/strengthening-supply-chains.
4. "National Average Charge for a Complex Hospital Stay for COVID-19 Is $317,810," FAIR Health press release, September 21, 2021. https://www.fairhealth.org/press-release/national-average-charge-for-a-complex-hospital-stay-for-covid-19-is-317-810-fair-health-finds.
5. "COVID-19 Cost Tracker: States by the Numbers," FAIR Health website, https://www.fairhealth.org/states-by-the-numbers/covid19-heatmap.

References

Africa CDC (Centres for Disease Control and Prevention). 2021. "The Critical Role of Community Health Workers in COVID-19 Vaccine Roll Out." Africa CDC, Addis Ababa, July 26, 2021. https://africacdc.org/download/the-critical-role-of-community-health-workers-in-covid-19-vaccine-roll-out/.

Africa CDC (Centres for Disease Control and Prevention). 2022. "Role of CHWs in Pandemic Preparedness and Response: Discussion on the Integration of Community Health Workforce into the Broader Health System." Africa CDC, Addis Ababa, March 23, 2022. https://africacdc.org/wp-content/uploads/2022/03/Concept -note-Role-of-CHWs-in-Pandemic-Preparedness-and-Response-Webinar.pdf.

Bala, Analisa R., Adam Behsudi, and Anna Jaqueiry. 2021. "A Life Well Lived." *IMF Finance and Development*, December 2021. https://www.imf.org/Publications /fandd/issues/2021/12/Countries-lessons-life-well-lived-Bala-Behsudi-Jaquiery.

Bali, Sulzhan Rameshwari, Andre L. Carletto, John Paul Clark, Sara Halstead Hersey, Alicia J. Hetzner, Hadia Nazem Samaha, Nicholas George Studzinski, and Mazvita Zanamwe. 2019. *Lessons Learned in Financing Rapid Response to Recent Epidemics in West and Central Africa: A Qualitative Study.* Washington, DC: World Bank Group. http://documents.worldbank.org/curated/en/241811559646029471/Lessons -Learned-in-Financing-Rapid-Response-to-Recent-Epidemics-in-West-and -Central-Africa-A-Qualitative-Study.

Bo, Yacong, Cui Guo, Changqing Lin, Yiqian Zeng, Hao Bi Li, Yumiao Zhang, Md Shakhaoat Hossain, Jimmy W. M. Chan, David W. Yeung, Kin On Kwok, Samuel Y. S. Wong, Alexis K. H. Lau, and Xiang Qian La. 2021. "Effectiveness of Non-pharmaceutical Interventions on COVID-19 Transmission in 190 Countries from 23 January to 13 April 2020." *International Journal of Infectious Diseases* 102 (January 2021): 247–53. https://www.sciencedirect.com/science/article/pii /S1201971220322700#sec0035.

Branas, Charles C., Andrew Rundle, Sen Pei, Wan Yang, Brendan G. Carr, Sarah Sims, Alexis Zebrowski, Ronan Doorley, Neil Schluger, James W. Quinn, and Jeffrey Shaman. 2020. "Flattening the Curve before It Flattens Us: Hospital Critical Care Capacity Limits and Mortality from Novel Coronavirus (SARS-CoV-2) Cases in US Counties." *medRxiv*, posted April 6, 2020. https://www.medrxiv.org/content /10.1101/2020.04.01.20049759v1.

Burwell, Sylvia Mathews, Frances Fragos Townsend, Thomas J. Bollyky, and Stewart M. Patrick. 2020. *Improving Pandemic Preparedness: Lessons from COVID-19.* Independent Task Force Report 78. New York: Council on Foreign Relations.

Collins, Téa, Svetlana Akselrod, Ashley Bloomfield, Amiran Gamkrelidze, Zsuzsanna Jakab, and Erika Placella. 2020. "Rethinking the COVID-19 Pandemic: Back to Public Health." *Annals of Global Health* 86 (1): PMC7546103.

COVID-19 National Preparedness Collaborators. 2022. "Pandemic Preparedness and COVID-19: An Exploratory Analysis of Infection and Fatality Rates, and Contextual Factors Associated with Preparedness in 177 Countries, from Jan. 1, 2020, to Sept. 30, 2021." *The Lancet* 399 (10334): 1489–512.

Dalberg. 2021. "Leveraging Covid-19 Investments to Strengthen Health Systems in Africa." Dalberg, New York, June 2021. https://dalberg.com/wp-content/uploads /2021/06/Strengthening-Health-Systems-in-Africa-Report.pdf.

Dyer, Paul. 2021. "Policy and Institutional Responses to COVID-19: South Korea." *Brookings Research,* June 14, 2021. https://www.brookings.edu/articles/policy-and -institutional-responses-to-covid-19-south-korea/.

Edoka, Ijeoma, Heather Fraser, Lise Jamieson, Gesine Meyer-Rath, and Winfrida Mdewa. 2022. "Inpatient Care Costs of COVID-19 in South Africa's Public Healthcare System." *International Journal of Health Policy and Management* 11 (8): 1354–61. doi:10.34172/ijhpm.2021.24.

Gatome-Munyua, Agnes, Henok Yeman, Allyson English, and Nivetha Kanna. 2020. "Coordinating, Financing, and Paying for COVID-19 Health Services: A Synthesis of Lessons and Best Practices from Country Experience." Joint Learning Network for Universal Health Coverage, September 2020. https://www.jointlearning network.org/wp-content/uploads/2021/03/JLN-PHC-Financing-and-Payment -Case-Studies.pdf.

Global Innovation Hub for Improving Value in Health. 2020. "Value-Based Health Care in the Midst of the COVID-19 Pandemic Response: Lessons from Health System Innovations Responding to the Pandemic in 12 Countries." Global Innovation Hub for Improving Value in Health, Riyadh. https://www.g20hub .org/files/Value-Based-Health-Care-in-the-Midst-of-the-COVID-19-Pandemic -Response-1.pdf.

GPMB (Global Preparedness Monitoring Board). 2021. *From Worlds Apart to a World Prepared: Global Preparedness Monitoring Board Report 2021.* Geneva: World Health Organization.

Greene, Linnie. 2023. "Taking the Pulse of Data and Technology in Modern Healthcare." *Arcadia,* September 6, 2023. https://arcadia.io/resources/taking-the -pulse-of-data-and-technology-in-modern-healthcare#:~:text=Today%2C% 20approximately%2030%25%20of%20the,for%20healthcare%20will%20 reach%2036%25.

Ha, Bui Thi Thu, La Ngoc Quang, Tolib Mirzoev, Nguyen Trong Tai, Pham Quang Thai, and Phung Cong Dinh. 2020. "Combating the COVID-19 Epidemic: Experiences from Vietnam." *International Journal of Environmental Research and Public Health* 17 (9): 3125.

IMF (International Monetary Fund). 2020. "Rwanda Harnesses Technology to Fight COVID-19, Drive Recovery." *IMF News,* August 6, 2020. https://www.imf.org/en /News/Articles/2020/08/06/na080620-rwanda-harnesses-technology-to -fight-covid-19-drive-recovery.

Jung, Julia, Tine Mejdell Larsen, Abdifatah Hussein Beledi, Emi Takahashi, Abdirahman Omer Ahmed, Jenny Reid, and Ida Anine Kongelf. 2024. "Community-Based Surveillance Programme Evaluation Using the Platform Nyss Implemented by the Somali Red Crescent Society—A Mixed Methods Approach." *Conflict and Health* 18: Art. 20. https://conflictandhealth.biomedcentral.com/articles/10.1186 /s13031-024-00578-5.

Kieny, Marie-Paule, David B. Evans, Gerard Schmets, and Sowmya Kadandale. 2014. "Health-System Resilience: Reflections on the Ebola Crisis in Western Africa." *Bulletin of the World Health Organization* 92 (12): 850. doi:10.2471/BLT.14.149278.

Kovacevic, Rialda, Marisi Mwencha, Ahmed Ouma, Moji Christianah Adeyeye, Olamide Folorunso, Ken Legins, and Souleymane Kone. 2021. "Challenges and Opportunities of Supply Chain in the Time of COVID-19." Health, Nutrition, and Population Global Practice Knowledge Brief, June 2021, World Bank, Washington, DC. https://openknowledge.worldbank.org/server/api/core/bitstreams/487c090e -033a-5b19-aa89-a29bb7258e04/content.

Lal, Arush, Ngozi A. Erondu, David L. Heymann, Githinji Gitahi, and Robert Yates. 2020. "Fragmented Health Systems in COVID-19: Rectifying the Misalignment between Global Health Security and Universal Health Coverage." *The Lancet* 397 (10268): 61–67. doi:10.1016/S0140-6736(20)32228-5.

Le, Lam. 2022. "Vietnam Vaccinates 90% of Its Population against COVID-19." *Gavi's Vaccines Work* (blog), February 28, 2022. https://www.gavi.org/vaccineswork /vietnam-vaccinates-90-its-population-against-covid-19.

Lee, Vernon J., Calvin J. Chiew, and Wwi Xin Khong. 2020. "Interrupting Transmission of COVID-19: Lessons from Containment Efforts in Singapore." *Journal of Travel Medicine* 27 (3): taaa039. doi:10.1093/jtm/taaa039.

Marani, Marco, Gabriel G. Katul, William K. Pan, and Anthony J. Parolari. 2021. "Intensity and Frequency of Extreme Novel Epidemics." *Proceedings of the National Academy of Sciences* 118 (35): e2105482118. https://doi.org/10.1073/pnas .2105482118.

Mukoa Wabuge, Esther. 2021. "JLN Kenya: Facilitating Joint Learning between National and County Health Authorities in the Fight against COVID-19." Joint Learning Network for Universal Health Coverage. https://www.jointlearningnetwork.org

/news/jln-kenya-facilitating-joint-learning-between-national-and-county -health-authorities-in-the-fight-against-covid-19/.

Oh, Seung-Youn. 2020. "South Korea's Success against COVID-19." *Regulatory Review*, May 14, 2020. https://www.theregreview.org/2020/05/14/oh-south-korea-success -against-covid-19/.

Pires, Fernanda. 2021. "How Countries on Five Continents Responded to the Pandemic, Helping Shape Future of Health Policy." *Michigan News* (University of Michigan), April 19, 2021. https://news.umich.edu/how-countries-on-five-continents -responded-to-the-pandemic-helping-shape-future-of-health-policy/.

Ratnayake, Ruwan, Meghan Tammaro, Amanda Tiffany, Anine Kongelf, Jonathan A. Polonsky, and Amanda McClelland. 2020. "People-Centred Surveillance: A Narrative Review of Community-Based Surveillance among Crisis-Affected Populations." *The Lancet Planetary Health* 4 (10): e483–e495.

Resolve to Save Lives. 2021. "Epidemics That Didn't Happen: Case Study; COVID-19 in Senegal." Resolve to Save Lives, New York. https://preventepidemics.org /epidemics-that-didnthappen/covid-19-senegal/.

Shortland, Neil. 2020. "Doctors Are Making Life-and-Death Choices over Coronavirus Patients—It Could Have Long-Term Consequences for Them." *The Conversation,* April 6, 2020. https://theconversation.com/doctors-are-making-life-and-death -choices-over-coronavirus-patients-it-could-have-long-term-consequences-for -them-134728.

Sirleaf, Ellen Johnson, and Helen Clark. 2021. "Report of the Independent Panel for Pandemic Preparedness and Response: Making COVID-19 the Last Pandemic." *The Lancet* 398 (10295): 101–03. https://www.thelancet.com/journals/lancet /article/PIIS0140-6736(21)01095-3/fulltext.

Sousa-Pinto, Bernardo, João A. Fonseca, Altamiro Costa-Pereira, and Francisco N. Rocha-Gonçalves. 2020. "Is Scaling-Up COVID-19 Testing Cost-Saving?" *medRχiv*, posted March 27, 2020. https://doi.org/10.1101/2020.03.22.20041137.

Swanson, Robert Chad, Rifat Atun, Allan Best, Arvind Betigeri, Francisco de Campos, Somsak Chunharas, Tea Collins, Graeme Currie, Stephen Jan, David McCoy, Francis Omaswa, David Sanders, Thiagarajan Sundararaman, and Wim Van Damme. 2015. "Strengthening Health Systems in Low-Income Countries by Enhancing Organizational Capacities and Improving Institutions." *Global Health* 11 (2015): Art. 5. https://doi.org/10.1186/s12992-015-0090-3.

Thornton, Jacqui. 2022. "Covid-19: Trust in Government and Other People Linked with Lower Infection Rate and Higher Vaccination Uptake." *BMJ* 376: o292. doi:10.1136/bmj.o292.

United Kingdom, FCDO (Foreign, Commonwealth, and Development Office). 2021. "Health Systems Strengthening for Global Health Security and Universal Health Coverage." FCDO Position Paper, UK FCDO, London, December 2021. https:// assets.publishing.service.gov.uk/media/61b093eae90e0704423dc07c/Health -Systems-Strengthening-Position-Paper.pdf.

United States, CDC (Centers for Disease Control and Prevention). 2020. "10 Essential Public Health Services." US CDC, Atlanta, GA. https://www.cdc.gov /publichealthgateway/publichealthservices/essentialhealthservices.html.

United States, Department of Health and Human Services. 2021. "Hospitals Reported That the COVID-19 Pandemic Has Significantly Strained Health Care Delivery." Results of a National Pulse Survey, Office of the US Inspector General, Washington, DC, February 22–26, 2021. https://oig.hhs.gov/oei/reports/OEI-09-21-00140.pdf.

Waldman, Annie, Al Shaw, Ash Ngu, and Sean Campbell. 2020. "Are Hospitals Near Me Ready for Coronavirus? Here Are Nine Different Scenarios." *ProPublica*, March 17, 2020. https://projects.propublica.org/graphics/covid-hospitals.

WHO (World Health Organization). 2018. *Building the Economic Case for Primary Health Care: A Scoping Review*. Geneva: WHO.

WHO (World Health Organization). 2020a. *Global Spending on Health: Weathering the Storm.* Geneva: WHO, December 2020. https://www.who.int/publications/i /item/9789240017788.

WHO (World Health Organization). 2020b. "Role of Primary Care in the COVID-19 Response." WHO, Regional Office for the Western Pacific, Geneva. https://apps .who.int/iris/handle/10665/331921.

WHO (World Health Organization). 2021. "21st Century Health Challenges: Can the Essential Public Health Functions Make a Difference?" Discussion Paper. WHO, Geneva. https://www.who.int/publications/i/item/9789240038929.

World Bank. 2017. *From Panic and Neglect to Investing in Health Security: Financing Pandemic Preparedness at a National Level.* Washington, DC: World Bank.

World Bank. 2022. *Change Cannot Wait: Building Resilient Health Systems in the Shadow of COVID-19.* Washington, DC: World Bank. https://openknowledge.worldbank.org /handle/10986/38233.

Yip, Wanfren, Lixia Ge, Andy Hau Yan Ho, Bee Hoon Heng, and Woan Shin Tan. 2021. "Building Community Resilience beyond COVID-19: The Singapore Way." *The Lancet Regional Health–Western Pacific* 7 (February): 100091.

Zhao, Feng, Sulzhan Bali, Rialda Kovacevic, and Jeff Weintraub. 2021. "A Three-Layer System to Win the War against COVID-19 and Invest in Health Systems of the Future." *BMJ Global Health* 6 (12): e007365.

2

An Implementation Pathway to Build Resilience in Health System Layers

David Bishai and Karima Saleh

IN SUMMARY

This chapter describes pathways to building health system resilience—that is, a system's ability to respond to crises and to adapt and learn from internal and external shocks.

- Postponing investments in resilience threatens efficiency. The tension between resilience and efficiency comes from an inappropriate focus on short-term results.

- Investing in a resilient public health system not only generates benefits for a crisis in the far-off future but also furthers the short-term achievement of the Sustainable Development Goals.

- There is no need to create new "resilience agencies" and "resilience workers." The current health workforce is available and desperately in need of attention and support. Helping health workers to perform their essential functions better is a step to achieving resilience.

- Using measurements of essential public health functions (EPHFs) in a continuous quality improvement paradigm can improve resilience in the health system; moreover, recognizing the relationship between EPHFs and resilience opens the door to a vast toolkit produced by decades of work on EPHFs.

- The workforce of public health professionals needs to be the focal point for measuring EPHFs—that is, the way these functions are financed, informed, and governed.

- The practical measurement of resilience supports accountable investments in resilience. For example, resilience is measured in terms of the health system's ability to rely on partnerships and trust so that it can be aware of and responsive to possible challenges and needs.

- The EPHF quality improvement framework is the foundation of multiple efforts to form checklists and performance improvement plans for public health. The practical tools used to improve EPHFs align with an agenda of improving resilience. The full program to build resilience has the following elements: (a) a high-level commitment to build and sustain resilience; (b) embedded teams of resilience measurement and performance improvement squads marshaled

(continued)

IN SUMMARY *(continued)*

from the public health cadre at peripheral, middle, and central levels; (c) collaborative and participatory consensus by the affected public health cadre on which resilience measures to assess; (d) ongoing, perpetual cycles of resilience measurement, feedback, and planning for improvement by performance improvement squads; and (e) secure funding and financing mechanisms to sustain or stabilize the system.

Introduction

Resilience is a highly desirable property of all systems. Crises are common, and the ability to handle a crisis is a necessity, not a luxury. Resilience refers to a system's ability to respond to crises and to adapt and learn from internal and external shocks (Barasa, Cloete, and Gilson 2017; Kruk et al. 2017; Meyer et al. 2020; Thomas et al. 2020). In a framework of three layers—where layer 1 focuses on maintaining population health, layer 2 focuses on responding to early stages of disease, and layer 3 focuses on responding to late stages of disease—all layers need to be resilient. Building resilience must be a daily investment across the system even in ordinary times; it is not something to start after a crisis breaks (World Bank 2022).

Yet in ordinary times it is easy to deprioritize resilience investment on the grounds of short-term efficiency. It is all too common for budget-makers to reassign staff and resources from activities that should be part of the normal routine (but also considered as resilience activity) to achieve short-term gains.

For example, budgets seldom provide support for district health officials to cultivate links with community leaders and nongovernmental organizations or to support a bottom-up participatory planning process. Partnerships are important to build community trust and are an important ingredient in providing access to services and sharing information. Given budget constraints, community liaison staff might be considered a luxury and be replaced by health care workers who can provide direct medical care. This substitution happens all the time, but it is based on an incorrect view of long-run efficiency.

There is a myth that resilience only pays off during a crisis and carries no benefit during ordinary times. This chapter urges systems to measure resilience in terms of their ability to rely on partnerships and trust and to be aware and responsive. The immediate benefits of partnerships and trust are a "resilience dividend" that pays off every day. Realizing that resilience in health systems corresponds to essential public health functions ties resilience to a specific subset of the health workforce (that is, persons in the public health profession). There are decades of experience in getting the public health professional workforce to do its job, which is and always has been the work of resilience.

The staff responsible for essential public health functions are the public health specialists assigned to national, regional, and district-level health departments.

EPHF professionals (a) assess health and health threats, (b) engage the community in developing policy responses, and (c) find solutions to arising health problems. Essential public health functions are defined and contextualized locally and are used to develop metrics and performance plans that build these capabilities. An EPHF-strengthening agenda is a resilience-building agenda that pays dividends across all layers and all geographic levels of the health system. It focuses on upstream interventions that promote health and prevent disease for the entire community.

Defining Resilience

In 2019 Turenne and her coauthors identified 41 definitions for health system resilience in the published literature and synthesized them to a common core: "Health systems resilience emphasizes the capacity of health systems to maintain their essential functions during a crisis" (Turenne et al. 2019, 171).

The Turenne definition reflects a common view that resilience is a property best revealed by crisis, which may be generated through everyday challenges or more severe factors, such as pandemics or natural disasters. However, resilience is attractive even in the absence of a crisis, as it is likely to prevent a crisis from escalating.

Kruk et al. (2017) focus on five characteristics of resilience, claiming that a resilient system is aware, diverse, self-regulating, integrated, and adaptive. Similarly, Blanchet et al. (2017) observe that resilience requires the capacity to manage knowledge, cope with uncertainty, engage in interdependency, and develop legitimate contextual norms. Boiling it down even further, resilience means that a system can "absorb" knowledge, diverse perspectives, and shocks and then "adapt" by marshaling resources and assets and solving new challenges (Biddle, Wahedi, and Bozorgmehr 2020).

Building Resilience Requires Investment in Core Capabilities

There is a misconception that resilience must incur the expense of redundant and idle resources waiting for a crisis. Redundancy is one pathway to resilience, but resilience does not always need to be achieved by padded payrolls, large stockpiles, and extra everything.

For example, building partnerships and trust with a community is an everyday job under the EPHFs because such relationships can help to achieve results in communities that adopt health-promoting interventions (for example, child immunization, growth monitoring). Building trust before a crisis pays off when a crisis requires the urgent mobilization of community facilitators, in-kind resources, facilities, and goodwill. Because of the high cost of maintaining excess staff, capital, and supplies at all times, a more reasonable approach to resilience is to build partnerships and prepare flexible mechanisms and plans to hire or relocate internal staff rapidly or form public-private partnerships and procure supplies, including outsourcing or leasing, if needed in a crisis. At the very least, building resilience requires administrative surge capacity to execute procurement, hiring, and budgeting rapidly.

In Ghana, for example, decentralized levels did not have the autonomy to hire and fire health workers. At Ghana Health Services, the human resource directorate had to contend with the lack of a standardized human resource information system. Ghana adopted several strategies to address these challenges: (a) improving health worker retention in the public sector; (b) redressing inequitable distribution of health workers; (c) improving access to health workers; and (d) improving competencies and staffing distribution (Saleh 2013). For example, a discrete-choice experiment by Kruk et al. (2010) found that a "supportive management" environment at the facility level in rural areas (including opportunities for career development) was considered a top incentive that would motivate health workers to work in those areas. To achieve this end, interventions may be required to give existing facility managers more management capacity and autonomy. Box 2.1 describes Ghana's approach to capacity assessment.

A complementary approach devotes some workforce activity to strengthening core public health capabilities every day because doing so helps to realize broad people-centered health objectives in normal times as well as in crisis times. Core public health capabilities build partnerships between the health organization and the community and improve the ability of staff to communicate, to be trusted, and to acquire and make sense of health data (DeSalvo and Kadakia 2021; DeSalvo et al. 2016).

Resilience requires years of investment in human and social capital. A more short-term approach is not feasible. Resilience investments can take the form of building institutional norms around maintaining and using health data systems coupled with staff trained to turn data into policy-relevant information. Resilience investments can be made in training and retaining qualified staff so that adaptive skills are honed and ready in the event of a crisis. Core public health capabilities support service delivery even in the absence of a crisis because they make the organization data-driven, people-centered, and thus tied to a community's goals and able to rely on its assets in ordinary and extraordinary times (Bishai et al. 2015).

In Tanzania, a self-assessment of public health capability found that the allocation of human resources at the district level did not follow a needs-based logic that would address gaps in equity. Two regional assessments showed wide and unexplained variations in per capita budget allocation across local areas (Couttolenc 2016). Budget allocation rules and formulas had been in place for several years, seeking to redress historical inequities. Unfortunately, the equity allocation formula applied only to the nonpersonnel budget and not to the personnel budget, which generally is a significant part of the budget. Budgetary reform is needed to create incentives for staff to remain where they are needed. Assessment is a precondition for policy reform, and ongoing, regular assessments can help to monitor the impact of policy reform.

> **Box 2.1**
>
> ### Capabilities Assessment of District and Regional Health Authorities: A Case from Ghana
>
> Ghana conducted an assessment of capabilities at the central, regional, district, and facility levels and used that information to create a plan to improve performance. The assessment was based on information from 7 regional health authorities and 26 district health authorities.
>
> Information was gathered in an in-country consultative workshop in three ways. First, the study tabulated and analyzed the frequency and distribution of responses to 78 questions about the different functions or dimensions of decentralization. Second, participants were encouraged to provide comments and details about the questions asked. And third, the discussions held during the group sessions and the final debate were organized and summarized to highlight major findings.
>
> A preliminary assessment was conducted of strengths and weaknesses for decentralizing particular functions to different levels of the health system, based on the rapid assessment conducted after the workshop. It would be useful to pursue this exercise using more detailed data from Ghana's local political bodies (known as district assemblies), as such information would help to improve planning and the decentralization process.
>
> However, the 2006 Ghana public expenditure tracking survey found various problems in decentralized resource management at the central and district assembly levels, including inconsistencies in financial data regarding transfers from central government to districts, substantial delays in effecting these transfers, inconsistent recordkeeping at the district level, poor accountability of funds received and significant leakages, and weak overall managerial capacity. The survey findings showed that local governments suffered from significant weaknesses regarding their devolved responsibilities.
>
> Ideally, a health system could maintain ongoing, regular cycles of self-assessment while planning ways to improve. However, outside support can catalyze a process of self-assessment that moves from having no self-assessments to having one cycle and then to having ongoing, regular cycles. Ghana's experience shows that tools exist. When used, those tools can highlight weaknesses in specific geographies and across specific capabilities, giving rise to more informed action of reform and institution building (Couttolenc 2012).

A pandemic preparedness plan and adequate capacity to conduct epidemiological surveillance response are critical for a quick response when needed. The Philippines was not ready for the COVID-19 pandemic, as it faced a critical shortage of epidemiologists for managing a community-based surveillance system. Several months into the pandemic, the country struggled to catch up and had to rely on more costly measures, such as enhanced community quarantine through city and regional lockdowns (Monsod and Gochoco-Bautista 2021). While many neighboring countries imposed targeted lockdowns after the initial phases, the Philippines imposed wider lockdowns between March 15 and April 30, 2020, for Metro Manila, which were then expanded to Luzon. This crisis response was costly. The failure to be resilient in the face of the pandemic had many causes, but the human resource constraints were paramount, with shortages of workers skilled in public health.

Relative to the entire health workforce, the public health management component is extremely small. Spending on public health core capability accounts for a few percentages, at most, of any national health budget. Improving this one sliver of the health workforce can pay far-reaching dividends, as public health managers can help their more numerous counterparts in direct service delivery to gain resilience capabilities.

Achieving Resilience by Measuring Essential Public Health Functions

Realizing that the public health workforce equals the resilience workforce and helping health workers to perform their essential functions creates an agenda for achieving resilience. The implementation tools developed for measuring EPHFs and improving performance are available for restoring a more resilient health system and realizing an immediate resilience dividend.

EPHF metrics are useful for putting the concept of resilience into practice (Martin-Moreno et al. 2016). The focal point for EPHF measurement is the workforce of public health professionals and the way they are financed, informed, and governed. It is time to consider the staff of public health departments as resilience professionals and to reorient them to their core mission of carrying out EPHFs. There is no need to create new "resilience agencies" and "resilience workers." The existing workforce is available and desperately in need of attention and support.

In the late 1990s, EPHF frameworks were developed by the US Centers for Disease Control and Prevention (United States, CDC) and the World Health Organization (WHO) to codify expectations for the essential functions that public health departments must do. The EPHF framework is the foundation of multiple efforts to create checklists and performance improvement plans for public health. There is a remarkable confluence between the elements of resilience in a "resilience index" (Kruk et al. 2017) and the essential public health functions. Thus, the practical tools used to improve EPHFs align with an agenda of improving resilience.

Table 2.1 offers a skeleton outline of the essential public health functions. For example, EPHF 7—link people to personal health services—encompasses capability in health care financing, overcoming stigma, and managing or contracting with health service delivery agencies. Any contextual application of the framework would tailor the details to the type of public health worker involved and to the local system architecture.

Communication is a function of resilience that will vary across settings. In 2020, Thailand, for example, promoted the use of teleconsultation services for nonurgent, stable chronic cases and provided drug delivery services. It also conducted an online survey to monitor perceptions about information,

Table 2.1   Comparison of Essential Public Health Functions and the Resilience Index

Essential public health functions	Resilience index
1. Monitor the health status of a population	Awareness—knows risks and population Awareness—knows health service utilization
2. Diagnose and investigate health problems and hazards	Presence of an active epidemiologic surveillance system
3. Inform, educate, and empower people about health issues	Breadth of functioning communication channels Platforms for dialogue with the community
4. Enforce laws and regulations that protect health	Agreements on delegation of authority in crises
5. Mobilize partnerships to identify and solve health problems	Engagement with citizens and communities to build trust
6. Develop policies and plans to support health needs	Promotion of rapid decision-making
7. Link people to personal health services	Link between health care provision to public health Coordination of primary and referral care
8. Assure a competent public health workforce	Availability of district staff with public health training
9. Evaluate the quality of public health programs	Evaluation to improve
10. Research new solutions to health problems	Management capacity of district health teams

Sources: The column on the left is based on Khaleghian and Das Gupta 2005. The column on the right is based on Kruk et al. 2017.

misinformation, and knowledge, attitudes, and behaviors of residents regarding COVID-19 and to assess communication capacity. The government deployed more than 1 million village health volunteers to disseminate and amplify messages in communities (Haldane et al. 2021). The system proved to be resilient, with effective precrisis preparedness and appropriate responses during the crisis, which limited unnecessary and costly tertiary-level treatments.

Recognizing the correspondence between EPHFs and resilience opens the door to a vast toolkit from decades of work on EPHF investment. This recognition can advance the cause of resilience without having to create new tools from scratch. The next section discusses how EPHF measurements can be combined with continuous quality improvement efforts to improve resilience in the health system.

Implementing a Pathway for Resilience

The truth of the proverb "what gets measured gets managed" depends on how measurements are used. Acquiring measurements of a system's resilience is only one of many steps. Ultimately, the measurements must be used to drive performance, which requires building commitments, staffing, trust, and a culture of quality.

Measurements are necessary, but not sufficient. They need to emerge from and feed a quality feedback loop where all members of the system are striving to improve their capability. In the absence of an institutional commitment to resilience and a widely shared consensus supporting more resilience, simply having measurements and checklists will not succeed. It is necessary to combine measurements with systems: staff need to be held accountable for responding to the measurements and need to have the authority and the means to improve the system.

With managers and professionals attuned, empowered, and incentivized to seek improved resilience, the measurements can help to spur policy changes, staffing changes, and strategic investments. However, if the resilience measures are filed away or kept at headquarters, they will be less effective.

The full program to build resilience has the following elements:

- A high-level commitment to build and sustain resilience;
- Embedded teams of resilience measurement and performance improvement squads marshaled from the public health cadre at peripheral, middle, and central levels;
- Collaborative and participatory consensus by the affected public health cadre on which resilience measures to assess;
- Ongoing and perpetual cycles of resilience measurement, feedback, and planning for improvement by performance improvement squads; and
- Secure funding and financing mechanisms to sustain or stabilize the system.

This section discusses these elements sequentially.

High-Level Commitment

Like any change in a human system, a program to build resilience will threaten people who are comfortable with the status quo. A high-level commitment to building resilience will help to counter the inevitable resistance that can scuttle any initiative. The power dynamics vary by context, but, in general, no natural forces rally for resilience. Resilience is abstract and difficult to see. In the face of tight budgets, funds are rarely allocated toward "resilience" activities, and, when they are, the funds that go to resilience and quality are some of the easiest to cut because no constituency feels the immediate harm of eroding system preparedness.

Without a high-level champion, resilience will disappear from the agenda. Furthermore, the tension between efficiency and resilience prepares a ready-made, though short-sighted, argument toward putting off investments and initiatives in resilience. Leaders need to understand that an immediate "resilience dividend" will ripple throughout the health system as it becomes more aware, self-regulating, and community engaged.

For a resilience initiative to survive, it needs to be more than an idea embraced by a small task force. Staff turnover can mean that even small steps are tentative and not sustainable. Committing a system to quality and resilience requires multiple redundant layers of institution building and even statutory reform so that the initiative can outlive the tenure of a few enlightened reformers.

Resilience Centurions

The confluence between resilience and public health practice means that there is no need to recruit and pay a new cadre of resilience workers—the system already has them in the form of public health professionals. However, these public health professionals have often been co-opted to perform tasks in service delivery. A service delivery paradigm rooted in measuring counts of vaccines given, screening tests conducted, and patients counseled has denied many public health professionals the skills and even the consciousness to realize the full scope of their practice.

Catalytic investments can awaken the preexisting public health workforce without a commitment to large-scale creation of new job postings. The Roman Army was administered at a ratio of 1 centurion per 100 legionnaires. Similarly, a resilience agenda can be built on retooling or hiring 1 percent of the public health workforce as "centurions" to collect data, share report cards, and coach fellow workers based on data about the public health resilience of the public health departments that the workers create together. The 1:100 ratio of supervisors to workers can be adapted to local settings. The staffing ratio needs to permit at least monthly contact that could combine assessment, mentoring, and coaching.

These EPHF quality supervisors (the "centurions") need to be seasoned professionals who know the practice of public health and have a coaching mindset built on respect for and service to colleagues. They are needed at central, middle, and peripheral units of the public health system. The amount of staffing should be enough to maintain the listening, measurement, and coaching that can help public health workers to improve their EPHF performance continuously and strengthen the resilience of the system.

Financial considerations are modest because, numerically, EPHF quality supervisors will represent only 1 percent of the public health workforce. The need to create new posts is small because these public health workers fill posts that are already budgeted.

In many countries, human resource strategies have created such posts and allocated positions for district health officers and assistant district health officers. Formalizing the expectation that a health officer's scope of work includes continuous quality improvement of the public health workforce may be necessary to motivate more activity in this area. In other countries, the district health officer post remains unfilled, or the public health worker is consumed by other tasks, is untrained, or is underbudgeted to fulfill his or her terms of reference.

The resilience centurions need to be recruited and trained or retrained. Training institutions could include local schools of public health, divisions of a national or provincial health ministry, or national public health institutes (Frieden 2022). The length of training could be as short as a few weeks or as long as a few years, depending on the context. The competencies that EPHF quality supervisors need to acquire can be drawn from lists that public health educators have already compiled. These competencies include data analysis, leadership, communication, partnering, management, finance, advocacy, and ethics.

In some settings, the EPHF supervisors' job posts will need to be created or reconfigured. The terms of reference for what they will do revolve around becoming coaches for their 100 or so public health staff. They will collect locally sourced measurements of EPHFs and repeatedly share these measurements directly with workers to develop and execute collaboratively a locally feasible performance improvement plan. They need to develop the trust of their team members as aids to professional growth and avoid the pitfall of becoming disciplinarians or quality police. They also need to develop cycles of measurement that can show quick wins. To quiet the ever-present concerns for efficiency, the EPHF quality supervisors' data can show how progress on EPHF measures support service delivery goals.

This workforce will need to be supported with training opportunities. For example, an update of the Lancet Human Resources Commission for the post-COVID-19 era found disparities in public health training. Between 2008 and 2018, the number of schools of public health grew 100 percent in high-income countries but only 10 percent in Sub-Saharan Africa, from 46 to 51 (Frenk et al. 2022).

Consensus on Measures

Resilience defies a cookie-cutter approach because each context comes with a preexisting set of strengths and cultural values as well as preexisting assignments of who is responsible for which elements of public health practice. Consequently, measurement tools for EPHFs will need to be adapted to the local context.

Developing measures will begin with open-ended listening to the concerns of local staff about resilience and local enabling and obstructive factors. The listening phase collects insightful suggestions about ways to improve performance and the reactions to suggestions about which domains of the EPHF list are relevant at the local level; this phase allows local workers to suggest modifying or adding elements from previous prototypes of the EPHF checklist.

Pilot testing the checklist is helpful for determining its ability to collect indicators of EPHFs and resilience. Showing workers the output of the checklist can initiate a new conversation about the priorities for a performance improvement plan that is feasible and has high impact at the local level. A cycle of coaching conversations and resource mobilization can help staff to enact their top priorities in the performance improvement plan.

The number of possible areas of performance improvement is large, and working on them all at once is not feasible. Local stakeholders' statements about prioritization should carry a lot of weight, but they will need to be tempered by the realities of what the available resources can achieve in the short term. Without short-term results, enthusiasm will wane.

An online appendix contains a curated bibliography of publicly available checklists for measuring EPHFs (refer to annex 2A). Past EPHF checklists contain scalable questions related to each of these elements.

Ongoing Feedback

When staff in public health are allowed to see their performance scores and are asked to respond by making performance improvement plans, the plans are better and the execution of the plans is more likely. As Jean-Jacques Rousseau once put it, "Obedience to the law one has prescribed oneself is freedom." Making one's own performance improvement plan and finding supportive resources is a pathway to tremendous job satisfaction if resources are forthcoming. Box 2.2 illustrates the process in three Southern African countries.

Box 2.2

Using Tools to Build Capacity of Layer 1 at District Health Departments in Angola, Botswana, and Mozambique

For more than two decades, efforts have been under way to build a system of regular self-assessment, follow-up, and coaching to improve the performance of national, state, and local public health departments. Regional offices of the World Health Organization (WHO) have developed checklists adapted for the Americas, Europe, the Middle East, South Asia, and Western Pacific. Many past efforts were one-off measurement exercises that led to national and regional reports but did not translate into ongoing efforts in continuous performance improvement. Having a professional workforce assess its own performance against expected benchmarks and then receive regular coaching and follow-up is a well-established method to institutionalize better quality. Three countries in Southern Africa launched initiatives to adapt international essential public health function (EPHF) checklist tools to local contexts and pilot them for use as regular guides to district-level performance improvement plans.

- *Step 1: national stakeholders meetings for consensus.* Lead agencies in Angola, Botswana, and Mozambique convened national-level stakeholders to embrace EPHF strengthening at the district level. These agencies were the Instituto Nacional de Saúde Pública in Angola, the Ministry of Health in

(continued)

Box 2.2

Using Tools to Build Capacity of Layer 1 at District Health Departments in Angola, Botswana, and Mozambique (*continued*)

Botswana, and the Instituto Nacional de Saúde in Mozambique. Conveners reviewed existing EPHF assessment tools that had been developed by the World Bank, the WHO, and the United States Centers for Disease Control and Prevention (United States, CDC). In each country, a day-long stakeholders' workshop reviewed possible EPHF priorities for each country and sought to reach consensus about possible indicators.

• *Step 2: pilot local checklist and performance improvement planning.* After participants came to a consensus about EPHF lists for each country, they developed a prototype for a guided self-assessment. The assessments involved gathering a district health department's health officer and executive team to collaborate on assigning self-ratings for about 100 EPHF indicators. The self-ratings were 0 ("not at all"), 1 ("partially"), and 2 ("fully"). The self-raters first assigned their ratings privately and then discussed the consensus score. Data were collected digitally and produced an instantaneous numerical rating as well as qualitative feedback from the group discussions.

• *Step 3: create performance improvement plans.* Immediately after seeing their self-ratings across each of the EPHFs, the local district teams met to prioritize their top three areas for performance improvement based on achieving the greatest impact and being the most feasible. The performance improvement plans were broken into tasks, actors, and deadlines. The national facilitator agreed to follow up every three months to coach the local team and work with them to mobilize resources for plans that needed outside resources.

District staff who participated often said that they had no prior knowledge of essential public health functions and expressed surprise that various elements of core public health capabilities were their responsibility. Most of the performance improvement plans endorsed by district staff were centered around improvements in the collection and use of data.

Each country experienced changes in its political leadership as well as in the leadership of the health ministry, and each country received variable amounts of stable support for EPHFs from partner agencies (United States Agency for International Development in Angola, United States CDC in Botswana and Mozambique). In each country, support for the central-level coach who would carry out the follow-up was not fully institutionalized as an ongoing budget item, posing a challenge to continuity.

However, this demonstration project showed that the resources required to catalyze increased professionalization of the public health workforce could require as little as adding 1 additional facilitator or coach for every 100 or so district public health staff. A project to improve layer 1 could be implemented by increasing staffing and spending on layer 1 by 1 percent. The critical change is to build sustained, high-level support for an ongoing program of supportive coaching and follow-up, with regular checklist-based self-assessment of performance on essential public health functions (Bellagio District Public Health Workshop Participants 2017; Bishai and Perreira 2019; Bishai et al. 2016).

Secure Funding

The new cadre of public health quality supervisors will need to have stable, secure funding. Collecting performance data takes time: time to collect the data, time for respondents to give answers in interviews and surveys, and time to analyze, interpret, and respond to data.

EPHF performance measurement can also incorporate administrative data by including counts of patients encountered, vaccines given, and hours worked, for example. Unfortunately, few surrogate markers carry information about the capabilities that constitute resilience. For this reason, both administrative data and EPHF checklist data are required. For example, a finding that 95 percent of children are vaccinated does not explain whether this was achieved by a system that is autonomous, data-driven, and community-engaged or by a system that relies on extensive outside contracts.

The performance improvement plans developed by local staff require resources, typically for staff training or communications or for data systems. Just like physical capital requires spending to keep up with depreciation, so too does human capital. Deferring the maintenance of public health systems is exactly the type of past-era thinking that led to the poor performance in so many countries during the COVID-19 pandemic.

Barriers to Measurement

Organizational culture—the shared beliefs and expectations of the workforce—can be one of the most significant barriers to improved performance. If, over time, workers in a local health department have come to see their role as merely delivering clinical services in vertical programs, then they will not see the importance of measuring resilience or being situationally aware or engaged with the community.

Even if the institutional culture is receptive to embracing resilience measurements, other obstacles arise. The boundary for what creates resilience does not stop with people and programs controlled by the public health department. Trust and partnerships involve external organizations and are affected by political movements, some of which may seek to erode community solidarity even when it is directed toward creating healthier lives. Historical, contextual, and social determinants constrain the system. Hence, the measurement project needs to be sensitive to what is under the control of the participants. For this reason, resilience and public health function measurement toolkits need to be adapted to the local context, and health workers need to be involved in designing local adaptations.

Staff turnover implies that having staff who are resilient this year is not a predictor that the level of resilient staff will be sufficient next year. Finding ways to measure not only what people do but also what the organization is capable of requires continual innovation.

Moreover, information on performance can be misused to punish or reward. Creating measures, collecting data, and distributing the information to drive decisions can also create and consolidate power (refer to box 2.3). Thus, the

Box 2.3

Comparing Top-Down and Bottom-Up Measurement

It is all too common for leaders to implement reforms without thinking about power dynamics. The incumbent managers who already have power typically determine a new organizational goal and seek to develop a strategy to attain it. They will try to take stock of their existing resources and learn what they need to move closer to the goal.

If leaders are not consultative, they will rely on their own vision and mental model of how the organization functions and set up a measurement framework based on what they think drives the system. They can start taking an inventory of the inputs they think are essential, go to their closed-door managerial suite to view the measured inventory, and devise a strategy to reform the organization based on identified gaps. They may prescribe hiring, purchasing, retraining, and creating new workflows as part of their strategy. As they proceed to implement the strategy, there could be resistance or sabotage by the rank and file. Resistance and resentment are common reactions to being excluded from decision-making.

By not engaging the broad workforce in setting goals, conducting measurement, and setting strategy, these top-down managers risk alienating members of the organization who joined based on an alternative understanding of the mission. If the workers who are the subject of the measures are not involved in creating the measures, they might find the measurement tools onerous and objectionable, and the quality of reporting will suffer. If the goal is to pursue "resilience," then a top-down strategy to measure resilience factors and then tell people what to do about creating resilience may be antithetical to creating self-motivating systems that can perpetually create resilience.

Gilson et al. (2017) collected in-depth data from health managers in Kenya and South Africa who embraced an inclusive approach. They describe a hospital superintendent who routinely involved unit managers in the annual budget process. One positive result was that there was better understanding of how limited resources were. According to the superintendent, "They understand why they cannot get what they ask for." In Mitchell's Plain, South Africa, subdistrict managers sought to encourage facility managers and their staff to develop locally specific priorities for their work and to use proactive and collaborative problem-solving during routine meetings. Role modeling inclusive managerial patterns helped other senior managers to adopt respectful language and behavior.

With inclusive approaches, the mental model of how the organization functions becomes grounded in the knowledge of people on the front line. The measurements needed emerge from the workers who suggest meaningful and actionable metrics under the belief that they will receive feedback based on them. Inclusive managers can ensure that the information derived by measurement is fed back to workers on a regular basis, along with opportunities to use the information to participate in joint decisions on how to close gaps. The chance that workers will resist the new direction is lower when every worker is tuned in to measures they created and repeatedly cycle through measuring-studying-planning-acting. The chance that the measurements will be acted on is higher when the subjects own the data.

However, a bottom-up approach requires managers who are open-minded about sharing power. It also requires staff whose professionalism ensures that they are intrinsically motivated to pursue goals on behalf of the organization. Neither precondition can be assumed in every context (Gilson et al. 2017).

act of measurement inside an organization is inherently political. Knowledge of organizational culture is crucial, as is knowledge of how measurements can be used most effectively in a particular context.

Challenges and Options for the Way Forward

The challenge in coming years is to capitalize on what we all have learned since 2020: local public health departments' lack of resilience left communities unprotected, and unnecessary deaths occurred. Investing in resilience will lead to a health system that is more successful at doing everything we want it to do. The reason to invest in more resilience in the public health system is not just to realize benefits that may only arise during some crisis in the far-off future. The payoff is immediate because improved public health capability furthers the short-term achievement of the Sustainable Development Goals (Sherry and Bishai 2020).

From their inception in the 19th century, local health departments were designed to identify and solve collective problems in health. Too many of them lack that capability today. Too many see their roles as nothing more than service delivery. The personal services they deliver are saving millions of lives, but restoring their capability to practice population-level public health could save millions more.

An unfortunate tension emerges between efficiency and resilience when budget planners fail to appreciate how powerful public health departments can be in promoting population-level health and their potential when they partner with multiple sectors of government, the community, and the private sector. This power to build trust and reserves of goodwill forms the core of a resilience dividend that pays off immediately for program operations now, preserves services, and enables adaptation when the next crisis comes.

The chapter has outlined the steps that can transform the public health workforce to become more resilient. The key lies in realizing that the existing public health workforce could carry out resilience tasks. An extensive set of tools is available to support resilience in practice: these tools are the checklists and interventions that revolve around improving the essential public health functions.

The missing catalyst is high-level leadership sufficient to build and embed a new cadre of public health quality supervisors who will constitute 1 percent of the current public health workforce. Local schools of public health around the world stand ready to become training partners in this transformation. Because the public health workforce is a tiny percentage of the total health workforce, the cost of improving their quality is small. The small price tag of these resilience investments in relation to what they can accomplish should appeal to policy makers concerned with efficiency. The cost of delaying a resilience transformation is the true threat to efficiency.

Annex 2A: Tools for Assessing Essential Public Health Functions

Table 2A.1 Tools for Assessing Essential Public Health Functions

Organization	Tool	Description
Association of State and Territorial Health Officials	State Health Improvement Plan	Designed for US state health officials. Provides guidance on setting up local health improvement coalitions and state-level quality improvement
China Centers for Disease Control and Prevention (CDC)	Cross-sectional assessment of county-level China CDC offices	Measures funding, functions, and capability of local offices
International Association of National Public Health Institutes	Peer-to-peer evaluation of public health institutes, functions, operations, and services	A framework for national public health institutes to assist each other in their quality improvement Derived from World Health Organization essential public health functions checklists for national public health institute to use
Pan American Health Organization	Public Health in the Americas National Assessments	Detailed assessment for national public health institutes in the Americas to self-assess; was used in 2000 and updated in 2020
Rockefeller Foundation, Johns Hopkins University, International Centre for Diarrheal Disease Research, Bangladesh	Health Systems Resilience Checklist	Developed with stakeholders in Bangladesh to allow facility-based assessment of resilience in 2019
United States Agency for International Development (USAID), United States Centers for Disease Control and Prevention (United States CDC), and Johns Hopkins University	Essential Public Health Functions Strengthening	A suite of tools for conducting assessments, setting priorities, and training coaches for EPHF strengthening
United States CDC	National Public Health Performance Standards Program	Tools for national, state, and local US-based public health departments to self-assess performance
USAID Measure Evaluation	Tools for Data Demand and Use	Focused on assessing data use by public health personnel
World Health Organization	Health Systems Resilience Toolkit	Crowdsourced directory of papers and initiatives directed to resilience
World Bank	Study of the organization and management of communicable disease prevention	Detailed checklists for essential public health functions at the local, state, and central levels

Source: Links to folders containing tools from each organization are available at https://office.sph .hku.hk/david-bishai/ke/.

Note: EPHF = essential public health function.

References

Barasa, Edwine W., Keith Cloete, and Lucy Gilson. 2017. "From Bouncing Back, to Nurturing Emergence: Reframing the Concept of Resilience in Health Systems Strengthening." *Health Policy and Planning* 32 (Suppl. 3): iii91–iii94.

Bellagio District Public Health Workshop Participants. 2017. "Public Health Performance Strengthening at Districts: Rationale and Blueprint for Action." Proceedings of a Bellagio Conference, November 21–24, 2016, Alliance for Health Policy and Systems Research, Geneva.

Biddle, Louise, Katharina Wahedi, and Kayvan Bozorgmehr. 2020. "Health System Resilience: A Literature Review of Empirical Research." *Health Policy Plan* 35 (8): 1084–109.

Bishai, David, Abdul Ghaffar, Ed Kelley, and Marie-Paule Kieny. 2015. "Honouring the Value of People in Public Health: A Different Kind of p-value." *Bulletin of the World Health Organization* 93 (9): 661–62.

Bishai, David, and Claudia Perreira. 2019. *Developing a Toolkit to Strengthen Essential Public Health Functions in Angola's Municipalities.* Project SOAR Final Report. Washington, DC: United States Agency for International Development and Population Council, Project SOAR.

Bishai, David, Melisssa K. Sherry, Claudia Pereira, Sergio Chicumbe, Francisco Mbofana, Amy Boore, Monica Smith, Leonel Nhambi, and Nagesh Borse. 2016. "Development and Usefulness of a District Health Systems Tool for Performance Improvement in Essential Public Health Functions in Botswana and Mozambique." *Journal of Public Health Management and Practice* 22 (6): 586–96.

Blanchet, Karl, Sara L. Nam, Ben Ramalingam, and Francisco Pozo-Martin. 2017. "Governance and Capacity to Manage Resilience of Health Systems: Towards a New Conceptual Framework." *International Journal of Health Policy Management* 6 (8): 431–35.

Couttolenc, Bernard F. 2012. *Decentralization and Governance in the Ghana Health Sector.* Washington, DC: World Bank. http://documents.worldbank.org/curated/en /106611468257682937/Decentralization-and-governance-in-the-Ghana-health -sector.

Couttolenc, Bernard F. 2016. "United Republic of Tanzania: Funding Flows and Cost Sharing in Health: The Case from Shinyanga and Geita Regions." Report no. 105368-TZ, World Bank, Washington, DC.

DeSalvo, Karen B., and Kushal T. Kadakia. 2021. "Public Health 3.0 after COVID-19: Reboot or Upgrade?" *American Journal of Public Health* 111 (S3): S179–S181.

DeSalvo, Karen B., Patrick W. O'Carroll, Denise Koo, John M. Auerbach, and Judith A. Monroe. 2016. "Public Health 3.0: Time for an Upgrade." *American Journal of Public Health* 106 (4): 621–26.

Frenk, Julio, Lincoln C. Chen, Latha Chandran, Elizabeth O. Groff, Roderick King, Afaf Meleis, and Harvey V. Fineberg. 2022. "Challenges and Opportunities for Educating Health Professionals after the COVID-19 Pandemic." *The Lancet* 400 (10362): 1539–56.

Frieden, Thomas. 2022. "What's a National Public Health Institute to Do?" *Health Affairs Forefront*, December 7, 2022.

Gilson, Lucy, Edwine Barasa, Nonhlanhea Nxumalo, Susan Cleary, Jane Goudge, Sassy Molyneux, Benjamin Tsofa, and Uta Lehmann. 2017. "Everyday Resilience in District Health Systems: Emerging Insights from the Front Lines in Kenya and South Africa." *BMJ Global Health* 2 (2): e000224.

Haldane, Victoria, Chuan De Foo, Salma M. Abdalla, Anne-Sophie Jung, Melissa Tan, Shishi Wu, Alvin Chua, Monica Verma, Pami Shrestha, Sudhvir Singh, Tristana Perez, See Mieng Tan, Michael Bartos, Shunsuke Mabuchi, Mathias Bonk,

Christine McNab, George K. Werner, Raj Panjabi, and Helena Legido-Quigley. 2021. "Health Systems Resilience in Managing the COVID-19 Pandemic: Lessons from 28 Countries." *Nature Medicine* 27 (6): 964–80.

Khaleghian, Peyvand, and Monica Das Gupta. 2005. "Public Management and the Essential Public Health Functions." *World Development* 33 (7): 1083–99.

Kruk, Margaret E., Jennifer C. Johnson, Mawuli Gyakobo, Peter Agyei-Baffour, Kwesi Asabir, S. Rani Kotha, Janet Kwansah, Emmanuel Nakua, Rachel C. Snow, and Mawuli Dzodzomenyo. 2010. "Rural Practice Preferences among Medical Students in Ghana: A Discrete Choice Experiment." *Bulletin of the World Health Organization* 88 (5): 333–41.

Kruk, Margaret E., Emilia J. Ling, Asaf Bitton, Melani Cammett, Karen Cavanaugh, Mickey Chopra, Fadi el-Jardali, Rose Jallah Macauley, Mwihaki Kimura Muraguri, Shiro Konuma, Robert Marten, Frederick Martineau, Michael Myers, Kumanan Rasanathan, Enrique Ruelas, Agnès Soucat, Amimg Sugihantono, and Heiko Warnken. 2017. "Building Resilient Health Systems: A Proposal for a Resilience Index." *BMJ* 357: j2323.

Martin-Moreno, Jose M., Meggan Harris, Elke Jakubowski, and Hans Kluge. 2016. "Defining and Assessing Public Health Functions: A Global Analysis." *Annual Review of Public Health* 37 (March): 335–55.

Meyer, Diane, David Bishai, Sanjana J. Ravi, Harunor Rashid, Shehrin S. Mahmood, Eric Toner, and Jennifer B. Nuzzo. 2020. "A Checklist to Improve Health System Resilience to Infectious Disease Outbreaks and Natural Hazards." *BMJ Global Health* 5 (8): e002429.

Monsod, Toby Melissa, and Maria Socorro Gochoco-Bautista. 2021. "Rethinking 'Economic Fundamentals' in an Era of Global Physical Shocks: Insights from the Philippines Experience with COVID-19." *Asian Economic Papers* 20 (1): 109–40. https://doi.org/10.1162/asep_a_00802.

Saleh, Karima. 2013. *The Health Sector in Ghana: A Comprehensive Assessment.* Directions in Development: Human Development. Washington, DC: World Bank.

Sherry, Melisssa, and David Bishai. 2020. "Continuity between Comprehensive Primary Health Care and Sustainable Development Goals." In *Achieving Health for All: Primary Health Care in Action,* edited by David Bishai and Meike Schlieff. Baltimore, MD: Johns Hopkins University Press.

Thomas, Steve, Anna Sagan, James Larkin, Jonathan Cylus, Josep Figueras, and Marina Karanikolos. 2020. "Strengthening Health Systems Resilience: Key Concepts and Strategies." European Observatory Policy Brief, European Observatory on Health Systems and Policies, Copenhagen.

Turenne, Charlotte Pailliard, Lara Gautier, Stéphanie Degroote, Etienne Guillard, Fanny Chabrol, and Valéry Ridde. 2019. "Conceptual Analysis of Health Systems Resilience: A Scoping Review." *Social Science and Medicine* 232 (July): 168–80.

World Bank. 2022. *Change Cannot Wait: Building Resilient Health Systems in the Shadow of COVID-19.* Washington, DC: World Bank.

3

Minding What We Spend on Resilience: Global Data, Local Examples

David Bishai, Katelyn Jison Yoo, Karima Saleh, and HuiHui Wang

IN SUMMARY

This chapter measures spending on three layers of a health system with a focus on layer 1, which is devoted to health promotion and public health. The chapter reviews past trends in health sector spending toward each of the three layers to reveal opportunities and gaps that must be corrected in the short, medium, and long terms.

- The evidence shows neglect of expenditure tracking for the public health functions that make up the first layer of protection. Many low-income and lower-middle-income countries are inconsistent in monitoring and compiling their spending patterns, especially for layer 1 public health functions. This gap in reporting is, in many countries, a result of weak public financial management and reporting systems and fragmented sources of financing and administration. An improved and consolidated reporting system, coupled with improved capabilities to capture spending for layer 1, will drive better understanding, planning, and monitoring at the country level.

- Spending on layer 1 functions (public health, prevention, and community preparedness) is estimated to be between US$2 per capita in low-income countries and US$4 per capita in lower-middle-income countries, based on national health accounts estimates. Spending on layer 1 functions could thus make up about 3–5 percent of total health spending. At the same time, about 25 percent of total health spending goes to layer 2 interventions (scaling disease detection and ensuring containment and mitigation). About 70 percent of total health spending goes to layer 3 needs (advanced case management and surge response). A better estimate of financial needs and gaps, especially for layers 1 and 2, would help policy makers to make timely decisions about how best to allocate development assistance for health.

- Leadership, managerial attentiveness, adequately skilled and staffed positions, and appropriate performance signals (for example, incentives), especially at local levels, are critical for a well-functioning health planning and delivery system.

- Failure to consider and prioritize human resource issues and challenges in strategic planning results in significant constraints in the effective delivery of health services. Policies creating an attractive environment for staff recruitment, distribution, retention, partnerships, and relevance are critical.

Introduction

For the coming decade, the health sector around the world requires invest-ments that can both restore past progress toward the Sustainable Development Goals (SDGs) and improve resilience against potential threats, including infec-tious pandemics, noncommunicable diseases, and the effects of climate change.

Chapter 1 made the case that a three-layer approach is required for success. This chapter reviews past trends in health sector spending on each of the three layers to reveal opportunities and gaps that must be corrected in the short, medium, and long terms. It shows that expenditure tracking for the public health functions that make up the first layer of protection has been neglected. Yet the available data show that the cost of improving public health operations devoted to prevention (layer 1) will be small relative to the total health budget.

The chapter begins by describing data on prevention spending from national health accounts (NHAs), which are a key resource for policy makers and researchers seeking to understand differences within and among countries over time. Severe limitations in the NHAs are blocking better health policy. COVID-19 highlighted the importance of tracking health spending for inform-ing responses to current and future pandemics. After describing why the health accounts are inadequate and looking at ways to improve them, this chapter examines the trends in expenditures on prevention versus clinical care for the past 10–15 years by country income level and region.

Global health expenditures have risen dramatically in the past two decades, from US$4.1 trillion (8.3 percent of global gross domestic product [GDP]) in 2000 to US$8.5 trillion (9.9 percent of GDP) in 2019, according to the Institute for Health Metrics and Evaluation (IHME) Financing Global Health database (Schneider et al. 2021). Inequalities loom: 90 percent of health spending serves the 3.6 billion residents of high-income countries, and 10 percent of health spending serves the 3.6 billion residents of low-income and lower-middle-income countries (Bishai and Cardona 2017). Of the roughly US$800 billion in health spending by lower-middle-income countries, development assistance for health (DAH) made up less than US$50 billion, or about 6 percent of the total in the years before 2020 (Global Burden of Disease Health Financing Collaborator Network 2019). These funds are tied mostly to vertical programs for specific diseases and populations, such as human immunodeficiency virus/acquired immunodeficiency syndrome (HIV/AIDS), tuberculosis, malaria, maternal and child health, and now COVID-19. About US$6 billion in DAH is allocated to sectorwide approaches and health sector support (Global Burden of Disease Health Financing Collaborator Network 2019).

Spending on health is expected to increase due to rising incomes and popu-lation aging. Although DAH has grown over the past few decades, it has never grown the way it did between 2019 and 2020. A new study tracking global health spending found that US$13.7 billion went toward COVID-19 in 2020, contributing to a 35.7 percent increase in DAH spending compared to 2019

(IHME 2020b). As shown in figure 3.1, DAH is a larger share of health spending in low-income countries (25 percent in 2018), while out-of-pocket spending is a larger share of health spending in lower-middle-income countries (55.9 percent in 2018) (IHME 2020b). However, DAH spending started to plateau in 2012. Due to recent shifts in the emphasis of development spending, DAH spending on malaria, HIV/AIDS, and tuberculosis declined from 2019 to 2020. This trend continued in 2021 as DAH investment in COVID-19 vaccination rose.

With growing spending comes growing urgency to know whether the funds are building a health system that is resilient against shocks and aligned with the goals of better health and health equity. For sustainability and resilience, mobilization and effective allocation of domestic resources are critical. By showing what is spent across the three layers, this chapter demonstrates ways in which financial oversight of health spending can help to achieve health goals.

"Prevention activities" are defined as measures that aim to avoid diseases and injuries and their complications. These measures include population-level health promotion to change the physical and social environment (for example, safer food, air, water, roads, buildings, and consumer products). Eradicating smallpox is an example, but so is enforcing sanitary and food safety regulations and changing social norms about exercise and smoking. Prevention also includes personal services given to one individual at a time to change health behavior before disease occurs. Vaccines are a personal preventive service and

Figure 3.1   Sources of Health Financing in Low-Income Countries and Globally, 1995–2022

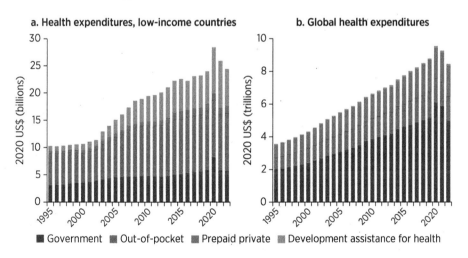

Source: Calculations based on data from Global Burden of Disease Collaborative Network 2024.

Note: Data after 2018 are forecasted.

so is a home visit to promote good nutrition and handwashing. Prevention spending also pays for personal services that modify a disease early in its course to prevent complications—for example, detecting and treating high blood pressure or latent tuberculosis infection (OECD, Eurostat, and WHO 2017; Szreter 1988).

According to the System of Health Accounts (SHA), preventive care can be divided into six subcategories: (1) information, education, and counseling; (2) immunization; (3) early disease detection; (4) healthy condition monitoring; (5) epidemiological surveillance and risk and disease control; and (6) preparing for disaster and emergency. A related area of spending is governance and health system administration, as proper governance can ensure that multiple components of the health system, including information technology systems, human resources, and financing, are facilitating prevention and resilience.

Reviewing past trends in health spending on the three layers of resilient health systems sets up possible scenarios for the future. In one scenario, countries revert to the systematic neglect of public health that left them vulnerable during the pandemic. In a more optimistic scenario, countries invest in oversight to measure spending on public health operations and prevention. With systematic efforts to track prevention activities and spending, countries are better able to set benchmarks for the specific investments that build resilience. Better measurement leads to better management of central and local public health departments, which historically have been the most highly productive elements of the health sector (Deaton 2013; Szreter 1988). Tracking prevention spending more adequately is a simple, efficient way for countries to spend more on priority areas that help them to progress toward the SDGs and achieve resilience.

Methods to Track Spending on the Three Layers

Data from the System of Health Accounts

In 2000, the Organisation for Economic Co-operation and Development (OECD) developed a System of Health Accounts, which is an internationally standardized framework that systematically tracks the flow of expenditures in the health system (OECD 2000). Soon thereafter, the World Health Organization (WHO) developed a producer's guide alongside investments by the US Agency for International Development, the World Bank, and others in building the capacity of government agencies to prepare NHAs. OECD published a major update to the SHA in 2011, and the term "SHA 2011" refers to those guidelines (OECD, Eurostat, and WHO 2017).

Countries reporting health expenditures using the SHA framework classify them in the three ways shown in figure 3.2. Each dollar spent in a health system comes from a health financing source (HF) and flows to a health provider (HP) for a health care function (HC). SHA 2011 classifies each health

Figure 3.2 The SHA 2011 Framework and Its Three Classifications

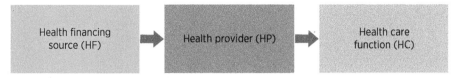

Source: Original figure for this publication.
Note: SHA = System of Health Accounts.

expenditure in all three ways, with codes for subclassifications within HF, HP, and HC. In theory, the sum of spending from all financial sources equals the sum of all spending received by all providers, which, in turn, equals the sum of all spending by purpose.

The SHA includes both domestic and external sources of finance. These systematic accounting classifications have enabled governments to compare themselves to global and regional benchmarks and to see historical time trends that inform planning. SHA 2011 has been widely used and adapted to the context of low- and middle-income countries.

NHA data are fundamental to progressing toward the SDGs and universal health coverage. The process of gathering and regularly reviewing health expenditures has itself become the means to achieve these goals (Rathe et al. 2021). Accounting for spending makes health system actors think about what they are doing and who is doing what. The result of accounting is not just data; it is a thoughtful and conscientious workforce that is aware of current and future resources.

Data Repositories

NHA data have been curated by the OECD, WHO, and IHME. The OECD database includes data on health care functions and health providers only from high-income countries (OECD 2022). The IHME offers a repository of NHA data extending from 2000 to 2017 (Schneider et al. 2021), based on the NHA data that countries report to the WHO, supplemented by an extensive search of country websites. WHO and IHME signed a memorandum of understanding in 2015 to set terms on which they will collaborate to improve the quality and use of global health estimates (Kieny and Murray 2015). Estimates from WHO and IHME diverge slightly, even though they extract data from the same source. This divergence is because WHO and IHME use different procedures to account for missing data. The WHO's Global Health Expenditure Database (GHED) holds NHA data for 193 countries for only four years, from 2016 to 2019,[1] and does not break down health care spending past HC6 for any other category except immunization (HC6.2). Due to the limited data on subcategorized spending in the GHED, the analysis here refers to the IHME database.

Regardless of where the NHA data are curated, all repositories share a basic limitation in that only a small number of low-income and lower-middle-income countries systematically track their health spending and, of those, even fewer track their prevention spending.

Mapping Health Accounts Data to the Three-Layer Framework

Using the SHA 2011 framework, data on past exenditures are disaggregated into the three-layer framework (Zhao et al. 2021). To understand the investment trends that promote health security and primary health care, a crosswalk was built from the three layers to high-level HC codes that classify the purpose of the spending.

Table 3.1 describes this mapping of the three layers and links to the HC functions of the SHA 2011 framework. In addition, a "sublayer" was included to improve links with the SHA 2011 framework. The sublayers shown in table 3.1 were recommended by accounting guidelines made especially for COVID-19 by OECD, Eurostat, and WHO (OECD, Eurostat, and WHO 2021). The guidance provided in this document supports the classification of the related COVID-19 expenditures with the aim of identifying all health expenses incurred by the COVID-19 crisis and ensuring to the maximum extent possible that a harmonized approach is adopted across European Union member states and countries participating in the Joint Health Accounts data collection.

The assignment of HC6.5 to layer 2 is arbitrary because, as noted in chapter 1, surveillance cuts across all three layers. The justification for assigning these costs to layer 2 comes from knowing how little contact NHA data collection teams have with layer 1 agencies and systems. Especially in low- and lower-middle-income countries, the expenditure data going into the health accounts come from care providers in the private sector and under the ministry of health. The estimates of HC6.5 that appear in the most recent NHA files were surveillance activities taking place in health care service delivery facilities that are more in line with layer 2 than with other layers of the health system.

Data Availability

In general, NHA reports are incomplete. Fifty-five United Nations member states have never reported any NHA data (Global Burden of Disease Collaborative Network 2024). Among countries reporting NHA data, most data reports on categories of health care function are incomplete. When HC functions are reported, reports on HC6 for preventive care are mostly blank, and the breakdown within HC6 is even more incomplete. In 2017, as shown in figure 3.3, 95 countries reported any NHA data to the WHO, 67 countries reported any HC data, and 60 countries reported data on

Table 3.1   Linking the Three-Layer Framework and the SHA 2011 Framework

Layer	Sublayer	Code	Description
Layer 1: risk reduction by promoting prevention and community preparedness	Public health function, administrative function	HC6.1	Information, education, and counseling programs
		HC6.2	Immunization programs
		HC6.4	Healthy condition monitoring programs
		HC6.6	Preparing for disaster and emergency response programs
		HC7.1	Governance and health system administration
		HC7.2	Administration of health financing
	Protective equipment	HC5.1.3	Medical nondurable goods
Layer 2: scaling detection and ensuring containment and mitigation	Testing	HC1.3	Outpatient curative care
		HC4.1	Laboratory services
		HC4.2	Imaging services
		HC6.3	Early disease detection programs
		HC6.5	Epidemiological surveillance and risk and disease control programs
Layer 3: advanced case management and surge response	Treatment	HC1.1	Inpatient curative care
		HC1.2	Day curative care
		HC1.3	Outpatient curative care
		HC1.4	Home-based curative care
		HC4.3	Patient transportation
		HC5.1	Pharmaceuticals and other medical nondurable goods

Source: Original table for this publication.
Note: SHA = System of Health Accounts.

Figure 3.3 Incompleteness of NHA Data Sets Based on Reporting up to 2017

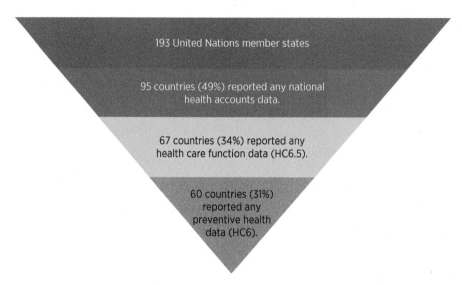

Source: Based on an analysis of the expenditure data in Global Burden of Disease Collaborative Network 2024.
Note: HC = health care spending; NHA = national health account.

HC6 (total preventive care). Nineteen countries (all of them high income) reported data on HC6.5 (epidemiology and surveillance spending). No lower-middle-income country reported spending on HC6.5 (layer 2) in 2017.

Between 2016 and 2017 the situation had improved, but reporting on population-level prevention activities (HC6) remained incomplete (table 3.2).

This incompleteness makes it difficult to obtain accurate data on gaps and trends in health spending on layer 1 (risk reduction by promoting prevention and community preparedness). Because the measurement is a precondition of investing and managing a component of the health system, incomplete data on layer 1 spending reflects inattention to this critical component of population health protection.

National income level is strongly associated with whether a country reports prevention spending (HC6). Figure 3.4 shows prevention spending reports by income for the most recent year available in the IHME file of originally reported data. Even among high-income countries, almost half do not keep track of prevention spending. Upper-middle-income countries have less than half the probability of reporting prevention spending data in an NHA than high-income countries.

Data capacity constraints are well known to be associated with differences in national income. Higher incomes allow countries to maintain a workforce of government accountants and recordkeeping systems. It may often appear luxurious to invest in government accountants (and auditors) when

Table 3.2 Number of Countries Reporting Any NHA Data, by Health Care Function, 2016 and 2017

Year	HC1 (curative care)	HC2 (rehabilitative care)	HC6 (preventive care)	HC7 (governance and administration)
2016	90	75	96	96
2017	55	50	60	60

Source: World Health Organization, Global Health Expenditure Database, https://apps.who.int/nha/database.

Note: Covers any data reported for spending on health care functions (HC). NHA = national health account.

Figure 3.4 Proportion of Countries That Reported Spending on Prevention, by Country Income Level, 2017

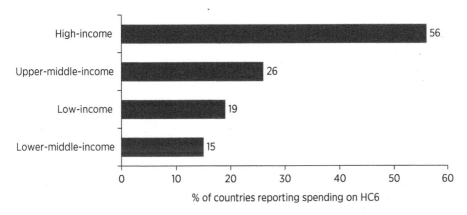

% of countries reporting spending on HC6

Source: Based on analysis of expenditure data in Global Burden of Disease Collaborative Network 2024.

people-centered services are wanting. Yet the lack of data on prevention spending enables a syndrome of neglect of prevention itself. Focusing on "people-centered" care after people become sick from preventable illnesses is not really people-centered after all. Spending on curative care is also easier to track when treatments get reimbursed through national and private health insurance programs. Public health functions, in contrast, are financed through multiple sources, including government budgets (central, state, or local government authorities in decentralized environments) and external financing, especially in low-income countries. While external financing may be better documented for donor-reporting purposes, government spending may not be (refer to the case of Nigeria in box 3.1). In a country that does not report spending on prevention, the health system is unable to prioritize all three layers.

Tracking Primary Health Care Spending in Nigeria

The government of Nigeria has not been able to track information reliably on how much is spent on primary health care services by the various levels of government and off-budget means. This inability is partly due to (a) the inability to capture granular information given the overly broad classification of expenditure in the health sector; (b) the fragmented nature of the resource flows (both in cash and in kind) toward primary health care services; and (c) the absence of a system to aggregate and track spending (including reporting and consolidating out-of-pocket payments) in the context of a highly decentralized federation. Several studies have identified governance challenges and weak monitoring and accountability structures at primary health care facilities and local governments in Nigeria.

A public expenditure tracking survey (PETS) showed that resources for primary health care came from multiple sources. Overall, primary health care services in Nigeria are financed through three main sources: (a) public budgets at various government levels; (b) international donors; and (c) private financing and internally generated revenue within primary health care facilities. Facilities could be receiving resources (in cash and in kind) from at least six direct official sources. Additional official financing flows could come indirectly. These multiple flows of financing limit planning, coordination, and monitoring.

The PETS also showed that primary health care services in Nigeria receive very low allocations from public sources and are highly dependent on off-budget sources for nonsalary recurrent spending. Local government authorities are the primary source for financing primary health care in the states of Niger and Ekiti. Federal government allocations in these states are negligible. Niger State received about US$4.60 per capita for primary health care, while Ekiti State received about US$3.20 per capita in 2015. The government financed most of these resources: 90 percent for Niger State and 96 percent for Ekiti State. The balance of financing came from internally generated revenue and external financing. More than 90 percent of primary health care expenditures were for personnel emoluments. However, when excluding salaries, per capita spending for primary health care operations was only US$0.12 for Ekiti State and US$0.47 for Niger State, coming mostly from internally generated revenue, followed by external financing, rather than from public sources. Possibly 50–65 percent of the resources (salary and nonsalary) are retained at the local government level for public health functions and other administrative functions, while the rest is sent to the primary health care facility level.

Source: Saleh, Gauthier, and Pimhidzai 2020.

Until countries improve their financial data systems, researchers and policy makers will have to use models to fill data gaps. However, models of health system data are limited by the quality of the underlying assumptions and are an inadequate substitute for primary data. The IHME used a Bayesian model to leverage the patterns in countries that did report NHA data and to fill in missing pieces for countries that did not. The modeled data for any single country might suffer from distortions. However, for overall inferences about aggregate trends and levels of spending, examining a global data set of partly original and partly modeled data is at least as good as confining the analysis to a small group of reporting countries.

The method used to track global spending on prevention draws on IHME modeled data on spending by subcategory for 195 countries from 2000 to 2017. The analysis aggregated spending into layer 1, layer 2, and layer 3 spending using the definitions from table 3.1 and then studied trends and levels by World Bank income categories: low-income, lower-middle-income, upper-middle-income, and high-income countries.

Results: Levels and Trends in the Three Layers of the Health System

Table 3.3 shows the average spending on each of the three layers of the health system by country income group. Layer 2 and 3 spending rises far more rapidly by country income level than layer 1 spending. For example, high-income countries spend US$1,628 per capita, while low-income countries spend US$24 per capita on layer 3, which implies a ratio of 68 to 1. By contrast, high-income countries spend US$42 per capita on layer 1, while low-income countries spend US$2 per capita, which implies a ratio of 21 to 1. Therefore, income growth will lead to larger increases in layer 3 spending than layer 1 spending. The Lancet Global Health Commission found that spending on primary health care in high-income countries (US$1,312) outpaced spending on primary health care in low-income countries (US$24) by 54 to 1 (Hanson et al. 2022). However, the Lancet Commission's definition of primary health care spending

Table 3.3 Average Primary Health Care Spending per Capita, by Layer and Country Income Level, 2017

US$ per capita

Country income level	Layer 1: risk reduction by promoting prevention and community preparedness	Layer 2: scaling detection and ensuring containment and mitigation	Layer 3: advanced case management and surge response
Low-income (N = 27)	2	9	24
Lower-middle-income (N = 55)	4	29	80
Upper-middle-income (N = 53)	14	116	317
High-income (N = 59)	42	613	1,628

Source: Based on analysis of data from the Institute for Health Metrics and Evaluation (IHME) Global Health Expenditures by Services and Providers 2000–2017 (data set), https://ghdx.healthdata.org /record/ihme-data/global-health-expenditures-services-and-providers-2000-2017.

spans all three layers and includes substantial out-of-pocket spending for direct medical services, so the estimates are not comparable.

One finding is that the resources required for layer 1 are relatively low. A low-income country could achieve the level of layer 1 protection of a lower-middle-income country by doubling its spending from US$2 to US$4 per capita, but it would have to more than triple layer 3 spending from US$24 to US$80 per capita to raise layer 3 protection to the level of a lower-middle-income country. Given the outsize benefits for population health from investments in layer 1 compared to investments in layer 3, these results could help to reorient new spending priorities for years to come. Unfortunately, without accurate data on layer 1 expenditure, most low- and middle-income countries will face obstacles in identifying where to focus investments on the layer 1 system.

Figure 3.5 shows time trend data on spending for prevention as defined by all spending on HC6. It reveals a more rapid pace of growth in spending for

Figure 3.5 Per Capita Spending on Health, by Country Income Level and Layer of the Health System, 2002–17

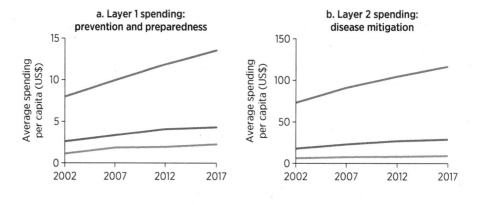

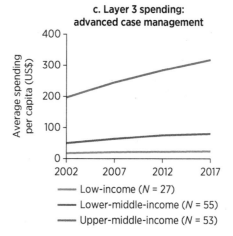

Source: Based on analysis of data from the Institute for Health Metrics and Evaluation (IHME) Global Health Expenditures by Services and Providers 2000–2017 (data set), https://ghdx.healthdata.org /record/ihme-data/global-health-expenditures-services-and-providers-2000-2017.

prevention in upper-middle-income countries as opposed to lower-middle-income and low-income countries. Figure 3.5 shows the trends in spending by layer over time as averages for country income groups; it is not scaled well to show that spending is growing across all three layers. Between 2012 and 2017, spending growth for low-income countries was 3.1 percent, 2.3 percent, and 1.2 percent (inflation-adjusted) for layers 1, 2, and 3, respectively (IHME 2020a). For upper-middle-income countries, spending growth was 2.9 percent, 2.3 percent, and 2.3 percent for layers 1, 2, and 3, respectively. Box 3.2 discusses a package of universal health coverage health benefits and financial needs in select countries in Sub-Saharan Africa.

Box 3.2

Financial Needs and a Package of Universal Health Coverage Health Benefits in Select Countries of Sub-Saharan Africa

Moving toward universal health coverage generally requires significant additional public financing, and each country must determine which services to provide. However, for low-income countries to provide a minimum health benefits package (or a universal health coverage benefits package) with comprehensive primary health care services would cost approximately 5 percent of gross domestic product (GDP) or US$86 per capita (McIntyre, Meheus, and Røttingen 2017). A study of low-income and lower-middle-income countries found that many countries are currently spending considerably less: an average of about 1.4 percent of GDP, or US$39 per capita (Cotlear et al. 2015).

No country can publicly finance all of the health services offered by modern medicine to all of its citizens. Constructing a minimum health benefits package that contains priority services recognizes this limitation by channeling available financing to priority services. The adoption of a minimum health benefits package, however, does not mean that service delivery and health financing are limited to those priority interventions. Other services of lower priority, such as referral care or treatment of less common diseases, are likely to continue to be delivered and to receive some public financing, in addition to financing from patients and their families. For example, many low- and middle-income countries in Latin America, such as Argentina, El Salvador, Guatemala, and Nicaragua, have explicitly defined a minimum health benefits package that focuses on maternal and child health services and is targeted to low-income families. Hospital services, not contained in the package, continue to be offered universally to all citizens, or to the poor, but with considerable rationing through queues, demand deflection, and low quality of care. Services covered in the minimum health benefits package receive the funding needed to achieve the coverage targets set by the ministry of health, while hospital and other services excluded from the minimum health benefits package receive residual funding.

Financing for a minimum health benefits package is not simply for commodities and programs. It must also be sufficient to ensure strong health systems, including information systems, governance and regulation, and infrastructure support. These costs (not included within program costs) are significant

(continued)

Box 3.2

Financial Needs and a Package of Universal Health Coverage Health Benefits in Select Countries of Sub-Saharan Africa *(continued)*

(and can be between 40 percent and 46 percent of the minimum health benefits package). When dissecting the "systems costs" of a minimum benefits package (using the breakdown used by the One Health Tool model), human resources (other than those related directly to the included programs) represent the larger part, with around 40 percent of the total cost, followed by infrastructure (around 30 percent) and logistics (25 percent). Governance, information systems, and health financing together represent between 5 percent and 10 percent of the total.

Universal health coverage will require much more funding than the amounts currently provided through public finance. In Côte d'Ivoire, Kenya, and Tanzania overall, total health expenditure is between 5 percent and 6 percent of GDP (Saleh, Bitran, and Couttolenc 2018). However, most health expenditure comes not from public spending but from household out-of-pocket spending. Government health spending only accounts for a small amount of GDP, with Kenya on top at 1.6 percent of GDP. Financial protection remains low in Côte d'Ivoire. Protection in Kenya and Tanzania is better, and both countries benefit from significant external financing. None of these countries has an explicit minimum health benefits package that is subsidized by public financing.

All three countries will continue to devote a significant share of their GDP to funding a minimum health benefits package, ranging between 3.7 percent in Côte d'Ivoire to 5 percent in Kenya and 6 percent of GDP in Tanzania, especially if they are to achieve universal health coverage by 2030. Given that the ability to achieve universal health coverage has a lot to do with sustainable commitment and the need for government to take on a lot more of this commitment, spending for a minimum health benefits package will likely be allocated from government health spending (from both on-budget and off-budget spending). None of the three countries was spending enough on health as of 2015. The study's cost estimates for an explicitly defined minimum health benefits package under universal health coverage principles were within the range of what appears in the literature. Saleh, Bitran, and Couttolenc (2018) estimated that the average costs for a minimum health benefits package range between US$33 per capita and US$34 per capita in Côte d'Ivoire and Tanzania and US$47 per capita in Kenya in 2015.

The costs of a country's minimum health benefits package can seem higher or lower compared to those of other nations, depending on several factors: differences in the services included in the costing exercise; differences in the relative prices of drugs; differences in the number of people covered; and whether the cost numbers are presented in numbers per capita or in numbers per covered person. For example, Côte d'Ivoire and Tanzania have similar costs measured in per capita terms; however, measured on a per person covered basis, Côte d'Ivoire's costs are significantly higher, given different levels of service coverage.

Discussion: Layered Spending Priorities in the Health System

Data on past spending on the three layers of health systems show the expected variation across countries by income level. It has long been known that most health spending grows at least as fast as, if not faster than, national income (Fleisher, Leive, and Schieber 2013). That said, there may be a differential effect: health care spending is least responsive to changes in income in low-income countries and most responsive to changes in income in middle-income countries, with high-income countries falling in the middle (Farag et al. 2012). Unfortunately, preventive health spending does not always keep pace with a nation's economy, which creates divergence. When an economy grows faster than the health system's capability in the first layer of prevention, problems outpace solutions.

In the case of vaccine spending, it has been shown that income elasticities are lower for spending on prevention than for spending on general health care (Alfonso, Ding, and Bishai 2015). Donors have played and could continue to play an important role in supplementing health financing in low-income countries as well, given the low elasticity of health spending for this country income group. Organizations devoted to health service delivery and financing (for example, health insurance) and to leadership and governance also play an important role in driving health expenditures.

Although the analysis of spending on each of the layers relies on models, it shows that spending is growing across all three layers. One of the contributions of the analysis has been to reveal a disparity in the growth of resources devoted to each layer. The slow 2–3 percent growth of health spending on layer 1 will not close the gap in basic protections in low-income countries, where layer 1 spending constituted only US$2 per capita in 2017. Layer 1 spending does not require the extensive capital and human resources required for advanced clinical services in layer 3, and small investments can help a country to punch far above its weight.

Equally important, there is a shocking absence of data on the prevention spending essential to expanding layer 1 capabilities and identifying deficiencies in the basic operations of the public health services that higher-income countries take for granted. No lower-middle-income country has data on how much is spent on epidemiological surveillance and risk and disease control programs.

The very process of identifying the resources devoted to elements of layer 1 helps to reorient existing workers to their assigned tasks in delivering layer 1 public health functions. Advocating for investments to track what is spent on public health functions is not a sterile appeal to generate data for irrelevant reports and charts. Tracking spending leads to the right questions being asked, which can help to improve performance.

A variety of tools are already available to help countries to track their performance and the resources being used in layer 1. Efforts to develop a systematic approach to assessing layer 1 spending go back to 1998 when the WHO developed a list of essential public health functions (Bettcher, Sapirie, and Goon 1998). This list led to regional efforts to track activities in layer 1 systematically, first in the Americas (PAHO 2001) and subsequently in India (Das Gupta and Rani 2004), the Middle East (Alwan, Puska, and Siddiqi 2016), and Europe (WHO 2012). Each of these initiatives yielded toolkits that can be adapted for local use and then used to assess performance, identify resource needs, and monitor public health infrastructure over time.

Investment Stewardship

Budget Constraints and Limited Understanding of Resource Use for Layers 1 and 2

In many low-income countries and decentralized country settings, several resource inputs for layer 1 are not captured, as they are fragmented and often off-budget. DAH contributes significantly toward public health goods and maternal and child health programs in low-income countries, and internally generated revenue does the same in lower-middle-income countries. Some resources are allocated through on-budget spending, while others are allocated off-budget, including those from internally generated revenue. Often, the fragmentation of financing sources coming through various administrative tiers (central, state, local) and inconsistencies in the development of public financial management (PFM) systems across these tiers create an added challenge. Some resources are allocated in cash, while others are allocated in kind. Limited mechanisms are available for capturing in-kind contributions and aggregating them correctly in administrative data. Some resources bypass government administrative tiers (whether central, state, or local) and are transferred directly to the point-of-service delivery, such as health facilities. Sometimes off-budget sources make one-time contributions to vertical programs.

These resources are helpful, but they are difficult to monitor. Improved accounting systems can help to track these contributions and improve resource planning. Some resource inputs also are not captured because of the fragmented nature of responsibilities, financing, flows, and PFM reporting. Meanwhile, the World Bank and the other partners have sought to capture spending patterns through income-expenditure household surveys, public expenditure reviews, public expenditure tracking surveys, and private sector spending surveys. Ultimately, given the weakness in country systems, limited information is captured within NHAs on an ongoing basis.

Investments in resource tracking reduce waste and improve performance. Often governments do not have decentralized bottom-up planning to identify resource needs. Historical budgeting processes prevail rather than needs-based or performance-based budgeting mechanisms. More often than not, insufficient operations budgets hamper effective implementation. Some of the PFM system challenges are systemic, such as lack of or limited considerations given to a comprehensive PFM system, including a chart of accounts, enforcement of reporting, auditing, reporting mechanisms, and capacity building at both local government authorities and primary health care facilities. These mechanisms could strengthen PFM systems all the way to the facility level. Providing appropriate incentives would be extremely important to ensure the likelihood of reliable reporting of both patient profile data but also financial and nonfinancial data. Organizational structures that result in effective decision-making and accountability can keep people motivated.

In countries where the responsibility for the health of the population is decentralized to local government authorities (for example, districts), fiscal decentralization does not follow. Districts need to invest in their capacity for making and implementing decisions so that they have the fiscal authority they need to carry out their responsibility for health. Even at the national level, without dedicated public health institutions taking leadership, public health functions are scattered across different departments within the ministry of health and are often neglected among competing priorities. Many local authorities are hampered by their small scale or their remoteness and have little leverage for attracting capable staff. Another bottleneck is the lack of reliable information for decision-making, monitoring, and evaluation. The space in which to make effective decisions with respect to most health functions and subfunctions remains narrow.

Finally, local authorities could face several challenges and problems in accountability. Engaging local communities and convening local partners are important. In many low-income countries, local councils and committees have mostly advisory or consultative roles. In many areas, they do not function as an effective channel of participation in decision-making and planning. One option to improve transparency at the local level is to engage citizens with the use of tools and scorecards, which monitor quality and could be used to hold local officials accountable and improve the quality of primary health care services (Das Gupta and Rani 2004).

Evidence Around the Attention for Managerial Effectiveness

Reports like this can be predictable. The diagnosis is always too little spending. The cure is always more money. However, the resources needed for layer 1 are minuscule. An average low-income country could double layer 1 spending on prevention for US$2 per person. This is an important point, but not the main one.

What is needed in layer 1 is managerial attentiveness much more than financing. The simple act of observing the resources being devoted to population-level prevention goes a long way toward closing the resource gaps. The sine qua non of prevention is paying attention to people's needs, coming health threats, and how money is spent. The main lesson of the COVID-19 pandemic is that countries that had the worst time containing the pandemic were inattentive and lost people's trust (COVID-19 National

Preparedness Collaborators 2022). Careful attention, greater accountability, and more transparency are needed—not just the amount of money raised, but also how it is spent and who it benefits. Such attention is needed to ensure that the needs of recipient countries remain at the forefront.

Attention and the resources to supply it are scarce everywhere. However, in every district with a population of 100,000 to 500,000, there is a public health officer whose job description includes paying attention to the health threats facing the population. The job of a leader of the public health department is to convene local resources in other sectors like education, agriculture, housing, transportation, and the private sector and then use them to devise and implement local strategies that are endorsed by the community. Unlike layer 3, where the medical care of a sick person is wholly a cost to the health sector, in layer 1 the responsibility to protect the community is ready to be shouldered by many outside the health sector. When the health sector fails to exercise its convening role in public health, pent-up resources and political will remain unused. People want to live in healthy and resilient communities, and they will donate their time, their land, and their skills only if they are convened and shown how their efforts can actually succeed.

Managerial attention to the performance of district-level public health departments and systems to track their spending do not require new tools. Existing tools just need to be adapted locally. Box 3.3 describes an experiment to improve recordkeeping in Nigeria.

Box 3.3

Findings from an Experiment on Social Recognition to Improve Recordkeeping in Public Health Care Clinics in Select States in Nigeria

Bureaucratic performance is a crucial determinant of economic growth. Little is known about how to improve it in resource-constrained settings. Gauri et al. (2018) describe a field trial of a social recognition intervention to improve recordkeeping in clinics in two Nigerian states, replicating the intervention—implemented by a single organization—on bureaucrats performing identical tasks in both states. Social recognition improved performance in one state, but had no effect in the other, highlighting both the potential and the limitations of behavioral interventions. Differences in observables did not explain cross-state differences in impacts, illustrating the limitations of observation-based approaches to external validity.

The randomized control trial took place in two states that have very different levels of human capital and bureaucratic organization. Across a number of indicators, Ekiti State has higher capacity than Niger State. According to figures from the 2013 Demographic and Health Survey, such as data on birth registration rates, bureaucratic capacity is higher and adult literacy rates are much higher in Ekiti than in Niger. This finding suggests, tentatively, that the incentive of social recognition requires higher levels of training and organization on the part of public

(continued)

Box 3.3

Findings from an Experiment on Social Recognition to Improve Recordkeeping in Public Health Care Clinics in Select States in Nigeria *(continued)*

sector health officials in order to be effective. It may be that social recognition was motivating for officials in Ekiti, but not in Niger, because in Ekiti health care workers believed that the bureaucracy had the capacity to use social recognition as a credible input into long-term career incentives. Ekiti and Niger differ along many dimensions; in addition to many demographic differences, the drug procurement systems for the public health systems in the two states depend on different fractions of public funding (Saleh, Gauthier, and Pimhidzai 2020).

As in many low- and middle-income countries, in Nigeria the bureaucratic and managerial environment for service providers is highly heterogeneous, varying between states and even within a single state (Rogger 2018). That an intervention was successful in one state, but not in another, speaks to the importance of considering this variation when translating successful findings to a new context—even when the implementers in both cases are the same.

In Ekiti, the social recognition intervention significantly improved the quality with which facilities filled out the cash book form and sustained the improved performance over the intervention period. Naturally, this analysis does not say anything about the long-term effects of similar approaches or, in particular, whether there is potentially either adaptation to the recognition or, on the flip side, habit formation regarding the desired activity. It would be valuable to know more about the effects of the intervention on the overall performance of bureaucrats in a multitasking environment. Future work may be able to speak to these and other questions concerning the establishment of effective organizations in low- and middle-income countries.

Source: Gauri et al. 2018.

Setting an Agenda for the Future

This chapter has demonstrated the challenges in estimating how much low-income and lower-middle-income countries spend on the three layers of the health system. The System of Health Accounts has established coding for distinguishing spending between the three layers; when data are available, the SHA could be used to trace country spending patterns on each of the three layers. However, the biggest challenge lies in countries' capacity to report their health spending patterns, especially for layers 1 and 2. NHA country reporting on layer 1 health spending, in particular, is incomplete for both low-income and lower-middle-income countries. Layer 2 information, too, is quite limited for countries at both income levels. The primary challenge is to build a comprehensive PFM system and to sustain it. Among the prerequisites for improved reporting, countries must develop a chart of accounts at all administrative levels and improve the capabilities and motives for compiling, accounting, analyzing, and reporting health spending information on a regular basis. Such data will help policy makers to make timely decisions on how many resources to allocate, for what, and from what sources and to assess the effectiveness of spending.

Spending on layers 1 and 2 is limited. Layer 1 spending accounts for 3–5 percent of total health spending. Layer 1 consists mostly of public health functions, which are highly cost-effective and should be financed primarily from public resources. Per capita spending for layer 1 is not high (US$2 to US$4), but even that small amount is often not allocated, given the low visibility of this subsector, coupled with funding challenges, capability challenges, and inequitable distribution of staffing. Country case studies reveal significant challenges in planning, implementing, monitoring, and supervision.

Setting an Agenda for Effective Country Engagement

The following are activities for countries to consider:

- Conduct staff and system capabilities assessments and planning at all administrative levels for the three layers;
- Prioritize packages of services and functions explicitly for public health and primary health care, plan financial needs and equitable allocations, and track spending against results, especially for layers 1 and 2;
- Prioritize institution building around systems and capabilities for PFM at all administrative levels;
- Identify mechanisms to improve motives (for example, social recognition and others), including monitoring and reporting of results and performance, and establish a clear accountability framework with a focus on primary health care; and
- Reassess policy goals by including efficiency and resilience as part of institutional strengthening.

Note

1. WHO, Global Health Expenditure Database, https://apps.who.int/nha/database.

References

Alfonso, Y. Natalia, Guiru Ding, and David Bishai. 2015. "Income Elasticity of Vaccines Spending versus General Healthcare Spending." *Health Economics* 25 (7): 860–72.

Alwan, Ala, Pekka Puska, and Sameen Siddiqi. 2016. "Essential Public Health Functions for Countries of the Eastern Mediterranean Region: What Are They and What Benefits Do They Offer?" *Eastern Mediterranean Health Journal* 21 (12): 859–60.

Bettcher, Douglas W., Steve Sapirie, and Eric H. T. Goon. 1998. "Essential Public Health Functions: Results of the International Delphi Study." *World Health Statistics Quarterly* 51 (1): 44–54.

Bishai, David, and Carolina Cardona. 2017. "Aggregate Health Spending." *The Lancet* 390 (10095): 647.

Cotlear, Daniel, Somil Nagpal, Owen Smith, Ajay Tandon, and Rafael Cortez. 2015. *Going Universal: How 24 Developing Countries Are Implementing Universal Health Coverage from the Bottom Up.* Washington, DC: World Bank.

COVID-19 National Preparedness Collaborators. 2022. "Pandemic Preparedness and COVID-19: An Exploratory Analysis of Infection and Fatality Rates, and Contextual Factors Associated with Preparedness in 177 Countries, from Jan. 1, 2020, to Sept. 30, 2021." *The Lancet* 99 (10334): 1489–512.

Das Gupta, Monica, and Manju Rani. 2004. "India's Public Health System: How Well Does It Function at the National Level?" Policy Research Working Paper 3447, World Bank, Washington, DC. https://hdl.handle.net/10986/14215.

Deaton, Angus. 2013. *The Great Escape: Health, Wealth, and the Origins of Inequality.* Princeton, NJ: Princeton University Press.

Farag, Marwa, A. K. NandaKumar, Stanley Wallack, Dominic Hodgkin, Gary Gaumer, and Can Erbil. 2012. "The Income Elasticity of Health Care Spending in Developing and Developed Countries." *International Journal of Health Care Finance and Economics* 12 (2): 145–62.

Fleisher, Lisa, Adam Leive, and George Schieber. 2013. *Taking Stock of Fiscal Health: Trends in Global, Regional, and Country Level Health Financing.* Health, Nutrition, and Population (HNP) Discussion Paper. Washington, DC: World Bank. https://open-knowledge.worldbank.org/handle/10986/18695.

Gauri, Varun, Julian C. Jamison, Nina Mazar, Owen Ozier, Shomikho Raha, and Karima Saleh. 2018. "Motivating Bureaucrats through Social Recognition: Evidence from Simultaneous Field Experiments." Policy Research Working Paper 8473, World Bank, Washington, DC.

Global Burden of Disease Collaborative Network. 2024. *Global Health Spending 1995–2022.* Seattle, WA: Institute for Health Metrics and Evaluation.

Global Burden of Disease Health Financing Collaborator Network. 2019. "Past, Present, and Future of Global Health Financing: A Review of Development Assistance, Government, Out-of-Pocket, and Other Private Spending on Health for 195 Countries, 1995–2050." *The Lancet* 393 (10187): 2233–60.

Hanson, Kara, Nouria Brikci, Darius Erlangga, Abebe Alebachew, Manuela De Allegri, Dina Balabanova, Mark Blecher, Cheryl Cashin, Alexo Esperato, David Hipgrave, Ina Kalisa, Christoph Kurowski, Qingyue Meng, David Morgan, Gemini Mtei, Ellen Nolte, Chima Onoka, Timothy Powell-Jackson, Martin Roland, Rajeev Sadanandan, Karin Stenberg, Jeanette Vega Morales, Hong Wang, and Haja Wurie. 2022. "The Lancet Global Health Commission on Financing Primary Health Care: Putting People at the Centre." *Lancet Global Health* 10 (5): e715–e772.

IHME (Institute for Health Metrics and Evaluation). 2020a. *Financing Global Health 2019: Tracking Health Spending in a Time of Crisis.* Seattle, WA: IHME. https://www.healthdata.org/research-analysis/library/financing-global-health-2019-tracking-health-spending-time-crisis.

IHME (Institute for Health Metrics and Evaluation). 2020b. *Financing Global Health 2020: The Impact of COVID-19.* Seattle, WA: IHME. https://www.healthdata.org/research-analysis/library/financing-global-health-2020-impact-covid-19.

Kieny, Marie-Paule, and Christopher J. Murray. 2015. "Memorandum of Understanding between WHO and IHME." World Health Organization, Geneva; Institute for Health Metrics and Evaluation, Seattle, WA.

Mcintyre, Di, Filip Meheus, and John-Arne Røttingen. 2017. "What Level of Domestic Government Health Expenditure Should We Aspire to for Universal Health Coverage?" *Health Economics, Policy, and Law* 12 (2): 125–37.

OECD (Organisation for Economic Co-operation and Development). 2000. *A System of Health Accounts.* Paris: OECD Publishing. https://doi.org/10.1787/9789264181809-en.

OECD (Organisation for Economic Co-operation and Development). 2022. "Health Expenditure." OECD, Paris.

OECD (Organisation for Economic Co-operation and Development), Eurostat, and WHO (World Health Organization). 2017. *A System of Health Accounts 2011: Revised Edition.* Paris: OECD Publishing. https://doi.org/10.1787/9789264270985-en.

OECD (Organisation for Economic Co-operation and Development), Eurostat, and WHO (World Health Organization). 2021. "Accounting Guidelines for COVID-19 Related Activities under the 2021 Joint OECD, Eurostat and WHO Health Accounts (SHA 2011) Data Collection." OECD, Paris; Eurostat, Luxembourg; WHO, Geneva.

PAHO (Pan American Health Organization). 2001. *Public Health in the Americas: Instrument for Performance Measurement of Essential Public Health Functions.* Washington, DC: PAHO.

Rathe, Magdalena, Patricia Hernandez, Cornelis Van Mosseveld, Claudia Pescetto, and Nathalie Van de Maele. 2021. "Health Accounts from Past to Present for a Political Arithmetic." *Pan American Journal of Public Health* 45: e72.

Rogger, Daniel. 2018. "The Consequences of Political Interference in Bureaucratic Decision Making: Evidence from Nigeria." Policy Research Working Paper 8554, World Bank, Washington, DC.

Saleh, Karima, Ricardo Bitran, and Bernard Couttolenc. 2018. *The Financial Sustainability of HIV/AIDS and Universal Health Coverage in Selected Countries of Sub-Saharan Africa.* Washington, DC: World Bank. https://documents.worldbank.org/curated/en /608031532356993332/The-financial-sustainability-of-HIV-AIDS-and-universal -health-coverage-programs-in-Sub-Saharan-Africa.

Saleh, Karima, Bernard Gauthier, and Obert Pimhidzai. 2020. "Resource Tracking for Primary Health Care in Selected States in Nigeria: Findings from a Prospective Public Expenditure Tracking Survey." In *Tracking Resources for Primary Health Care: A Framework and Practices in Low- and Middle-Income Countries,* ch. 7, edited by Hong Wang and Peter Berman. World Scientific Series in Global Health Economics and Public Policy, vol. 8. Waltham, MA: World Scientific. https://doi.org/10.1142 /9789811212413_0007.

Schneider, Matthew T., Angela Y. Chang, Abigail Chapin, Catherine S. Chen, Sawyer W. Crosby, Anton C. Harle, Golsum Tsakalos, Bianca S. Zlavog, and Joseph L. Dieleman. 2021. "Health Expenditures by Services and Providers for 195 Countries, 2000–2017." *BMJ Global Health* 6 (7): e005799.

Szreter, Simon. 1988. "The Importance of Social Intervention in Britain's Mortality Decline c. 1850–1914: A Reinterpretation of the Role of Public Health." *Social History of Medicine* 1 (1): 1–38.

WHO (World Health Organization). 2012. "Strengthening Public Health Services and Capacity: An Action Plan for Europe: Promoting Health and Well-Being Now and for Future Generations." WHO, Regional Office for Europe, Copenhagen. https:// iris.who.int/handle/10665/340447.

Zhao, Feng, Sulzhan Bali, Rialda Kovacevic, and Jeff Weintraub. 2021. "A Three-Layer System to Win the War against COVID-19 and Invest in Health Systems of the Future." *BMJ Global Health* 6 (12): e007365.

PART 2

Country Case Studies

To complement the more conceptual framework, a range of experts provided snapshots of health system resilience in a variety of countries. Although there are commonalities among them, each country faces opportunities and challenges unique to its own context. There is no one-size-fits-all solution to strengthening health care system resilience, and the three-layer framework offers a broad set of strategies that each country will execute in its own way. The following are some of the main conclusions.

Chapter 4 builds on chapter 3 by illustrating the insight that can emerge from examining national health accounts. Pakistan spends only 4 percent of total government health expenditure on public health, and most of this spending is for staff salaries, leaving few resources for core public health activities such as disease preparedness and response. An analysis of health spending in one urban district in Pakistan found that immunization management accounts for more than 50 percent of the district health office's activity. While immunization is a foundational intervention, public health capability requires urgent attention. Pakistan needs not only to expand public health spending but also to strengthen local resilience.

Chapter 5 examines digital health interventions for pandemic preparedness. As COVID-19 strained health systems around the world, many countries developed or adapted digital health tools to detect and respond to the novel coronavirus. Burkina Faso used the existing scale and familiarity with CommCare, a health app, to deploy COVID-19 modules for triage, counseling, and e-learning for health workers across the country. To address the pandemic, Sri Lanka scaled the use of modules of DHIS2 (District Health Information Software 2), a digital health information systems management tool built on an underlying data infrastructure, local information technology expertise, and health care workers' familiarity. Nigeria used the modular design of SORMAS— the Surveillance Outbreak Response Management and Analysis System—to accommodate new disease outbreaks quickly and easily. The Indian state of Uttar Pradesh used collaboration between public and private stakeholders to develop and adopt the Unified COVID-19 Data Platform.

Chapter 6 describes the Republic of Korea's experience in promoting prevention, pandemic preparedness and response, and advanced case management and surge response. Korea used the lessons learned from a deadly outbreak of Middle East respiratory syndrome (MERS) in 2015 and policy and institutional reforms implemented before the COVID-19 pandemic hit to prepare and respond to COVID-19. It subsequently adopted legislative and regulatory reforms that enhanced the public health preparedness and response system, showing the benefits of making predictable and sustained investment in essential public health functions in an integrated health system over time.

Chapter 7 examines Thailand's success in addressing the challenges posed by the COVID-19 pandemic. The second country in the world to detect a case of COVID-19, Thailand was effective in its ability to assess, adapt, and respond to the many complex challenges that presented during the COVID-19 pandemic. This success was due, in large part, to the country's strong network of village health volunteers; coordinated, demand-driven approach; and high level of public trust.

Chapter 8 describes the Dominican Republic's response to the pandemic and ability to mobilize the entire country toward a common goal. The country also benefited from previous investments in building trust between communities and health care workers to ensure rapid uptake of public health interventions. It also encouraged strong public-private alliances, which provided the health system with the resources and funding needed to avoid saturating the health system during pandemic surges.

Chapter 9 looks at Costa Rica's highly integrated health care system. During the COVID-19 pandemic, Costa Rica's integrated health system allowed one entity, the Costa Rican Social Security Fund (CCSS), to implement changes across the health system to maintain essential health services during the pandemic and respond to urgent health system needs. In particular, the country's prior experience with transferring patients from overwhelmed hospitals to less-affected hospitals proved invaluable in relieving pressure on the system. Moreover, the use of EDUS, an electronic medical record system, facilitated the gathering of data. A contingency fund provided the funding needed to adjust protocols and staffing.

Finally, chapter 10 describes Uganda's early and aggressive actions to limit the spread of COVID-19. Immediately after the World Health Organization declared COVID-19 a public health emergency of international concern, the Ministry of Health activated its Public Health Emergency Operations Center and National Task Force—shifting from preparedness to response when the first case was recorded in March 2020. Building on experience gained in previous outbreaks of epidemic-prone disease, Uganda employed innovative strategies such as shifting tasks to community health workers, leveraging technology for telemedicine and supervision, establishing special clinics for essential health services, and providing medicines in higher quantities.

4

Financial Analysis of Local Public Health Activity in Urban Pakistan

Cynthia Wang, David Bishai, Ammarah Ali, and Shehla Zaidi

IN SUMMARY

- Public health spending is low in Pakistan, accounting for only 4 percent of total government health expenditure exclusive of staff salaries, and it has changed little despite an incremental rise in government health spending overall.

- District health systems are the administrative units where public health functions are integrated. However, staff salaries account for the lion's share of public health expenditure, leaving few resources for core public health activities such as disease preparedness and response.

- An analysis of an urban district in Pakistan found that immunization management accounts for more than 50 percent of the district health office's activity. While immunization is a foundational intervention, its financing dominates and distorts the public health capability of health workers.

- Because public health spending on capabilities at the district level is so low, it is necessary to tie the expansion of public health spending with the adoption of an agenda to strengthen local resilience.

- One solution is to impose a 20 percent surcharge on vertical disease program budgets held at federal and provincial levels to be dedicated for nonsalaried and noncommodity expenditures to expand public health capability in early tracking and response to diseases.

Introduction

Past Research on Local Public Health Spending on Capability

Little is known about local public health spending on capability. The major obstacle is that accounting systems for local health departments do not use a chart of accounts that ties spending to categories of public health capabilities. One study in the United States, a higher-income country, showed that the state of Ohio spent a median of US$7.67 per capita on foundational capabilities in public health (Singh, Bekemeier, and Leider 2020). To date, an extensive search for similar studies from low- and middle-income countries has not been successful. Because national data on spending for public health activities are scarce in low- and middle-income countries, formative research was conducted in urban Pakistan both to assess the feasibility of costing public health activity and to validate the impressions gained from national health accounts (NHA) data. The data were collected in an urban setting where the team was implementing an action-learning pilot on immunization delivery.

Context of Pakistan's Health Spending

Pakistan spends 3.2 percent of the gross domestic product (GDP) on health care, amounting to US$48 per capita, of which approximately US$17 per capita is spent by the government and the remainder by households, nongovernmental organizations, and parastatals (Pakistan, Bureau of Statistics 2018). NHAs map health expenditure by levels of health care and type of spending. The recent round of Pakistan's NHAs provided data on national health spending by the public sector. These results showed that spending on health constitutes only 4 percent of total government spending, with hospitals accounting for the largest share (76 percent), followed by the administration of peripheral district health infrastructure (19 percent), as shown in table 4.1. Salaries for staff involved in public health spending are counted under general administration. While government health expenditures increased 49 percent between 2015–16 and 2017–18, countering inflationary erosion, there has been little change in spending patterns over time.

Under Pakistan's devolved health system, the federal government is only responsible for setting national targets and for coordinating and administering health care in the federal territories. Provincial governments direct planning and programming, and districts are the administrative hubs of service delivery (Zaidi et al. 2019). Districts are the largest consumers of the budget, although they are only responsible for managing district spending for frontline health

Table 4.1   Government Health Expenditures in Pakistan, by Function, 2017–18

Function[a]	Expenditure (Pakistani rupees, millions)	Share of total (%)
Medical products, appliances, and equipment	268	0.08
General services	797	0.2
Outpatient services	1,332	0.4
Public health services	12,210	4
Health administration	63,155	19
Hospital services	246,619	76
Total	**324,381**	

Source: Pakistan, Bureau of Statistics 2018.

a. Function is according to the chart of accountants.

staff and consumables for field operations. The main district expense consists of salaries of doctors, equipment, and commodities and is borne by the province (figure 4.1). Pakistan has a long history of implementing vertical disease control programs, most of which originated because of similar global initiatives. While donors have been the most powerful advocates for public health in Pakistan, they have been criticized for supporting vertical disease control activities as opposed to creating synergies for core public health functions (Zaidi et al. 2019). Immunization consumes the largest share of vertical program budgets across all programs. The next section provides more granular data on spending for public health functions in one district of Pakistan.

Methods

Data are from Karachi, which is the largest city of Pakistan, with a population of more than 16 million, according to the 2017 census (Pakistan, Bureau of Statistics 2017).

Figure 4.1   Government Health Expenditures in Pakistan, by Source of Financing, 2017–18

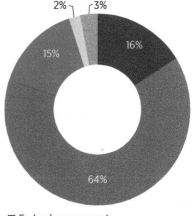

■ Federal government
■ Provincial government
■ District or tehsil government
▨ Social security funds
▨ Autonomous bodies and corporations

Source: Pakistan, Bureau of Statistics 2018.

Although Karachi is the provincial capital of Sindh Province and the commercial hub of the country, approximately 45 percent of its population lives in urban slums. There are five districts within the metropolis of Karachi. The study focused on one district with a population of 2.9 million, providing a mix of low- and middle-income populations. Each district is headed by a district health officer backed up by an additional district health officer and four assistant district health officers.

District governments are important financial intermediaries, as 60 percent of total health expenditures is spent in district budgets. The flow of funds for salaries is from the provinces and goes directly into employee accounts. Expanded Program on Immunization vaccines, Lady Health Worker kits, and other preventive program supplies are supplied directly to the districts; medicines are purchased partially by the provinces and partially by the districts based on reapproved tenders. While the district is the largest consumer of the budget, it manages only part of its budget; the rest is controlled by the province.

Public health capacity is weak across provincial and district health personnel, with leadership-governance and access to medicines scoring the weakest across the six health systems. While considerable effort has gone into building the capacity of provincial health officers and district officers of rural districts through a combination of short courses and full master's degrees, urban Sindh districts have not benefited from similar training (figure 4.2).

Figure 4.2 Average Self-Assessed Capacity Scores of Provincial and District Public Health Personnel in Sindh Province, Pakistan, 2014

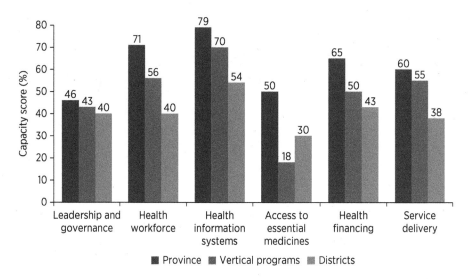

Source: JSI 2014.

More recently, as part of provincial disease surveillance efforts, monitoring and evaluation hubs have been established in all districts, including the urban districts of Karachi, assisted by a dashboard, information technology staff, and a data analyst; however, a field-based real-time data system is yet to be implemented.

Data Source

Secondary data were collated and their interpretation was supported by insights from local district health stakeholders. Data were collected on allocations by staff grade, salary range by staff grade, time allocation across different public health functions, categorization of functions by district versus provincial responsibility, and annual health budget managed by the district health office.

Key informant interviews were held with district health officer leadership to discuss the staffing and allocation of staff time to the various projects and to the various public health activities run by the health office. Time allocations were also categorized into four exclusive public health capacities: organizational management, partnerships, surveillance, and communication. The motivation for this four-way categorization came from the RESOLVE framework for building a chart of accounts for public health (Public Health Leadership Forum 2014).

The time spent by each staff member was allocated across these capabilities to add up to 100 percent of their effort. Each worker's time allocation was also attributed to the various public health activities, adding up to 100 percent.

The salary classification for each public health staffer was determined, and the high, low, and midpoint salaries were determined by reference to official government pay scales.

Analysis

For each worker, the expenditure on each public health activity was calculated as follows:

$$Spending \ on \ Activity \ i = \sum_{j} Wage_j \times \% \ Effort_{ji},\tag{4.1}$$

where subscript "i" is for activities, and subscript "j" is for the type of worker.

$$Spending \ on \ Capability \ i = \sum_{j} Wage_j \times \% \ Effort_{ji}.\tag{4.2}$$

The total costs of all activities in the health department were computed by summing over all activities. All spending is given in 2022 currency values, with conversion to US dollars at the commercial bank rate as of June 2022.

Results

Personnel of District Health Department

The local district health department in Karachi in 2022 was made up of 47 staff with a mean monthly salary of PRs 61,510 (US$302.13). The total estimated monthly cost of salaries for the health department was PRs 3,790,460 (US$18,609). Positions held in the department were broken down into different basic pay scale (BPS) or grade levels, ranging from 11 to 20, with a greater number indicating a higher ranking in the system. As table 4.2 shows,

Table 4.2 Descriptive Data on District Health Personnel in Karachi, Pakistan, by Basic Pay Scale and Median Income, 2022

Designation	Number of posts	Basic pay scale	Median income (PRs)
Accounts officer	1	16	53,980
Additional district health officer—curative	1	19	115,690
Additional district health officer—planning, administration, and accounts	1	19	115,690
Additional district health officer—preventive	1	19	115,690
Assistant district health officer, CDD, EPI, and polio	1	17	68,890
Assistant district health officer, CDD, nutrition and noncommunicable diseases	1	17	68,890

(continued)

Table 4.2 *(continued)*

Designation	Number of posts	Basic pay scale	Median income (PRs)
Assistant district health officer, CDD-II	1	17	68,890
Assistant district health officer, CDD-I	1	17	68,890
Assistant district health officer, curative	1	17	68,890
Assistant district health officer, reproductive, maternal, neonatal, and child health	1	17	68,890
Data analyst	1	16	53,980
Deputy district health officer, curative	1	18	86,610
Deputy district health officer, management information system	1	18	86,610
Deputy district health officer, planning and development	1	18	86,610
Deputy district health officer, CDD-I (tuberculosis, HIV/AIDS, and perinatal death surveillance and response)	1	18	86,610
Deputy district health officer, EPI and polio	1	18	86,610
Deputy district health officer, nutrition and noncommunicable diseases	1	18	86,610
Deputy district health officer, CDD-II (typhoid, hepatitis, and CDD)	1	18	86,610
Deputy district health officer, reproductive, maternal, neonatal, and child health	1	18	86,610
Deputy district health officer, vector-borne disease	1	18	86,610
Deputy town or taluka officer, preventive	3	18	86,610
Deputy town or taluka officer, curative	3	18	86,610
District malaria superintendent	1	16	53,980
District EPI focal person	1	17	68,890
District health officer	1	20	129,740
District superintendent, vaccination	1	16	53,980
District surveillance coordinator	1	17	68,890
District tuberculosis coordinator	1	17	68,890
Emergency or disaster focal person	1	18	86,610
Epidemiologist	1	17	68,890
Health education officer	1	17	68,890
Medical superintendent, hospitals	2	19	115,690
Procurement officer, needs-based local procurement	1	17	68,890
Town superintendent, vaccination	3	11	33,390
Town surveillance officer, urban	3	17	68,890
Town or taluka health officer	3	19	115,690

Source: Tabulation of administrative data from a district health department in Sindh Province, Pakistan.

Note: CDD = childhood disintegrative disorder; EPI = Expanded Program on Immunization; HIV/AIDS = human immunodeficiency virus/acquired immunodeficiency syndrome.

workers were mostly in the higher categories of 16 to 18; 16 workers were in BPS 18 (34.0 percent), followed by 15 workers in BPS 17 (31.9 percent), 8 workers in BPS 19 (17.0 percent), and 4 workers in BPS 16 (8.51 percent). The health officer was in the highest BPS, at BPS 20.

Staff Spending Distributed by Public Health Activity

Figure 4.3 shows the allocation of spending for full-time equivalent (FTE) staff across the main public health activities undertaken by the department. Total monthly expenditure for FTE staff was PRs 1,834,794 (US$9,008). Immunizations constituted the greatest proportion of this budget, at 52.6 percent per month (PRs 965,115 or US$4,738), while tobacco contributed only 1 percent per month (PRs 18,391 or US$90).

Figure 4.3 Share of Total Spending on District Full-Time Equivalent Staff in Karachi, Pakistan, by Public Health Activity, 2022

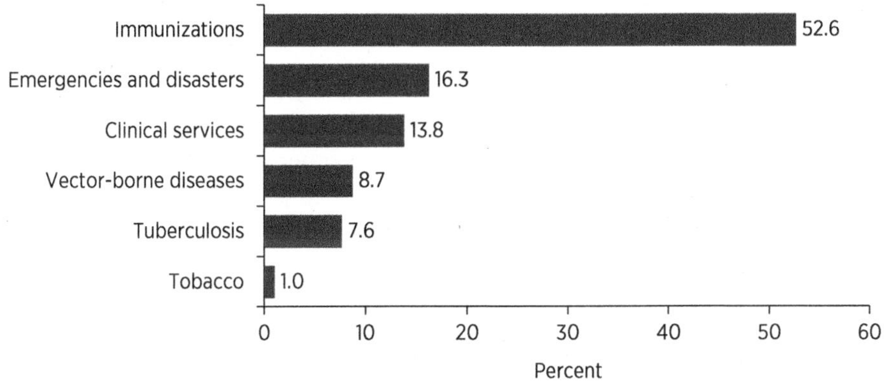

Source: Analysis of data from a district health office in Sindh Province, Pakistan.

District Health Office Spending by Public Health Capability

The annual district health budget was analyzed, and allocations by activities were categorized against four main public health capabilities: communication, surveillance, partnerships, and organizational management. The district health office budget is only a portion of total district health spending and solely includes allocation for district frontline staff, local monitoring, risk communication, and field support activities. Organizational management was the greatest contributor to spending, making up 50.2 percent of the expenditures, followed by surveillance, with 31.4 percent (figure 4.4). Communication and partnerships both contributed less, with 8.4 percent and 10.0 percent, respectively.

Figure 4.4 Allocation of the District Health Budget in Karachi, Pakistan, by Public Health Capability, 2022

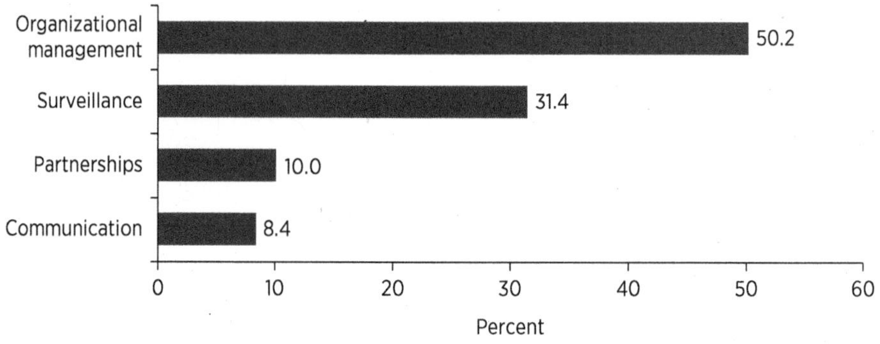

Source: Analysis of data from a district health office in Sindh Province, Pakistan.

Discussion

The allocation of public health spending at the district level is strikingly low for an urban health district: US$223,308 per year (US$18,609 × 12) divided by 2.8 million people, which equals just US$0.08 per person per year. Total health spending in Pakistan was US$48 per capita in 2017–18, amounting to US$17 per capita in government health spending and to only 4 percent on public health (Pakistan, Bureau of Statistics 2018). If this district's health spending reflects the national average, the public health allocation managed at the district level would account for a mere 0.05 percent of government health spending.

This finding highlights two important issues: first, overall national public health funding is limited, and allocations at the district level are insufficient to manage core public health functions (communication, surveillance, organizational management, and partnerships); second, immunization consumes the lion's share of scant allocations, severely constraining the ability to respond to other diseases.

Fragmentation and Distortion

Immunization activities consume more than half of the effort of the public health department, excluding the costs of frontline vaccinators, syringes, needles, waste management, and acquiring and storing vaccines.

Immunization is indeed one of the most cost-effective public health interventions, and this activity, which includes polio eradication efforts, is extremely important to the health of Karachi residents. Nevertheless, the dominant role of immunization financing distorts the public health capability of Karachi's district-level public health workers, as shown in figure 4.4. Immunization work demands organizational management of logistics and personnel, and it demands surveillance. These two public health capabilities account for 81 percent of the effort of public health staff and have crowded out capabilities in communication and partnerships.

Challenges to Becoming More Resilient

Even though Sindh Province assessed its public health capability in 2014 and invested in training its workforce in public health in rural areas, it continues to face challenges in maintaining a well-rounded set of public health capabilities. The funding sources flowing through this urban health district have prioritized badly needed immunization activities, and the work of this one activity dominates the department.

The goals of resilience would be well served if urban health departments could autonomously allocate some of their workforce to partnerships, communication, and surveillance of health determinants and to priorities other than immunization. Given the low share of public health in overall government spending, there is clearly room to expand public health spending by investing in overall capability and not just in capability tied to immunization. The range of public health threats facing Karachi encompasses far more than vaccine-preventable diseases. Karachi and other urban areas of Pakistan experienced the highest concentration of COVID-19 cases early in the pandemic (TDEA 2021). Moreover, outbreaks of dengue and typhoid are common, alongside endemic diseases such as tuberculosis, malaria, and hepatitis and the rise of noncommunicable diseases (WHO and Alliance for Health Policy and Systems Research 2017). While scant resources are available for public health functions at the district level, little effort has been made to create cost-efficiencies between disease programs. Capabilities built for immunization can be applied to other programs if supported with additional resources. Obtaining additional resourcing—based on incremental costs—is likely to be more cost-efficient than fully resourcing public health functions for each disease program, assuming a zero-cost base.

Protected financing is required for essential public health functions at the district health offices to assess and respond to old threats as well as emerging threats such as noncommunicable diseases and aging, antimicrobial resistance, climate emergencies, and sexual and reproductive health problems. The goal is for Karachi's urban health districts and all districts to marshal community members to identify and respond to whatever threatens health, in addition to maintaining high levels of immunization as they do now.

Conclusion

An analysis of an urban district health office in Pakistan found that its allocations for public health functions accounted for just 0.05 percent of all of government health spending. Furthermore, immunization management accounted for more than 50 percent of the district health office's public health activity. Immunization dominated the workplan because it is highly cost-effective and because financing is often leveraged by donor contributions.

The dominance of immunization activity in the public health workflow may have crowded out the public health department's ability to allocate staff time to resilience-building activities related to building partnerships, communicating with the public and others, and conducting local surveillance of emerging health threats not related to immunization. Capabilities developed for immunization surveillance, risk communication, field monitoring, and organizational management somehow must be pivoted toward other disease programs. Achieving cross-system benefits when one unit develops heightened capacity is a managerial dilemma if staff are tied to acting only within their own programs. New costing models need to embrace cost-efficient synergies across programs.

Because public health's share of government health spending is so minuscule, it may be possible to expand public health spending while intertwining it with an agenda centered around resilience measures. Existing tools that measure public health capability could be used to take stock of current capabilities. They also could tie new expenditures to activities that promote population health and emphasize less-developed capabilities such as communication and partnerships as well as monitoring the population for emerging health threats.

A more innovative idea would be for financing of peripheral district health offices in Pakistan to sequester a public health system surcharge of 20 percent on federal and provincial vertical programs inclusive of donor finance tied to vertical programs. The surcharge would be used to expand the competencies of public health staff and to cover the operations costs for core field and management activities. Spending on competency development could be made accountable if the districts would collect measurements of essential public health functions and track them over time, as described in chapter 2. If public health funds are spent on measurable improvements in essential public health functions, they would pay a resilience dividend to municipal residents and help vertical programs to improve their delivery of services. More important, districts' public health operations would be resilient and able to build trust and partnerships to achieve shared public health objectives.

Note

The authors acknowledge Dr. Lala Aftab of Aga Khan University for coordination and fieldwork.

References

JSI (John Snow International). 2014. "Capacity Development in Sindh Province." Report funded by US Agency for International Development in partnership with the Department of Health, Sindh Province, Pakistan. JSI, Berkeley, CA. https://www.jsi.com/resource/capacity-development-in-sindh-province/.

Pakistan, Bureau of Statistics. 2017. *Population and Housing Census–2017.* Islamabad: Ministry of Planning, Development, and Special Initiatives. https://www.pbs.gov.pk/content/final-results-census-2017.

Pakistan, Bureau of Statistics. 2018. *National Health Accounts 2017–18.* Islamabad: Ministry of Planning, Development, and Special Initiatives. https://www.pbs.gov.pk/sites/default/files/national_accounts/national_health_accounts/national_health_accounts_2017_18.pdf.

Public Health Leadership Forum. 2014. "Defining and Constituting Foundational 'Capabilities' and Areas." RESOLVE, Washington, DC.

Singh, Simone R., Betty Bekemeier, and Jonathan P. Leider. 2020. "Local Health Departments' Spending on the Foundational Capabilities." *Journal of Public Health Management and Practice* 26 (1): 52–56.

TDEA (Trust for Democratic Education and Accountability). 2021. "Pakistan's Pandemic Governance Framework: FAFEN's Monitoring and Assessment of the Government's COVID-19 Response." TDEA and Free and Fair Election Network (FAFEN), Islamabad, April 2021. https://phkh.nhsrc.pk/sites/default/files/2021-08/FAFEN%20Monitoring%20and%20Assessment%20of%20the%20Government%20COVID-19%20Response%20%20Pakistan%202021.pdf.

WHO (World Health Organization) and Alliance for Health Policy and Systems Research. 2017. *Primary Health Care Systems (Primasys): Comprehensive Case Study from Pakistan.* Geneva: WHO. https://iris.who.int/handle/10665/341143.

Zaidi, Shehla Abbas, Maryam Bigdeli, Etienne V. Langlois, Atif Riaz, David W. Orr, Nasir Idrees, and Jesse B. Bump. 2019. "Health Systems Changes after Decentralisation: Progress, Challenges, and Dynamics in Pakistan." *BMJ Global Health* 4 (1): e001013.

5

Three-Layer Health Sector Investment: Digital Health Interventions for Pandemic Preparedness in Low- and Middle-Income Countries

Siobhan Lazenby, Caitlyn Mason, Rachel Stuhldreher, Meredith Kimball, and Rebecca Bartlein

IN SUMMARY

- As COVID-19 strained health systems around the world, many countries developed or adapted digital health tools to detect and respond to the novel coronavirus. The following examples from Burkina Faso, India, Nigeria, and Sri Lanka offer insights on the implementation factors that led to the rapid launch and scale-up of digital tools in low- and middle-income countries during the COVID-19 pandemic.

- While clients, health care providers, and health system managers used the digital tools described in this chapter for a range of tasks (including surveillance, contact tracing, case management, risk communication, health worker training, lab management, and vaccine certification), common lessons emerged about the importance of user-centered design, strong country-led partnerships, and the leveraging of existing and adaptable digital tools.

- The lessons learned from implementing and adapting digital tools quickly during the COVID-19 pandemic can inform the use of digital tools for health applications beyond pandemic preparedness, such as bolstering primary health care, reaching vulnerable and marginalized populations, and empowering health workers with the real-time information necessary to optimize their work and improve the health of their target populations.

(continued)

Exemplars in Global Health (EGH), which sponsored the research for this chapter, has a mission to identify positive global health outliers, analyze what makes countries successful, and disseminate core lessons so they can be adapted in comparable settings. EGH is a global coalition of partners including researchers, academics, experts, funders, country stakeholders, and implementers. A small, core team supporting EGH is based at Gates Ventures, the private office of Bill Gates, and closely collaborates with the Gates Foundation. For the full case studies, refer to Exemplars in Global Health (2021a, 2021b, 2021c, 2022).

IN SUMMARY *(continued)*

Burkina Faso[a]

- The existing scale of and familiarity with CommCare in Burkina Faso enabled the rapid deployment of COVID-19 modules for triage, counseling, and e-learning across the country.

- Strong partnerships between the government, Terre des hommes, Dimagi, and other organizations contributed to the success of the Integrated e-Diagnostic Approach.

- CommCare's offline functionality and intuitive interface enhanced support for decision-making and improved the quality of care delivered.

- The large amount of data generated by the app provided health officials at the district and national levels with access to near real-time information for decision-making.

- By leveraging an established digital platform with a proven capacity for scale, the Ministry of Health and Terre des hommes could focus on the scope and content of the app rather than on the platform itself, which improved their ability to comply with regulations related to collecting and storing the health data of individuals.

Sri Lanka[b]

- Sri Lanka responded early and quickly—within two days—to scale modules of DHIS2, a digital health information systems management tool, for COVID-19 nationwide, before the country recorded any cases of the disease.

- Developers began building on the existing DHIS2 platform, which enabled them to leverage underlying data infrastructure, local information technology expertise, and health care workers' familiarity with the system to deploy the new module rapidly.

- The Ministry of Health had already invested in digital infrastructure and established strong relationships with the Health Information Systems Programme (HISP) Sri Lanka team; these factors enabled the Ministry of Health to take decisive action and launch work on the initial port-of-entry module.

- The existing global network enabled HISP to turn Sri Lanka's innovation into the basis for a global DHIS2 COVID-19 surveillance package, which other countries were quick to adopt.

Nigeria[c]

- The modular design of SORMAS (Surveillance Outbreak Response Management and Analysis System) allows it to accommodate new disease outbreaks quickly and easily. The system incorporated a COVID-19 module in February 2020, before Nigeria had confirmed its first case of the disease.

(continued)

IN SUMMARY *(continued)*

- Joint ownership of the development process gave local stakeholders the tools and experience they needed to adapt and scale up the system.
- Nigerian health authorities used the system to monitor real-time data for tracking cases and identifying clusters and to establish and update COVID-19 policies and public health measures.
- SORMAS enables health care providers and community members to report suspected cases of disease easily and creates standardized workflows to ensure that action is taken to limit further spread.

Uttar Pradesh, India[d]

- Collaboration between public and private stakeholders drove quick statewide development and adoption of the Unified COVID-19 Data Platform.
- The medium- to long-term thinking and support from technical support partners, such as the Uttar Pradesh Technical Support Unit, enabled the quick development, implementation, adaptation, and rollout of the digital platform.
- The platform's modular design integrates the needs of various stakeholders, including tracking teams, testing laboratories, and patients in home quarantine.
- The decision-making dashboard shows policy makers the data they need—such as information on contact tracing, transmission patterns, and clusters of cases—to develop, adapt, and evolve pandemic-response policies and practices.

a. The Burkina Faso case study is based on Exemplars in Global Health 2021a.
b. The Sri Lanka case study is based on Exemplars in Global Health 2021b.
c. The Nigeria case study is based on Exemplars in Global Health 2021c.
d. The Uttar Pradesh case study is based on Exemplars in Global Health 2022.

Layer 1: Risk Reduction—Promoting Prevention and Community Preparedness

Burkina Faso: How an Existing App, Designed for Child Health, Was Rapidly Adapted for COVID-19

Burkina Faso's Enabling Environment

More than a decade ago, Burkina Faso introduced a digital health solution to improve the health of children under five across the country. The Ministry of Health, in collaboration with the Swiss nonprofit Terre des hommes, implemented the Integrated e-Diagnostic Approach (IeDA) to improve protocol adherence and quality of care at the primary health care level. Built on Dimagi's CommCare platform, the tablet-based app provides health workers with enhanced decision support and serves as a digital aid to support the integrated management of childhood illnesses (IMCI) and reduce child mortality (Jane, Foutry, and Sanou 2018; Terre des hommes and Dimagi n.d.).[1] What started as a pilot project in one district in 2010 has since been scaled up to more than 1,700 rural primary health care facilities, with 6,300 health workers using the app to deliver more than 250,000 IMCI consultations per month (as of December 2021).[2]

Since the initial pilot of IeDA in 2010, strong partnerships between the government, Terre des hommes, Dimagi, and other organizations contributed to the success of IeDA. The app is fully integrated with the country's health infrastructure and is considered a priority within the national digital health strategy.

When the first cases of COVID-19 were reported in Burkina Faso in 2020, the CommCare app was already in the hands of health workers at 67 percent of the country's primary health care facilities. Because the app was already in widespread use and familiar to health workers, the Ministry of Health and Terre des hommes were able to adapt it rapidly for COVID-19 (figure 5.1).

Generating Value across Burkina Faso's Health System

The app was originally designed for primary health care workers. Health workers are prompted to fill in the information requested before receiving an automated diagnosis (which they use to make their own diagnosis) and guidance for proper treatment. The app is designed to be user-friendly. It guides health workers through decisions step by step, ensuring that they follow the proper protocols to complete their consultations. Instructional videos, audio files, and enabled text fields are easy for all health workers to use, regardless of their digital literacy, and e-learning modules help to refresh knowledge and provide continuous training for health workers who use the app every day.

The app generates value for users at every level of the health system:

- *Primary health care level.* Health workers can access patient registries and the full medical history of a patient, which was previously impossible with the paper-based system (figure 5.2). They can also view reports and assess their own performance relative to that of their peers.
- *District level.* Dashboards enable district health management teams to visualize the data collected during consultations and use them for monitoring and disease surveillance. CommCare also generates time stamps on app usage, enabling district staff to see the date, time, and speed of data entry, which facilitates performance coaching, targeted supervision, and training tailored to address the real needs of health workers.
- *National level.* CommCare integrates directly with the government's national health information system (Entrepôt National des Données Sanitaires built on DHIS2), creating an automatic end-to-end data pipeline from data collection and aggregation to national-level monitoring and reporting on key indicators.

Figure 5.1   Timeline of Key Events for the Development and Scale-Up of CommCare in Burkina Faso

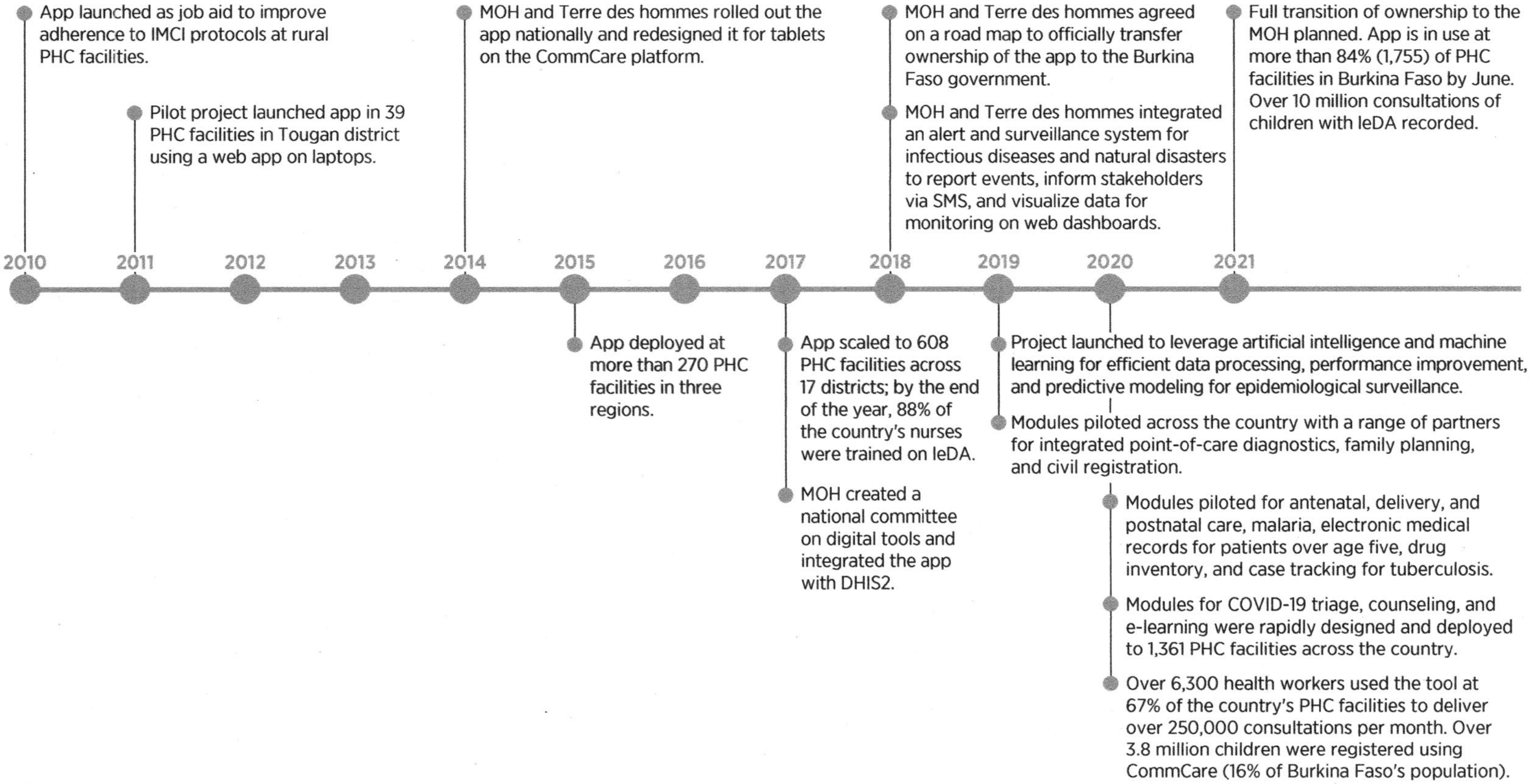

2010

2011   Pilot project launched app in 39 PHC facilities in Tougan district using a web app on laptops.

App launched as job aid to improve adherence to IMCI protocols at rural PHC facilities.

2012

2013

2014   MOH and Terre des hommes rolled out the app nationally and redesigned it for tablets on the CommCare platform.

2015   App deployed at more than 270 PHC facilities in three regions.

2016

2017   App scaled to 608 PHC facilities across 17 districts; by the end of the year, 88% of the country's nurses were trained on IeDA.

MOH created a national committee on digital tools and integrated the app with DHIS2.

2018   MOH and Terre des hommes agreed on a road map to officially transfer ownership of the app to the Burkina Faso government.

MOH and Terre des hommes integrated an alert and surveillance system for infectious diseases and natural disasters to report events, inform stakeholders via SMS, and visualize data for monitoring on web dashboards.

2019   Project launched to leverage artificial intelligence and machine learning for efficient data processing, performance improvement, and predictive modeling for epidemiological surveillance.

Modules piloted across the country with a range of partners for integrated point-of-care diagnostics, family planning, and civil registration.

2020   Modules piloted for antenatal, delivery, and postnatal care, malaria, electronic medical records for patients over age five, drug inventory, and case tracking for tuberculosis.

Modules for COVID-19 triage, counseling, and e-learning were rapidly designed and deployed to 1,361 PHC facilities across the country.

Over 6,300 health workers used the tool at 67% of the country's PHC facilities to deliver over 250,000 consultations per month. Over 3.8 million children were registered using CommCare (16% of Burkina Faso's population).

2021   Full transition of ownership to the MOH planned. App is in use at more than 84% (1,755) of PHC facilities in Burkina Faso by June. Over 10 million consultations of children with IeDA recorded.

Source: Exemplars in Global Health 2021a.

Note: DHIS2 = District Health Information Software 2; IeDA = Integrated e-Diagnostic Approach; IMCI = integrated management of childhood illnesses; MOH = Ministry of Health; PHC = primary health care; SMS = short message service.

Figure 5.2 Data Flow and Integration of CommCare with the Levels of Burkina Faso's Health System

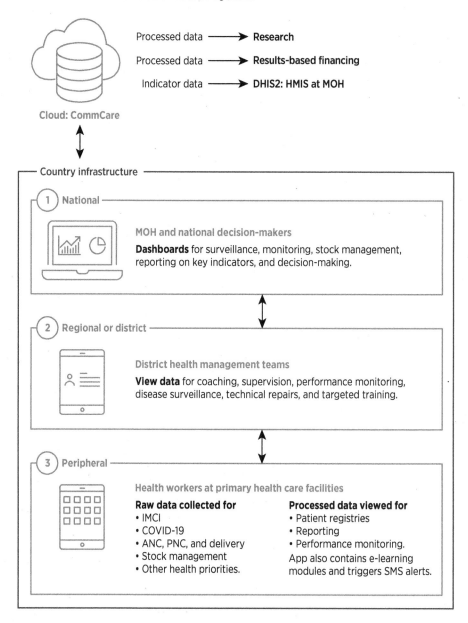

Source: Adapted from slides shared by Terre des hommes. Refer to Exemplars in Global Health 2021a.

Note: ANC = antenatal care; DHIS2 = District Health Information Software 2; HMIS = Health Management Information System; IMCI = integrated management of childhood illnesses; MOH = Ministry of Health; PNC = prenatal care; SMS = short message service.

Expanding Scale and Scope, Use in Other Countries and for Other Diseases

Before the COVID-19 pandemic, CommCare was a rare example of a digital health tool with widespread use in low- and middle-income countries. Throughout the pandemic, it was adopted or adapted by dozens of governments. For example, the governments of Togo and Zambia quickly equipped their contact tracers with a CommCare-based app. The government of Sierra Leone built a suite of CommCare tools, including quarantine compliance, supply management, and health facility readiness. The Instituto Nacional de Salud in Peru used it to deploy a home-based-care monitoring tool.

Burkina Faso's decade-long experience with one of the largest digital health projects in Sub-Saharan Africa demonstrates that it is possible to respond rapidly to an emerging health crisis with the help of strong digital infrastructure (map 5.1). The rapid adaptation of CommCare for COVID-19 in Burkina Faso illustrates the ease with which additional content can be deployed when digital solutions are running at scale in communities, and health workers are already familiar with the tool. By leveraging an established digital platform with a proven capacity for scale, the Ministry of Health and Terre des hommes could focus on the scope and content of the app rather than on the

Map 5.1   Deployment of the CommCare App in Primary Health Care Facilities across Health Districts of Burkino Faso, June 2020–December 2021

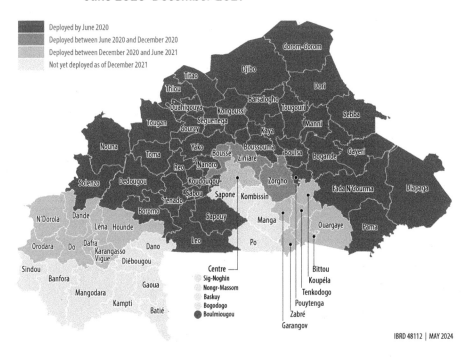

Source: Raw data provided by Terre des hommes. Also refer to Exemplars in Global Health 2021a.

platform itself, which helped them to comply with regulations regarding the collection and storage of the health data of individuals.

Moreover, implementation of the tool for child health—and an expanding list of other health areas, including malaria, nutrition, maternal health, tuberculosis, and pneumonia—offers important lessons on how to scale up and sustain digital health interventions for a variety of uses in low- and middle-income countries.

Layer 2: Focus on Detection, Containment, and Mitigation Capabilities

During a brief weekend workshop in Burkina Faso, three COVID-19 modules were designed and developed, and within three weeks the new content was deployed to health workers at primary health care facilities across the country:

- *Screening and triage*, which guides health workers through an algorithm to assess symptoms, map suspected cases, and trigger text alerts to health authorities for testing and follow-up;
- *Counseling and community sensitization*, which prompts health workers to share information, raise awareness, and coach caregivers on protective measures during IMCI consultations; and
- *E-learning for health workers*, which equips health workers with up-to-date information, guidance, and answers to frequently asked questions about COVID-19 in their communities.[3]

Rather than building and scaling up a new solution from scratch, COVID-19 content was integrated promptly into the existing CommCare app and deployed remotely to health workers at primary health care facilities that had the equipment and knowledge to begin using the app without the need for extensive training. The large amount of data generated by the app has provided health officials at the district and national levels with access to near real-time information for decision-making. Customizable and predictive dashboards facilitate monitoring, surveillance, and statistical analyses as well as performance coaching and targeted supervision of health workers.

Sri Lanka: Leveraging Existing Systems at Scale for COVID-19

When the COVID-19 outbreak began to spread throughout Asia at the beginning of 2020, Sri Lanka's health authorities moved quickly to keep it from spreading to their country. The Ministry of Health already used DHIS2 as its primary health information system to track and manage health data; within just a few days, partners from HISP Sri Lanka—a global network including independent HISP groups, universities, ministries of health, nongovernmental organizations, and global policy makers—developed and implemented new DHIS2 modules specifically for COVID-19 surveillance.

Sri Lanka's Enabling Environment

More than a decade of investment in digital health infrastructure in Sri Lanka made it possible for policy makers to assess their needs quickly in response to the emergence of COVID-19 in 2020, to identify the digital tools that could meet their needs, to define their requirements, and to mobilize support for their execution.

In 2011, some departments in the country's Ministry of Health implemented DHIS2 pilot programs to serve as the primary health information system for the country. DHIS2 is a web-based software platform for collecting, managing, and analyzing data. Today, DHIS2 is the world's largest health management information system platform, in use by ministries of health in 73 low- and middle-income countries.

Within Sri Lanka, many preventive health care institutes in the Ministry of Health use DHIS2 as the national information system. These are national-level implementations. Therefore, the country has developed capacity at the district and field levels to use DHIS2 to capture both aggregate and case-based data.

A few custom health information management systems based on DHIS2 were already operating at scale in Sri Lanka, including the electronic Reproductive Health Management Information System (eRHMIS). The eRHMIS is a DHIS2-based health information management system that was developed and implemented to manage data from reproductive, maternal, newborn, child, adolescent, and youth health programs in Sri Lanka since 2017. According to HISP Sri Lanka, "eRHMIS captures nearly 1,860 data elements in 25 data sets from 38,194 organization units. Around 100,000 data values are currently being recorded per day and nearly 3,000 users are registered in the system. Nearly 600 maternal and child health indicators are generated in the system."[4]

While Sri Lanka developed DHIS2 infrastructure, the country also focused on strengthening health information expertise; health authorities invested in a community of developers they could mobilize quickly to address emerging digital health challenges. In 2009, with support from Norway, the Sri Lankan government developed a master's program in health informatics to train local health care workers to operate DHIS2 systems. More than 200 doctors have completed the program and returned to work for the Ministry of Health at the national and district levels.

As the COVID-19 pandemic was beginning in early 2020, DHIS2 already had a strong foothold in Sri Lanka, including an HISP team based in Colombo that provides support and resources for the design and customization, development, implementation, and training of the DHIS2 platform, with support from the University of Oslo and the global HISP network that managed the existing DHIS2 infrastructure and new developments. The Ministry of Health, the Information and Communication Technology Agency, and HISP collaborated closely, and frequently exchanged information to enable rapid decision-making. Figure 5.3 describes the multisectoral approach employed.

Figure 5.3   Multisectoral Approach to Use of the DHIS2 COVID-19 Response Package in Sri Lanka

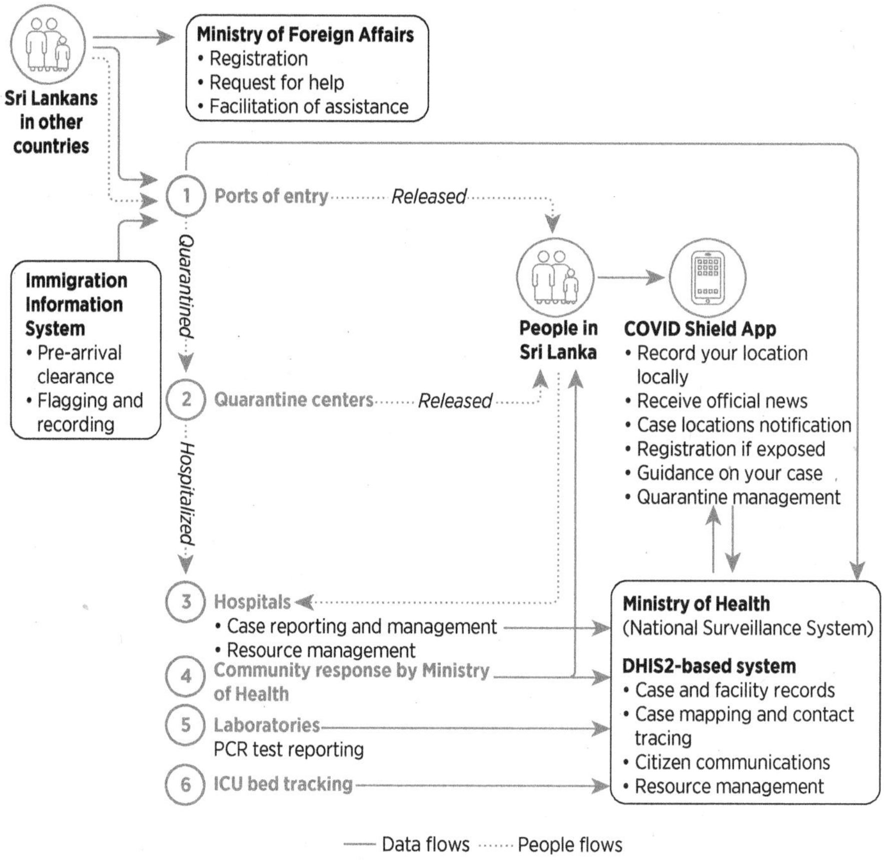

Source: Exemplars in Global Health 2021b.

Note: DHIS2 = District Health Information Software 2; ICU = intensive care unit; PCR = polymerase chain reaction.

The first module developed enabled Sri Lanka to monitor its borders by screening travelers for COVID-19 at ports of entry and then maintaining active disease surveillance for the entire 14-day incubation period.[5] Within five days, the module had been deployed at Colombo International Airport, which was the only port of entry in the early days of the COVID-19 pandemic; the initial user training was completed in two days. In part because of this effective port-of-entry tracking, Sri Lanka reported no cases of COVID-19 between May 2020 and October 2020.

Adapting to COVID-19

Health authorities sought to adapt the standard DHIS2 tracker model to register data for individual travelers from areas with high rates of COVID-19 as they entered the country and to enable health care workers to follow up with them twice over the course of their mandatory two-week quarantine.

The standard DHIS2 tracker data model already enabled case-based surveillance and contact tracing; however, Sri Lanka's Ministry of Health also wanted to build visualizations—for both public health interventions and epidemiological investigations—that could demonstrate the possible spread of disease across a cohort of cases and their contacts. Specifically, the team shared system dashboards with key decision-makers, including the director general of health services and the National COVID Centre.

Within days, the new DHIS2 system was operational at the country's airports, with training and support provided by HISP Sri Lanka. As individual travelers from areas with high rates of COVID-19 entered Sri Lanka, immigration officials collected data on "tracked entity attributes"—names, dates of birth, gender, email addresses, passport numbers, telephone numbers, and a few other sociodemographic factors—as well as any symptoms of COVID-19, contacts in Sri Lanka, and length of stay in the country.

In the second compulsory program stage, health care workers followed up with travelers during their 14-day quarantine to check for symptoms of COVID-19 and capture data on any action taken during the surveillance process. Finally, health care workers followed up for a third time at the end of the quarantine, marking the conclusion of the surveillance process. All the tracker data could be aggregated for national-level reporting and dashboards, while still protecting the privacy and security of individuals whose data are stored in the system.

Nigeria: Adapting a Fully Integrated Surveillance System to Track COVID-19

During the 2014–16 Ebola outbreak in West Africa, researchers and public health experts from Germany and Nigeria developed a digital early-warning and disease management system: the Surveillance Outbreak Response Management and Analysis System (SORMAS). Since then, SORMAS has expanded to accommodate other diseases, including monkeypox, Lassa fever, and now COVID-19.[6] At its core, SORMAS receives inputs from officials involved in surveillance (for example, health care workers, surveillance officers) and presents these data to users throughout the health system to inform a comprehensive strategy and response.

Nigeria's Enabling Environment
Nigeria's health system is decentralized across 36 states and the Federal Capital Territory and 774 local government areas. Its burgeoning digital health environment, however, enabled some aspects of the health system to be centralized. At least 24 information and communication technology and ehealth initiatives already had nationwide coverage, and the eHealth Strategy Toolkit, developed by the World Health Organization and the International Telecommunication Union, assessed the overall status of the country's enabling environment as

"developing and building up." In 2013, Nigeria adopted DHIS2 as its national health management information system, although there were initial gaps in its integration with the other tools in use. In addition, Nigeria has more than 125 million mobile phone users, so much of the population was already somewhat familiar with mobile technology (United Nations Foundation 2014).

How SORMAS Works

SORMAS is a comprehensive, customizable, user-friendly system that enables early detection of disease outbreaks and rapid mobilization of resources for containment and treatment. In addition to tracking cases, SORMAS addresses all aspects of disease response, including rumor management and validation, and is linked to Nigeria's existing data systems and strategies (for example, DHIS2 and the regional Integrated Disease Surveillance and Response Strategy) (Grainger 2020). Health officials can use SORMAS to visualize chains of transmission, analyze risk factors for infection, and change policies such as travel restrictions as pandemic outbreaks evolve over time. It can also provide workflow reminders to health care workers on the dashboard and via text messages (Grainger 2020). Figure 5.4 describes how SORMAS operates.

Figure 5.4 How SORMAS Operates in Nigeria

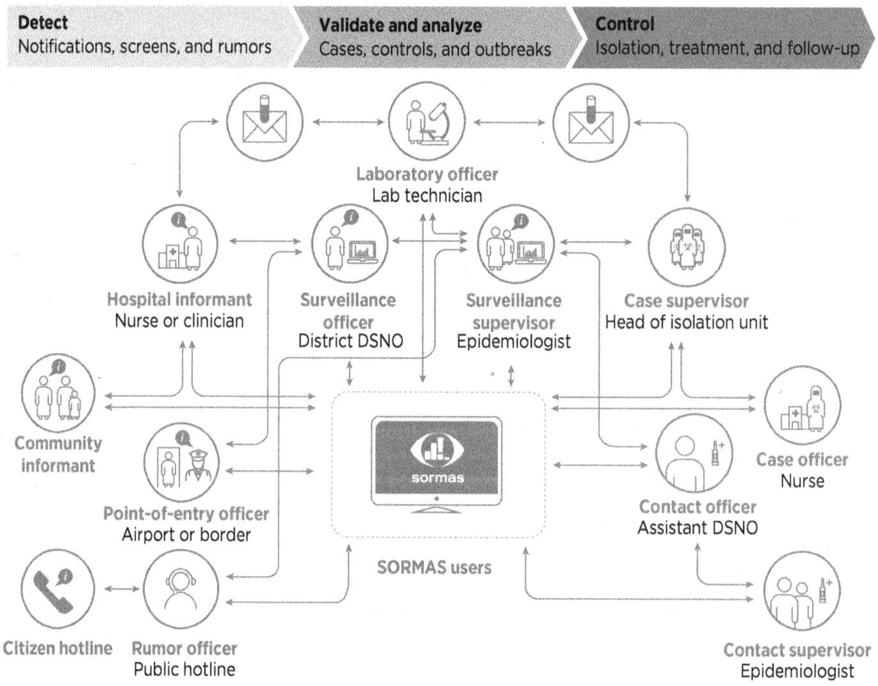

Source: Exemplars in Global Health 2021c.

Note: DSNO = disease surveillance and notification officer; SORMAS = Surveillance Outbreak Response Management and Analysis System.

SORMAS is modular, so it is quick to adapt and scale. Even before Nigeria reported its first case of COVID-19 in February 2020, SORMAS had begun to deploy a new COVID-19 module that would enable Nigerian authorities to track cases and contacts.[7] The 2017 monkeypox outbreak prepared Nigeria's Centre for Disease Control (CDC) for quick deployment during the COVID-19 outbreak (Nature Communications 2020). Because SORMAS was familiar to health care personnel working in 19 states where it was already in place, the new COVID-19 module required minimal training to scale up to the rest of the states. Between February and September 2020, SORMAS expanded its coverage quickly, from 19 Nigerian states to all 36 states and 74 local government areas.

Adapting to COVID-19

Early pilot tests focused on specific places and user groups, but SORMAS scaled up quickly, especially in 2017 and 2018, as Nigeria experienced outbreaks of monkeypox, Lassa fever, and meningitis. The system's adaptable design enabled developers to build and deploy new modules quickly for tracking Lassa fever, monkeypox, dengue fever, yellow fever, meningitis, and plague. Dr. Chikwe Ihekweazu, head of Nigeria's CDC, explained some of the benefits of deploying this multimodal version of SORMAS:

> Dealing with one outbreak can be difficult. Dealing with four concurrent outbreaks in a large country such as Nigeria presents far greater challenges. The use of SORMAS during 2017–2018 enabled us to adopt a more coordinated approach to data collection, analysis, and presentation for decision-making across all four diseases, reducing the need for multiple approaches in the context of limited resources (Grainger 2020, 16).

The new modules increased the utility of SORMAS and boosted support for its expansion throughout Nigeria. At the beginning of the COVID-19 pandemic, not every Nigerian state had access to SORMAS. It was more common in larger, more urban states such as Kano and Lagos. (Likewise, COVID-19 testing response and availability varied widely across the country's decentralized health system.) But by the end of 2020, SORMAS covered all 260 million people in Nigeria.

SORMAS streamlined and expedited Nigeria's response to COVID-19. Without it, health care workers would have had to use paper forms and multiple disconnected tools, causing delays in information reporting and large gaps in data. The system also supported contact-tracing efforts by reducing friction from paper forms and by linking the tracing tools to the case database. In 2021, Nigerian CDC representatives reported its usefulness in several ways: identifying case clusters, reducing the use of paper forms, and providing more actionable data for real-time decision-making. The system also continued to adapt to the COVID-19 response—for example, adding a feature to notify people of negative test results in early 2021.

Layer 3: Advanced Case Management and Surge Response

Uttar Pradesh, India: An Integrated End-to-End Surveillance Platform for COVID-19 Response

Uttar Pradesh's Enabling Environment

Approximately 235 million people were living in Uttar Pradesh's 107,000 villages and 75 districts in 2011. Of these, 78 percent lived in rural areas. The state also has more than 5 million migrant workers, a population that is particularly susceptible to infectious diseases. Consequently, last-mile health solutions have been a long-standing challenge in the state. Additionally, Uttar Pradesh's dispersed rural population is well suited for digital health solutions. Digital solutions can complement existing health system delivery models, although very few digital health interventions achieved scale in Uttar Pradesh before the COVID-19 pandemic. The pandemic provided an opportunity for the government of Uttar Pradesh to build its own solution from the ground up and to demonstrate a successful statewide scale-up.

Adapting to COVID-19

Under the guidance of the Uttar Pradesh chief minister's office, two departments—the Department of Health and Family Welfare and the Department of Medical Education and Training—led Uttar Pradesh's response to COVID-19. In March 2020, as COVID-19 cases in India began to rise, state officials and their partners at the Uttar Pradesh Technical Support Unit initiated development and deployment of the integrated Unified COVID-19 Data Platform.

By the end of March 2020, working in close coordination with the government, the Uttar Pradesh Technical Support Unit had developed an understanding of the surveillance team's needs and workflow across the entire life cycle of a COVID-19 case. Together they developed a comprehensive vision of a platform that could drive end-to-end case management of COVID-19 cases in Uttar Pradesh.

In addition to the surveillance module, links needed to be established with labs and health facilities across the public and private sectors to achieve three key objectives: (1) ensure timely screening and prompt clinical assistance, (2) drive absolute transparency and accountability across the value chain from detection through treatment, and (3) ensure that there is a single source of information for tracking cases across the entire state (figure 5.5).

What Does the Unified COVID-19 Data Platform Do?

The Unified COVID-19 Data Platform is designed to facilitate end-to-end digital case management for health workers and patients. It gives officials a real-time view of the status of the pandemic within or across local districts by collecting and aggregating data from its tracking and contact-tracing modules. It also incorporates information from a COVID-19 helpline call center

Figure 5.5   Key Design Principles of the Unified COVID-19 Data Platform in Uttar Pradesh, India

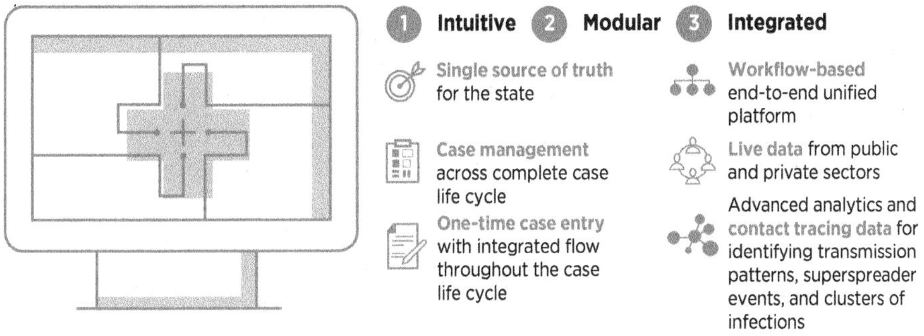

Source: Exemplars in Global Health 2022.

established to conduct disease surveillance and educate the public on COVID-19 symptoms and prevention. The data platform is Uttar Pradesh's authoritative source of information about the COVID-19 pandemic.

The Unified COVID-19 Data Platform enables comprehensive case management and provides a real-time view of the status of the COVID-19 pandemic across districts via:

- *End-to-end data visibility.* The digital platform makes it possible for data collected from the tracking platform, call center, surveillance teams, and self-quarantine app to flow into the system in near real time. As of July 31, 2021, the platform had enabled Uttar Pradesh to track nearly 49.6 million potential cases across the continuum of care and to manage 1.7 million positive cases.
- *Integrated modules for diverse stakeholders.* Key components of the platform include a surveillance module, a facility module, and a lab module, all built on a common backbone. The platform also includes mobile applications for field tracking, contact tracing, and home isolation. In addition, as protocols evolved over time, a death audit module and a home isolation module were added.
- *Digitally enabled decision-making.* Information collected via different interfaces and users can be viewed on the decision-making dashboard, the focus for all COVID-19 planning and monitoring. The dashboard includes information on case summaries and overviews, hot spots, contact-tracing status, availability of trained human resources or infrastructure, and facility preparedness for COVID-19—which equips administrative and departmental officials with the data they need to prioritize their efforts and enables proactive pandemic-response planning.
- The platform has three main functions, known as T3: tracking, testing, and treating.

- *Tracking* involved active surveillance of itinerant populations and the number of active and closed cases in real time. Over time, the platform evolved to identify individual cases across 17 types of cases; field teams were assigned to contact-tracing duties.
- *Testing* also involved understanding the shifting landscape of testing across districts in the state. Officials were able to adapt the platform's algorithms to account for changes in per capita testing levels and adjust to any delays.
- *Treatment* was determined depending on whether a case was linked to a facility or home isolation. Uniform treatment protocols were developed across the state.

Impact

Using the Unified COVID-19 Data Platform, the state was able to track digitally nearly 49.6 million (potential) COVID-19 cases across the continuum of care, conduct more than 67.1 million tests, and manage 1.7 million positive cases as of July 31, 2021. The comprehensive, end-to-end Unified COVID-19 Data Platform incorporated multiple dimensions of Uttar Pradesh's COVID-19 response: supporting government officials, developing digital tools, collecting data at the source, strengthening health workers' capacities, leveraging technology to manage surveillance and treatment efforts, ensuring actionable visualization via the COVID-19 dashboard, and providing strategic guidance for future pandemic response efforts. In particular, the most important and timely contribution of the statewide rollout of the Unified COVID-19 Data Platform was the ability to view and analyze case trends in real time.

Real-time data ensured that the state could proactively manage changing disease response strategies and infrastructure requirements, from increasing the number of facilities and availability of beds to earmarking paid facilities and the timely implementation of protocols for home isolation and quarantine. The digital platform also allowed health workers and government officials to compare and track caseloads, map the speed of a disease's spread, and build and compare epidemic curves—all tools that will likely be useful in the future.

Overall, the platform made it possible to support the Indian Council of Medical Research's "track, test, and treat" strategy, enabling real-time updates and analysis of data across all three areas. Last-mile delivery of health services has traditionally been a challenge for Uttar Pradesh, but with its comprehensive COVID-19 response, the government has successfully developed and scaled an end-to-end digital platform that works across the health care value chain and serves as the authoritative response to this emergency. The state's ability to engage partners across the public and private sectors to deliver on its ambitious vision demonstrates that even a large state can quickly and effectively build, adapt, and adopt digital tools at scale for managing health care in a fast-changing pandemic environment.

Notes

1. Also refer to "What Is Integrated Management of Childhood Illness?" World Health Organization website, https://www.who.int/teams/maternal-newborn -child-adolescent-health-and-ageing/child-health/integrated-management-of -childhood-illness/.
2. "IeDA—A Digital Solution to Save Children's Lives," Terre des hommes website (accessed February 2, 2021), https://www.tdh.org/en/projects/ieda.
3. "A Digital Revolution Fighting Infectious Diseases," Terre des hommes website, August 20, 2020, https://www.tdh.ch/en/press-releases/digital-revolution-fighting -infectious-diseases.
4. Electronic Reproductive Health Management Information System (database), Health Information Systems Programme (HISP), Sri Lanka website (accessed April 21, 2021), https://hisp.lk/our-projects/erhmis/.
5. "Innovative Management of COVID-19 Vaccine Delivery in Sri Lanka," District Health Information Software 2 (DHIS2) website, https://dhis2.org/sri-lanka-covid -vaccine/.
6. SORMAS flyer, SORMAS website, accessed January 21, 2021, https://sormas.org /wp-content/uploads/2021/01/SORMAS-Flyer_A4_PRINT_cwa_190701.pdf.
7. "WS 01—COVID-19 Pandemic Response Management," World Health Summit YouTube page, published October 25, 2020, https://www.youtube.com/watch?v =YF4-_frt6uM.

References

Exemplars in Global Health. 2021a. *CommCare in Burkina Faso: How an Existing App at Scale Was Adapted for COVID-19.* Seattle, WA: Exemplars in Global Health. https:// www.exemplars.health/emerging-topics/epidemic-preparedness-and-response /digital-health-tools/commcare-in-burkina-faso.

Exemplars in Global Health. 2021b. *Scaling DHIS2 in Sri Lanka: Early Action to Track and Prevent COVID-19.* Seattle, WA: Exemplars in Global Health. https://www.exem-plars.health/emerging-topics/epidemic-preparedness-and-response/digital-health-tools/sri-lanka.

Exemplars in Global Health. 2021c. *SORMAS in Nigeria: Adapting a Fully Integrated Surveillance System to Track COVID-19.* Seattle, WA: Exemplars in Global Health. https://www.exemplars.health/emerging-topics/epidemic-preparedness-and -response/digital-health-tools/sormas-nigeria.

Exemplars in Global Health. 2022. *An Integrated End-to-End Surveillance Platform for COVID-19 Response in Uttar Pradesh, India.* Seattle, WA: Exemplars in Global Health. https://www.exemplars.health/emerging-topics/epidemic-preparedness-and -response/digital-health-tools/goup-narrative.

Grainger, Corinne. 2020. *A Software for Disease Surveillance and Outbreak Response: Insights from Implementing SORMAS in Nigeria and Ghana.* Bonn, Germany: Federal Ministry for Economic Cooperation and Development. https://health.bmz.de/ghpc/case -studies/software_disease_surveillance_outbreak_response/index.html.

Jane, Enric, Guillaume Foutry, and Simon Sanou. 2018. "Using Digital Tools at Scale: The Integrated e-Diagnostic Approach in Burkina." Africa Health, Kampala, July 2018. https://africa-health.com/wp-content/uploads/2018/07/13.-July-Scaling -digitally-in-Burkina.pdf.

Nature Communications. 2020. "A Vision for Actionable Science in a Pandemic." *Nature Communications* 11 (1): Art. 4960. https://doi.org/10.1038/s41467-020-18056-w.

Terre des hommes and Dimagi. n.d. "Terre des hommes: The Integrated eDiagnostic Approach for Child Health Case Study." Dimagi Inc., Cambridge, MA. https://www.dimagi.com/case-studies/mhealth-tdh-burkinafaso/.

United Nations Foundation. 2014. *Assessing the Enabling Environment for ICTs in Nigeria: A Review of Policies.* Washington, DC: United Nations Foundation. https://ehealth4everyone.com/wp-content/uploads/2016/01/nigeria-policy-report.pdf.

6

From MERS to COVID-19: Building a Resilient Health System in the Republic of Korea

Huihui Wang, Patricio V. Marquez, and Inuk Hwang

IN SUMMARY

The Republic of Korea's experience in promoting prevention, pandemic preparedness and response, and advanced case management and surge response is based on lessons learned from a deadly outbreak of Middle East respiratory syndrome (MERS) in 2015 and policy and institutional reforms implemented before the COVID-19 pandemic hit (Wang, Hwang, and Marquez 2023).

- The adoption of legislative and regulatory reforms enhanced the public health preparedness and response system.
- Predictable and sustained investment in essential public health functions in an integrated health system over time were key to protecting lives and preventing severe social and economic disruption during Korea's health crisis.
- The Bloomberg COVID Resilience Ranking of 2022 placed Korea in first place among those countries most effectively controlling the pandemic. Korea suffered the fewest scars because it was able to reopen its borders and economies without a substantial spike in deaths.
- Universal health coverage, which is under the National Health Insurance (NHI) system, provides coverage to the entire population, encompasses all health care providers, and ensures access to testing and treatment without financial barriers.
- Decisive and data-driven leadership, strategic clarity (a focus on testing and contact tracing as well as on developing a triage system to manage the flow of patients to treatment facilities), and a willingness to be innovative were also crucial.
- Dedicated effort for providing transparent and open communication, fostering public-private partnerships, engaging in evidence-based deployment of public health measures, and using technology and data innovatively enhanced Korea's preparedness and response capacity.

Country Context: Demographic Profile and Health Risks

Asia's fourth-largest economy, Korea had a population of 51.8 million in 2020.[1] The demographic structure of the country has undergone major changes in the last few decades. In 2020, Korea's population declined for the first time in the country's history, with the number of deaths exceeding the number of births. While life expectancy increased from less than 80 years to more than 83 years in 2020, the total birth rate fell to 0.84 birth per woman, one of the lowest in the world.

Noncommunicable diseases account for most of the disease burden in Korea. The leading causes of mortality are stroke, ischemic heart disease, lung cancer, self-harm, and stomach cancer. Six leading behavioral and metabolic risk factors drive most of the country's death and disability, including tobacco use, high fasting plasma glucose, alcohol use, dietary risks, high blood pressure, and high body-mass index. In addition to the burden of noncommunicable diseases, the incidence of tuberculosis (TB) remains the highest among high-income countries (Kwak, Hwang, and Yim 2020).

Falling birth rates and an aging population pose large social and economic challenges for Korea. Shifting demographics, key lifestyle risk factors, especially among men, and an increasing burden of chronic disease require priority attention in health promotion and disease prevention (OECD 2020).

The rise in chronic disease is of critical importance in Korea, as major preexisting cardiometabolic conditions (diabetes mellitus, obesity, hypertension, and heart failure), separately and jointly, were shown to increase the risk of severe COVID-19 disease, and a substantial proportion of COVID-19 hospitalizations were attributable to them (O'Hearn et al. 2021).

The accumulated evidence on the role that noncommunicable disease comorbidities and risk factors played in increasing the burden of health care for COVID-19 and TB can help to inform public health prevention strategies in Korea. The dichotomy between communicable and noncommunicable diseases is false. For example, adoption of an integrated service delivery approach involving collaborative treatment of TB and noncommunicable diseases should be intensified.

Health System Structure and Features

Organization and Policy for Disease Surveillance and Response

At the central level, the Ministry of Health and Welfare (MOHW) plays a central role in system stewardship, policy formulation, health planning, and implementation nationwide (Wang, Hwang, and Marquez 2023). It directly manages several national hospitals (for example, the national cancer center and psychiatric hospitals) and implements various public health policies by collaborating with (or providing subsidies and grants to) local governments.

The MoHW and the Korea Disease Control and Prevention Agency (KDCA) play a crucial role in managing infectious disease through regulation, financial support, technical assistance, and training.

In collaboration with the MOHW, regional governments are responsible for regional medical centers (usually secondary hospitals) based on their own health planning. Municipalities are responsible for public health, vaccination, and prenatal care, mainly through public health centers (primary care).

Although the country's public health system is decentralized, the central government plays an important role in providing funding and technical support. In a health emergency like COVID-19, coordination among central and local governments can increase the government's capacity to respond more quickly than a bottom-up approach in a highly decentralized system, as in the United States (Marquez 2021).

Health Financing and Universal Health

The National Health Insurance (NHI) system, a single-payer system, covers more than 97 percent of the population and encompasses all types of care, including medical, dental, and traditional medical care, medicines, and laboratory testing. The other 2.8 percent of the population is covered by the Medical Aid Program. All citizens earning an income in Korea contribute a percentage of their monthly salary to the NHI system. Employers match employee contributions. The contributions paid by one working citizen cover health insurance for his or her entire family.

Private providers deliver the majority of health care services in Korea (that is, less than 10 percent of hospitals and 15 percent of beds are public). However, both public and private health care providers are mandated to contract with the NHI system and are subject to the same benefits package and reimbursement price set by law.

Public Health Reforms After the 2015 MERS Outbreak

The Korean experience with the Middle East respiratory syndrome (MERS) outbreak, a new virus to humans in 2015, brought to light serious inadequacies in the health system. The ineffective response was characterized by a lack of appropriate protocols for screening and isolation, limited scope of epidemiological investigations, inadequately prepared human resources and public health infrastructure, and absence of a robust information system and transparent communication.

However, once the MERS outbreak was controlled, the government transformed the health care system by introducing reforms to boost public health emergency preparedness. From 2015 to 2020, the Korean government implemented 48 reforms to improve the public health system based on a careful assessment of problems detected. With clearly defined targets, deadlines, lines of responsibility, coordination arrangements, and accountability, the reforms addressed five key areas: (1) elevating the roles and responsibilities of certain public health agencies; (2) investing in research and development (R&D) by domestic manufacturers; (3) designing rapid response processes for emerging infectious diseases; (4) creating a national stockpile to manage and distribute medical countermeasures; and (5) amending legislation to expand access to data and engender public trust (United States, FDA 2021). As a result of the successful implementation of these reforms, Korea's response to COVID-19 has been heralded as one of the most successful in the world (Park and Chung 2021).

Since MERS, the Infectious Disease Control and Prevention Act has been revised several times to facilitate rapid and effective health emergency responses and to give the central government the authority to implement top-down approaches during emergencies. The public health governance structure was transformed through a redefinition of roles and coordination arrangements. Networks of central and local government agencies were established to detect, contain, and treat illness during a pandemic. After several organizational changes, the KDCA became a stand-alone agency in September 2020, with full autonomy from the MOHW and with new units that expanded its functions and operational capacity for carrying out pandemic response activities.

The Korean government invested in innovative technologies to prevent and control infectious diseases and to support related R&D. Through public-private partnerships, the government developed screening and testing technologies, including laboratory and diagnostic devices, as well as information systems that allow organizations and government agencies to exchange real-time information for pandemic preparedness and response.

The reforms facilitated the implementation of countermeasure activities, further improving the capacity of the public health agencies and institutions. They also brought about enhancements to the infectious disease control and prevention workforce, which grew in size and capability. A significant number of personnel were added to national and local organizations in different public health areas, including surveillance, epidemiological investigation, laboratory testing, case confirmation, emergency response, treatment, risk communication, and R&D. Related training helped to improve the performance of existing and newly added personnel. Hospital facilities were equipped with negative pressure beds and with isolated patient rooms to prevent nosocomial infections.

The amended Infectious Disease Control and Prevention Act allows the MOHW to request and collect personal data from the Korean National Police Agency and telecommunication companies on confirmed and suspected cases of infection during a public health emergency, with a provision that the information collected must be destroyed when the relevant tasks for an outbreak are accomplished. These legal measures permitted extensive contact tracing in the case of COVID-19. The revisions to the act also required the government to disclose information about the path of confirmed cases to ensure the public's right to information, therefore allowing the MOHW to override certain privacy provisions at the onset of a serious infectious disease outbreak.

The changes in public health preparedness and response that the Korean government implemented between MERS and COVID-19 offer insights and lessons for other countries as they continue to deal with the ongoing pandemic and prepare for future public health emergencies. In particular, Korea's successful response to COVID-19 was the result of years of policy and institutional reforms and dedicated investment to strengthen infectious disease prevention and control.

Three Layers of Health System Pandemic Preparedness in Korea

Korea stands out in the global COVID-19 response. The Bloomberg COVID Resilience Ranking of 2022 places Korea in first place among countries most effectively controlling the pandemic; the country was able to reopen its borders and economies without a substantial spike in deaths.[2] Although the number of COVID-19 cases jumped significantly in early 2022 due to the spread of the more transmissible Omicron variant and a revamped testing regime that cast a broader net to detect infections, Korea has had a much lower rate of total confirmed COVID-19 deaths per million population than other countries. This result may be attributed to high vaccination rates, with 86 percent of the 51.8 million population fully vaccinated (Wang, Hwang, and Marquez 2023).

In contrast to the MERS experience, the government's response in the early phases of the COVID-19 pandemic illustrated its awareness of the emerging threat and its ability to respond quickly to the changing needs and expectations of the population.

Layer 1: Risk Reduction—Promoting Prevention and Community Preparedness

Primary Care Network

Public health centers are the dominant public health care provider in Korea, with 256 public health centers located throughout the country, roughly 1 center per 200,000 population. These centers, which are funded and managed by local governments, provide preventive and health promotion services such as immunization, maternal and child health services, screening, and health education. In addition, they act as local posts for surveillance of communicable diseases. Private clinics and hospitals provide similar services as well.

A comprehensive network of public-private laboratories spans the country. The laboratories are an essential part of the infectious disease surveillance system, providing diagnostic services and supporting monitoring and inspections. In addition, private laboratories are set up in 298 hospitals and other commercial health care facilities throughout the country to form a network of private laboratories working in partnership with public laboratories.

National Health Promotion Fund

In 1995, the Health Promotion Act led to the establishment of the National Health Promotion Fund, which is financed through earmarked tobacco taxes that comprise specific excise taxes and a general value added tax (World Bank 2018). While the overall goal of tobacco taxation is to increase the price of tobacco products and reduce their use, the proceeds are earmarked for the National Health Promotion Fund to support government health promotion programs, including tobacco cessation programs, to support KDCA's infectious disease control and prevention activities, and to subsidize NHI coverage. As of 2018, 54 percent of the fund was used to subsidize the NHI system, and about 46 percent was used for general health expenditures.

Disaster Management Fund

In accordance with the Framework Act on the Management of Disasters, sub-national governments allocate 1 percent of their general tax revenue to the Disaster Management Fund every year. The resources from the fund can help provincial and municipal governments to finance expenditures during emergencies and disasters. During the COVID-19 pandemic, the Disaster Management Fund was used to procure medical supplies for local government personnel and to provide income subsidies, among other uses.

Disease Surveillance

The KDCA operates the National Infectious Disease Surveillance System (NIDSS), which covers both the Mandatory Surveillance System and the Sentinel Surveillance System. The NIDSS integrates various data-reporting activities, such as monitoring of patients, pathogens, and mediums, diagnosis of pathogens, epidemiological investigation, vaccination, management of patients and their contacts, and quarantine management. It is linked to medical institutions and health facilities across the country and receives the infectious disease occurrence reports that are generated automatically by the electronic medical record system of the facilities.[3]

Level of Alerts and Response

Korea has a system of crisis management for prevention and preparedness against infectious disease outbreaks and prompt response to disasters and crises.[4] The system has four levels of crisis alert, from lowest to highest: blue (level 1, attention), yellow (level 2, caution), orange (level 3, warning), and red (level 4, serious). Levels 1 and 2 are determined and controlled by the KDCA, and levels 3 and 4 are controlled by the Central Disaster and Safety Countermeasures Headquarters (CDSCHQ) with recommendation of the KDCA.

Level 1, "attention" (blue), includes outbreaks and epidemics of new infectious diseases abroad and infections of unknown cause or reemergence of infections. Level 2, "caution" (yellow), responds to the domestic influx of new infectious diseases from abroad and the limited spread of infectious diseases of unknown cause and reemergence in Korea. Level 3, "warning" (orange), responds to the limited spread of new infectious diseases introduced into Korea and the domestic spread of infectious diseases of unknown cause or their reappearance in the country. Level 4, "serious" (red), responds to the spread of new overseas infectious diseases to the local community or their spread nationwide and the nationwide spread of infectious diseases of unknown origin and their reemergence.

The operation of the alert system is illustrated by the decisions adopted at the beginning of the COVID-19 pandemic. Korea was one of the first countries to experience a COVID-19 outbreak, with its first case, imported from Wuhan, China, reported on January 20, 2020. When the level of the crisis was changed to serious (red) on February 23, 2020, the Korean government activated the CDSCHQ within days and then met daily, with the prime minister attending at least three times a week.

The KDCA provides technical information to inform the decisions adopted by the CDSCHQ. The minister of health and welfare is the first deputy head of CDSCHQ and director of the Central Disaster Management Headquarters; the minister of the interior and safety is the second deputy head of CDSCHQ and director of the governmentwide Support Center, which provides assistance, including coordination between the central and local governments, to allocate patients across public hospitals in different localities.

Each local government also established a Local Disaster and Safety Countermeasures Headquarters, directed by the head of the local government, which ensures the availability of hospitals dedicated to COVID-19 patients. The central government provides support for hospital beds, personnel, and other supplies when local governments face shortages.

Surveillance of Emerging Zoonotic Diseases

The COVID-19 pandemic clearly shows that preventing future pandemics at source would cost a small fraction of the damage already caused by viruses that jump from wildlife to people. Governments, therefore, need to tackle the root causes of diseases and not focus solely on preventing the spread of new viruses once they have infected humans. To reduce the socioeconomic burden of emerging zoonotic diseases, it is necessary to address the importance of surveilling animals and their breeding environment, with the goal of detecting zoonotic diseases early and limiting their transmission.

Korea has developed surveillance systems for priority zoonotic diseases and pathogens (WHO 2017). The government has designated 10 priority zoonotic diseases in the country, including anthrax, severe acute respiratory syndrome (SARS), animal influenza with human infection, TB, enterohemorrhagic *Escherichia coli*, Japanese encephalitis, brucellosis, rabies, variant Creutzfeldt-Jakob disease, and Q fever.

Several ministries operate the surveillance system for zoonotic diseases. Coordination and communication between ministries are conducted electronically and through the Zoonotic Disease Committee.

Layer 2: Detection, Containment, and Mitigation Capabilities

The Korean government's COVID-19 response was anchored on implementation of the "4T" strategy: test, trace, treat, and transparency. Massive testing, isolation of cases, and extensive contact tracing as well as public participation in social distancing enabled Korea to control COVID-19 without disruptive and taxing lockdowns.

Detection

Post-MERS, several Korean government agencies—including the KDCA, the Korea Society for Laboratory Medicine, the Ministry of Food and Drug Safety, and the Korean Association of External Quality Assessment Service—designed rapid response processes for emerging infectious diseases. These processes included a program to expedite the authorization of certain products for emergency use, which was formally established through an amendment of the Medical Device Act in 2016. The Emergency Use Authorization program in Korea, which is modeled after the system used in the United States, allows the temporary production, sale, and use of test kits during a pandemic when no authorized product is available on the domestic market (United States, FDA 2021).

The Korean government also invested in R&D and commercial test production as well as in information technology infrastructure to support a sophisticated testing and contact-tracing regime. Since 2017, the Ministry of Science and Information and Communication Technology (MSIT) has invested almost ₩27 billion (approximately US$25 million) in technology to diagnose infectious diseases (Korea, MSIT 2020).

As a result of these investments and the expectations created through these partnerships, a subset of Korean commercial manufacturers was well positioned to develop and manufacture tests quickly (Shuren and Stenzel 2021). To encourage the development of diagnostic tests by commercial manufacturers, the Korean government guaranteed that it would purchase a minimum quantity of tests and would reimburse the costs of the tests once they were authorized for emergency use by the Ministry of Food and Drug Safety.

Additional measures were adopted to support the fast-track development of testing (Shuren and Stenzel 2021). The KDCA established a testing capability in selected laboratories to conduct clinical studies and evaluate commercial manufacturers seeking emergency use authorization for their tests. Korea also has a centrally coordinated, nationwide testing program that relies on a few dozen authorized tests commercially manufactured in high volumes. To expend its resources efficiently in support of its national testing strategy, the Korean government initially accepted emergency use requests from commercial manufacturers only for one month.

The government helped to make testing affordable, and the innovative testing facilities that were established made it easy for the public to get tested. The network of eligible locations with on-site COVID-19 diagnostic testing quickly expanded across the country, including three types of testing stations: stations in and around hospitals, drive-through stations, and walk-through stations. The testing results were entered into a sophisticated contact-tracing system.

The measures adopted in Korea to scale up testing at the start of the COVID-19 pandemic allowed rapid identification of cases and isolation of persons infected without requiring far-reaching mobility restrictions or business closures. The high rate of testing achieved may also explain the country's low fatality rate, as even mild cases were systematically tested and isolated.

Contact Tracing

Korea adopted a robust approach to contact tracing during COVID-19 using a scaled-up network of contact tracers, who had access to data beyond what they would have been able to learn from a typical patient interview (Kim et al. 2021). This approach also used public communications to empower citizens to assist the health system with contact tracing.

The Epidemiological Survey Support System, developed in March 2020 by the KDCA in collaboration with the MSIT, allowed epidemiological investigation officers to identify quickly the movement of confirmed COVID-19 cases and analyze transmission routes. This information was obtained through information on the patient's location, which was gathered from various sources:

- Patient and doctor interviews (SeungCheol 2020);
- Records of facility visits, including pharmacies and medical facilities;
- Global Positioning System data from cell phones;
- Credit card transaction logs; and
- Closed-circuit television.

KDCA developed a SMART Quarantine Information System in 2017, following the MERS outbreak, to detect and track (via overseas mobile phone roaming information) any potentially infected patient known to have traveled to a country with a nationwide outbreak of the disease (Kwon et al. 2020). Under this system, agencies collect information on incoming passengers from the Ministry of Justice, Ministry of Foreign Affairs, airline companies, and telecommunication companies. Through the Drug Utilization Review and NHI system, they also share with frontline health care facilities information on passengers from countries with an ongoing infectious disease outbreak during the incubation period of the disease of concern.

During COVID-19, smartphone apps were deployed for inbound international travelers who were undergoing the 14-day self-monitoring period and for others in mandatory self-isolation with suspected coronavirus cases. The facilitation of self-monitoring and reporting data to the government prevented the need to ban the entry of international travelers. Hospitals introduced remote diagnosis for patients with mild symptoms, freeing up medical professionals to focus on patients with more serious symptoms.

Screening

With the expansion of testing and contact-tracing capacity, the focus shifted to screening (Kim et al. 2021). For example, COVID-19 screening clinics were erected outside the entrances of hospitals to prevent infected people from entering. Anyone flagged based on their symptoms or responses to screening questions was tested and sent home to self-quarantine while they waited for results. Persons considered low risk received a day entrance pass. Screening stations were set up in various strategic locations, including at Incheon International Airport. To encourage the testing of migrant worker communities, where several clusters had emerged, the government announced that health workers no longer had to report known undocumented residents.

Social Measures (Reducing the Contact and Duration of Infection)

Social measures, including mask wearing, social distancing, and selective and temporary business closures, and an effective communications strategy helped to contain the spread of COVID-19 in Korea (Kim et al. 2021). Under current legislation, the government must provide masks at an affordable price to vulnerable populations in case of a health emergency. To this end, the government intervened in early March 2020 to purchase 80 percent of the mask supply from Korean manufacturers, fully ban exports, set a price limit on mask sales, and limit the number of masks sold weekly through retailers. Moreover, the government prioritized the distribution of masks to medical facilities. These interventions provided relief and averted further shortages, without forcing hospitals to issue policies about reusing personal protective equipment. Throughout the pandemic, the government widely shared information on proper mask wearing and distancing, and the Korea Communications Standards Commission addressed misinformation with cooperation from major websites like Google and Facebook. In October 2020, Korea amended the Infectious Disease Control and Prevention Act to introduce mandatory mask wearing, enforceable by fines.[5]

The government restricted large gatherings, closed schools and day-care centers, and asked employers to offer flexible work arrangements. But it largely avoided restricting or controlling the movement of people, and international borders remained relatively open to travelers from affected countries, except for an outright ban on travel from China's Hubei Province (Kim et al. 2021).

Isolation and Quarantine

Current protocols call on people who have been in contact with a confirmed case, traveled internationally, or suspect that they might be infected to self-quarantine. Each person under self-quarantine receives an official "Notice of Isolation/Quarantine," an assigned case officer to monitor twice a day for symptoms, access to the self-quarantine safety protection app that they are required to use for 14 days, and random on-site inspections. Under the Infectious Disease Control and Prevention Act amended in 2020, violators of self-quarantine risk imprisonment. Violators are required to wear "safety bands," electronic wristbands that connect to the app and alert case officers if they are not in the same location as their mobile devices.

In the early months of the pandemic, the Korean government transformed public facilities and retreat centers owned by private corporations into temporary isolation wards (Kwon et al. 2020). This measure was intended to relieve the shortage of hospital beds and to care for COVID-19 patients while preventing transmission within households.

Risk Communication

Korea offers a good example of open, transparent, and effective health communication. After MERS, the amended Infectious Disease Control and Prevention Act strengthened the accessibility and right of the population to obtain information during public health crises, including information on the routes of confirmed cases, their means of transportation and close contacts, and the history of visits to health care facilities (ADB 2021). Several organizational reforms were implemented as well. Within the KDCA, the Office of Communication was established in 2016 to improve public health and risk communication during public health emergencies.

Transparency and communication helped to allay fear and prevent panic during the COVID-19 pandemic (Chung and Sahib Soh 2020). The government rolled out a massive public information campaign on personal hygiene and social distancing. It conducted twice-daily press briefings, provided COVID-19 updates via social media such as Facebook and YouTube and television channels, including detailed information on the number of confirmed cases, people in self-isolation, and tests performed and the routes of confirmed cases. Combined with a massive rollout of testing and information on the results, such transparency helped to minimize fear and misinformation.

Vaccination

Korea overcame the early shortage of vaccines and quickly expanded vaccination coverage by setting evidence-based priorities and sharing transparent information using innovative technologies (Kwon and Oh 2022). Facing societal pressure, the Korean government announced a vaccination program in January 2021 that aimed to vaccinate 70 percent of the population by November 2021. KDCA was in charge of designing the program and procuring vaccines; it was assisted by other agencies, such as the Ministry of Trade, Industry, and Energy and the Public Procurement Service, following a whole-of-government approach. The Korean government also participated in the COVAX Facility and strengthened international diplomacy to extend vaccine supply globally (Lee et al. 2022).

This organized effort speeded the procurement of vaccines. By August 2021, the government had contracted roughly 194 million doses of vaccine, more than enough for the entire population of 51.8 million. In 2022, the government also expanded the coverage for vaccination to include children between 5 and 11 years of age (figure 6.1).

Figure 6.1   Number of COVID-19 Vaccine Doses Administered per 100 Population in Select Countries, as of November 20, 2022

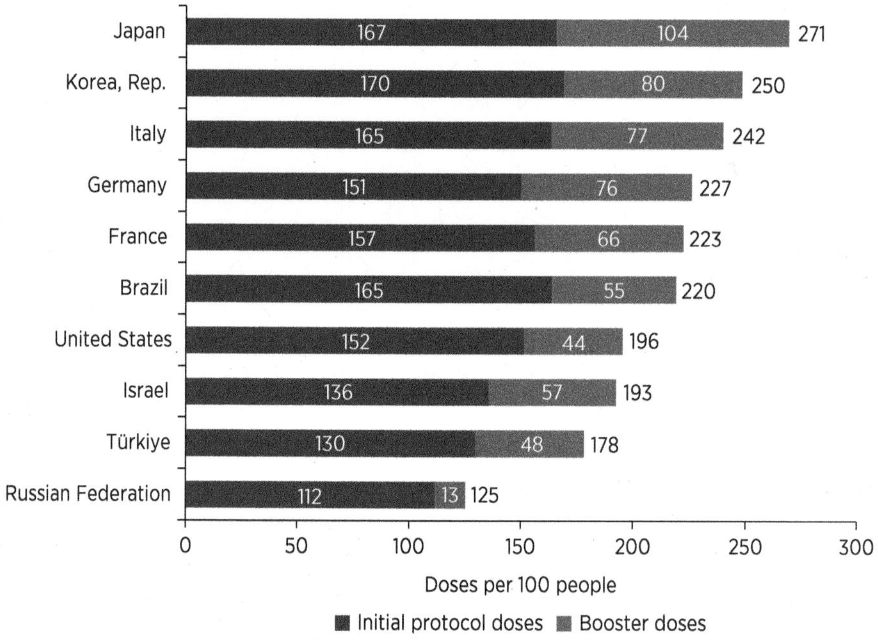

Japan: 167, 104, 271
Korea, Rep.: 170, 80, 250
Italy: 165, 77, 242
Germany: 151, 76, 227
France: 157, 66, 223
Brazil: 165, 55, 220
United States: 152, 44, 196
Israel: 136, 57, 193
Türkiye: 130, 48, 178
Russian Federation: 112, 13, 125

Doses per 100 people

■ Initial protocol doses   ■ Booster doses

Source: Official data collated by Our World in Data (https://ourworldindata.org).

Note: Total number of doses administered, broken down by whether they are part of the initial protocol or booster doses, divided by the total population of the country.

Along with the procurement efforts, the key to increasing the vaccination rate was to set priorities, reduce barriers to vaccination, and deploy innovative technologies (Kwon and Oh 2022). The government formed an expert committee on immunization practices to set priorities for vaccination for each quarter of 2021. In addition, 250 vaccination centers were installed at large auditoriums and sports facilities across the country, mobile vaccination teams were deployed to community welfare centers to vaccinate individuals with disability, and all citizens and foreigners were exempt from cost sharing, all of which lowered the barriers to vaccination. Innovative technologies, such as a real-time, no-show vaccine supply information system, which allowed anyone to be vaccinated ahead of his or her assigned schedule once leftover vaccine doses were registered to the system, and a specially manufactured low-dead-space syringe, which reduced the waste of residual vaccines up to 15 percent, helped to increase the vaccination rate. Lastly, the Korea Institute of Drug Safety and Risk Management, which is in charge of monitoring the safety of marketed vaccines and other medicines, ensured that drugs worked correctly and that their health benefits outweighed their known risks (Wang et al. 2023).

Layer 3: Advanced Case Management and Surge Response

Surge response and advanced case management included surge response interventions and secondary and tertiary hospital interventions for cases requiring advanced case management.

The key to managing COVID-19 mortality was to redesign the triage and treatment system and to transfer patients to appropriate levels of treatment, including designated hospitals and residential treatment centers (Kwon et al. 2020).

A severity-scoring system to classify patient illnesses as asymptomatic or mild, moderate, severe, or critical was established to deal with COVID-19 disease (Ariadne Labs 2020). Asymptomatic and mild cases were placed in one of five residential treatment centers instead of hospitals, where they were closely monitored; moderately ill patients were sent to community hospitals; and severely or critically ill patients were hospitalized at tertiary hospitals equipped to provide intensive care. Hospitals were designated National Safe Hospitals for people seeking non-COVID-19 treatment (Korea, Ministry of Foreign Affairs 2020).

Measures to prevent nosocomial infections were also adopted. These measures included developing procedures for separating infected patients in intensive care units, using portable negative pressure devices to expand the availability of temporary airborne infection isolation rooms across the country, increasing the number of health personnel, designating nurses as the main caregivers for infected patients, and ensuring the availability of personal protective equipment.

Lessons Learned

Korea's effective response to the COVID-19 pandemic was the result of a dynamic process of "adopt and adapt" or learning from the past and building on accumulated experience, new knowledge, and scientific and technological developments. In combination, the policy and institutional reforms and investments adopted after MERS transformed the Korean infectious disease control and prevention system into a resilient public health system that was able to adapt and respond effectively during the COVID-19 pandemic.

More specifically, the following factors and their interplay enhanced the resilience of the Korean public health system:

- Government leadership in planning and implementing policy and institutional reforms and related investments was critical.
- Reformed and strengthened public health institutions and systems for infectious disease control and prevention anchored the COVID-19 emergency response and the implementation of effective countermeasures.
- Development of human and medical resources and adoption of innovative technologies were essential for implementing the COVID-19 countermeasures.

- Korea's effective response to COVID-19 provides strong evidence that sustained financing for infectious disease control and prevention as well as for other essential medical and social services is a critical investment not only to reduce countries' vulnerability to health and other concurrent shocks but also to foster future development.

Korea stands out in the global COVID-19 response. Learning from prior public health emergencies, Korea was able to keep the COVID-19 death toll at a relatively low level and to do so without severe lockdowns and other highly restrictive measures.

Notes

1. Demographic and health data in this section are from "Korea, Rep.," World Bank DataBank, https://data.worldbank.org/country/Korea-Rep.
2. "Bloomberg COVID Resilience Ranking of 2022," Bloomberg website, https://www.bloomberg.com/graphics/covid-resilience-ranking/.
3. Information from the KDCA website, http://www.cdc.go.kr/contents.es?mid=a20301140000.
4. The information in this section is drawn from Kwon et al. (2020).
5. "Updates on COVID-19 in Republic of Korea: Mask Wearing to Become Mandatory," KDCA press release, November 13, 2020, http://cdc.go.kr/board/board.es?mid=a30402000000&bid=0030.

References

ADB (Asian Development Bank). 2021. *The Republic of Korea's Coronavirus Disease Pandemic Response and Health System Preparedness.* Manila: ADB.

Ariadne Labs. 2020. "Protecting Health Care Workers in Korea during the COVID-19 Pandemic." Global Learnings Evidence Brief, Ariadne Labs, Boston, May 12, 2020. https://covid19.ariadnelabs.org/global-learnings-south-korea.

Chung, Dawoon, and Hoon Sahib Soh. 2020. "Korea's Response to COVID-19: Early Lessons in Tackling the Pandemic." *World Bank Blogs, East Asia and Pacific on the Rise,* March 23, 2020. https://blogs.worldbank.org/eastasiapacific/koreas-response-covid-19-early-lessons-tackling-pandemic.

KDCA (Korea Disease Control and Prevention Agency). 2020. "Updates on COVID-19 in Republic of Korea: Mask Wearing to Become Mandatory." Press release, KDCA, Seoul, November 13, 2020. https://cdc.go.kr/board/board.es?mid=a30402000000&bid=0030.

Kim, June-Ho, Julia Ah-Reum An, SeungJu Jackie Oh, Juhwan Oh, and Jong-Koo Lee. 2021. "Emerging COVID-19 Success Story: Korea Learned the Lessons of MERS." *Our World in Data,* March 5, 2021. https://ourworldindata.org/covid-exemplar-south-korea.

Korea, Ministry of Foreign Affairs. 2020. "All about Korea's Response to COVID-19." Ministry of Foreign Affairs, Seoul. https://www.mofa.go.kr/viewer/skin/doc.html?fn=20201021031300238.pdf&rs=/viewer/result/202101.

Korea, MSIT (Ministry of Science and Information and Communication Technology). 2020. "How We Fought COVID-19: A Perspective from Science and ICT." MSIT, Seoul. https://www.mofa.go.kr/eng/brd/m_22591/down.do?brd_id=20543&seq=28&data_tp=A&file_seq=1.

Kwak, Nakwon, Seung-Sik Hwang, and Jae-Joon Yim. 2020. "Effect of COVID-19 on Tuberculosis Notification, South Korea." *Emerging Infectious Diseases* 26 (10): 2506–08. https://doi.org/10.3201/eid2610.202782.

Kwon, Seunghyun Lewis, and Juhwan Oh. 2022. "COVID-19 Vaccination Program in Korea: A Long Journey toward a New Normal." *Health Policy and Technology* 11 (2): 100601. https://www.sciencedirect.com/science/article/pii/S2211883722000077.

Kwon, Soonman, Hoonsang Lee, Moran Ki, Da Woon Chung, and Enis Baris. 2020. "Republic of Korea's COVID-19 Preparedness and Response." Korea Office Innovation and Technology Note Series 3, World Bank Group Korea Office, Seoul.

Lee, Taejin, Hongsoo Kim, Sung-il Cho, Myoungsoon You, Wankyo Chung, and Juhyeon Moon. 2022. "Country Case Study: The Republic of Korea." Korea–World Bank Group Partnership on COVID-19 Preparedness and Response, World Bank Group, Washington, DC. https://thedocs.worldbank.org/en/doc/214261388bdfa468bd8d180cb8ecb907-0070012023/original/Korea-case-study.pdf.

Marquez, Patricio V. 2021. "Understanding the COVID-19 Pandemic as a Preventable Societal Catastrophe." Patricio V. Marquez blog post, July 25, 2021. http://www.pvmarquez.com/index.php/covidasocialcatastrophe.

OECD (Organisation for Economic Co-operation and Development). 2020. *OECD Reviews of Public Health: Korea: A Healthier Tomorrow.* Paris: OECD Publishing. https://doi.org/10.1787/be2b7063-en.

O'Hearn, Meghan, Junxiu Liu, Frederick Cudhea, Renata Micha, and Dariush Mozaffarian. 2021. "Coronavirus Disease 2019 Hospitalizations Attributable to Cardiometabolic Conditions in the United States: A Comparative Risk Assessment Analysis." *Journal of the American Heart Association* 10: e19259. https://www.ahajournals.org/doi/10.1161/JAHA.120.019259.

Park, June, and Eunbin Chung. 2021. "Learning from Past Pandemic Governance: Early Response and Public-Private Partnership in Testing of COVID-19 in Korea." *World Development* 137 (January): 105198. doi: 10.1016/j.worlddev.2020.105198.

SeungCheol, Ohk. 2020. "Tracking Strategy in Korea." Oxford University MPP and SciencesPo MPA, Oxford, UK. https://covidtranslate.org/tracking-strategy-in-korea.pdf.

Shuren, Jeffrey, and Timothy Stenzel. 2021. "South Korea's Implementation of a COVID-19 National Testing Strategy." *Health Affairs Forefront* (blog), May 25, 2021. https://www.healthaffairs.org/content/forefront/south-korea-s-implementation-covid-19-national-testing-strategy.

United States, FDA (Food and Drug Administration). 2021. "South Korea's Response to COVID-19." US FDA, Center for Devices and Radiological Health, Silver Spring, MD. https://www.fda.gov/media/149334/download.

Wang, Huihui, Inuk Hwang, and Patricio V. Marquez. 2023. "Learning from the Republic of Korea: Building Health System Resilience." Pharmacovigilance and Essential Public Health Services Series, World Bank Group, Washington, DC. https://openknowledge.worldbank.org/handle/10986/40203.

Wang, Huihui, Patricio V. Marquez, Albert Figueras, and Kseniya Bieliaieva. 2023. "Overview of the Republic of Korea Pharmacovigilance System: Learning from Best Practices." Pharmacovigilance and Essential Public Health Services Series, World Bank Group, Washington, DC. https://openknowledge.worldbank.org/server/api/core/bitstreams/7114ee70-64e1-4095-a063-dbb27ae0af4a/content.

WHO (World Health Organization). 2017. "Joint External Evaluation of IHR Core Capacities of the Republic of Korea." WHO/WHE/CPI/2017.65, WHO, Geneva.

World Bank. 2018. "Reducing Tobacco Use through Taxation: The Experience of the Republic of Korea." World Bank Group, Washington, DC. https://documents1.worldbank.org/curated/en/150681529071812689/pdf/127248-WP-PUBLIC-ADD-SERIES-WBGTobaccoKoreaFinalweb.pdf.

7

Three-Layer Health Sector Investment in Thailand

Piya Hanvoravongchai, Paul Li Jen Cheh, Ham Suenghaitaiphorn,
Wasin Laohavinij, Aungsumalee Pholpark, Natchaya Ritthisirikul,
Melanie Coates, Moytrayee Guha, Arielle Cohen Tanugi-Carresse, Lucia Mullen,
Sara Bennett, Jennifer Nuzzo, William Wang, Siobhan Lazenby, and Anne Liu

IN SUMMARY

Thailand was the second country in the world to detect a case of COVID-19 and was relatively successful in its ability to assess, adapt to, and respond to the many complex challenges that presented during the pandemic. Several critical factors contributed to the effectiveness of the country's COVID-19 response:

- Investment in strengthening both the health care workforce, including a primary health care system supported by a strong network of village health volunteers, and the pandemic response infrastructure;

- A whole-of-government response coordinated by national-level governing bodies;

- An integrated health system to support strong subnational implementation efforts, collaboration among health care centers, and coordination across health system levels;

- Health service delivery innovations and adaptations across sectors including digital tools and repurposed infrastructure (for example, repurposed hotels, or "hospitels");

- Data-driven decision-making supported by strong academic and research networks within Thailand; and

- Public trust in the public health system and leadership, which led to high adherence to public health measures, such as hand sanitation and mask wearing.

This research was led by partners at the Thailand National Health Foundation in collaboration with Brown University School of Public Health and Johns Hopkins Bloomberg School of Public Health. It was supported and funded by the Rockefeller Foundation and by the Exemplars in Global Health (EGH) program at Gates Ventures. EGH has a mission to identify positive global health outliers, analyze what makes countries successful, and disseminate core lessons so they can be adapted in comparable settings. EGH is a global coalition of partners including researchers, academics, experts, funders, country stakeholders, and implementers. A small, core team supporting EGH is based at Gates Ventures, the private office of Bill Gates, and closely collaborates with the Gates Foundation. For the full case study, refer to Exemplars in Global Health (2023).

Country Context

Experience with Past Epidemics

Both epidemiologists in the field and scientists in the lab gained important experience responding to outbreaks of severe acute respiratory syndrome (SARS) in 2003, swine flu (H1N1) in 2009, and Middle East respiratory syndrome (MERS) in 2016. As such, Thai public health authorities at all levels recognize the need for comprehensive preparedness and rapid action to manage emerging communicable diseases. However, unlike SARS and MERS, COVID-19 was able to establish local transmission in Thailand.

Overall, Thailand has had a good track record in controlling the spread of disease, particularly when importation of a highly transmissible virus has been detected. For both SARS and MERS, there was no reported transmission to health care workers (Smith 2021). In fact, the coordination and collaboration of the Ministry of Public Health (MOPH) with hospital infection control teams led to the quick and successful diagnosis and management of these diseases and the rapid deployment of staff, which allowed hospital services to remain uninterrupted and minimized the impact on other patients.

These past experiences also led to the establishment of a national public health emergency incident command center and the strengthening of risk communication and community engagement efforts, all of which were essential elements of the health system's response to COVID-19. Lastly, in past epidemics, village health volunteers (VHVs) were mobilized to support community awareness, prevention, and control of various diseases, including dengue and avian influenza (H5N1). During the 2004 H5N1 epidemic, VHVs monitored abnormal death counts in domesticated birds and alerted health authorities to investigate. This early detection and control at the source supported the rapid containment of H5N1 (Rajatanavin et al. 2021).

The general public also learned from these experiences with past pathogens and recognized the need for public health measures such as handwashing, mask wearing, and physical distancing. In April 2020, a local survey conducted by MOPH in Nonthaburi Province just northwest of Bangkok reported that more than 90 percent of the population was following recommendations regarding the wearing of face masks (Nittayasoot et al. 2021).

Universal Health Coverage in Thailand

Before 2002, Thailand's health coverage was a patchwork of arrangements for different population groups; however, in 2002, with the passage of the National Health Security Act, the country achieved universal health coverage. Three public health insurance schemes cover the entire population:

- *The Civil Servant Medical Benefit Scheme* for civil servants and their dependents; under the Ministry of Finance, the scheme covers 5.7 million people (10 percent of the population).

- *The Social Security Scheme* for private sector employees; under the Social Security Office, the scheme covers 12.3 million people (18 percent of the population).
- *The Universal Coverage Scheme* for the population not covered by the first two schemes; under the National Health Security Office, the scheme covers 47.8 million people (72 percent of the population).

Beyond public health insurance for Thai citizens, Thailand also introduced health insurance schemes for migrant workers. Migrants who work in the formal sector are covered under the Social Security Scheme, with equal rights of access to social security benefits, including health services, as Thai citizens. Migrants who work in the informal sector are covered through the Health Insurance Card Scheme, which is open to all documented and undocumented migrants and their dependents.

In addition to these three government health insurance schemes, individuals with higher incomes can choose to buy private health insurance.

Health System Structure and Features

The MOPH is the main authority for public health in Thailand, responsible for health promotion, prevention, and disease control, treatment, and rehabilitation. It oversees national health policy, health service provision, regulation, and implementation of public health laws. Its administrative structure is divided into central and provincial levels, with the central administration also delegating roles to regional offices. Provincial health offices oversee each province's regional, general, and district hospitals and district health offices, which oversee health centers and coordinate with district hospitals.

Health care is provided in a multilevel health system. A health center, as the smallest unit of the health system, provides primary care in each subdistrict. A district hospital, staffed with medical doctors and other health care professionals, delivers services for secondary and some tertiary care.

Layer 1: Risk Reduction—Strong Existing Surveillance Systems

Infrastructure for Strong Surveillance Systems

Established in 2004, over 900 surveillance and rapid response teams are positioned across the country to detect and respond to emerging public health threats (figure 7.1). During the COVID-19 pandemic, many of these teams were deployed to isolate cases rapidly, provide treatment, and trace and quarantine contacts. Stationed at provincial health offices and district hospitals (and also networked with subdistrict health centers), surveillance and rapid response teams typically comprise public health nurses and officers, with some teams including epidemiologists. These teams are supported by Thailand's national network of infection control professionals and epidemiologists.

Figure 7.1   Contact-Tracing Efforts by Surveillance and Rapid Response Teams and Village Health Volunteers in Thailand

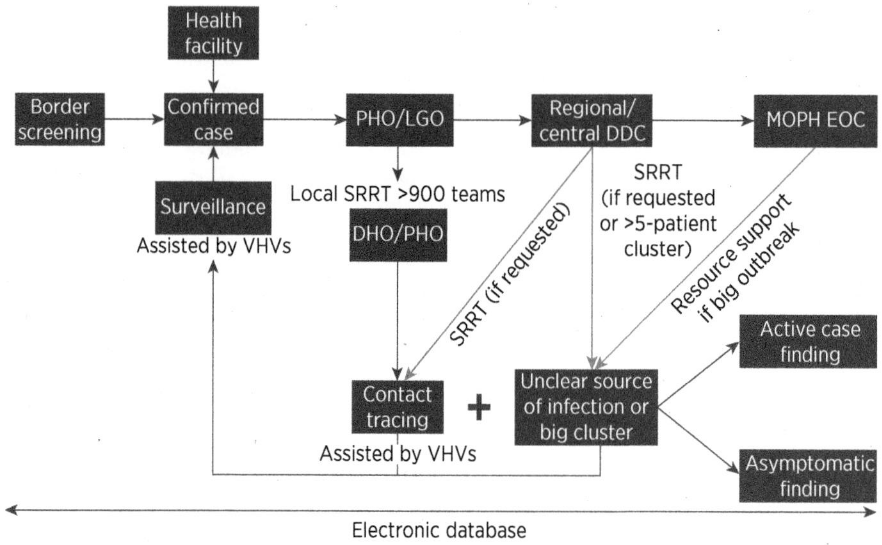

Source: Rajatanavin et al. 2021.

Note: DDC = Department of Disease Control; DHO = district health office; EOC = Emergency Operation Center; LGO = local government office; MOPH = Ministry of Public Health; PHO = provincial health office; SRRT = surveillance and rapid response team; VHVs = village health volunteers.

Additionally, a national Field Epidemiology Training Program (FETP) was established in 1980 with the United States Centers for Disease Control and the World Health Organization (WHO); it is the oldest FETP outside of the United States. The program has trained thousands of experts to investigate and control disease outbreaks, many of whom work at the provincial and district levels and were involved in managing the COVID-19 pandemic.

During the COVID-19 pandemic, critical personnel (including epidemiologists, laboratory technicians, and logisticians) were deployed rapidly to respond to COVID-19 clusters and local outbreaks. Staffing rosters were updated, and mechanisms were put in place to move people to where they were needed most. The network of FETP alumni proved to be a valuable resource for investigating clusters, tracing contacts, and analyzing epidemiological data (Thailand, MOPH and WHO 2020).

Moreover, the national network of VHVs played a significant role in COVID-19 surveillance, given their reach and familiarity with local communities. Laboratory and research capacity was strengthened significantly during the course of the pandemic, contributing to Thailand's strong surveillance system.

Lastly, early activation of the Emergency Operation Center and the Incident Command System at all levels of the health system also supported surveillance and reporting.

Mobilization of the Thai Health Workforce

The mobilization, deployment, and shifting of resources, particularly human resources, to address both COVID- and non-COVID-related health services have been critical to the overall response and resilience of the Thai health system over the last few years. As of 2019, the country had 8.1 doctors and 29.6 nurses and midwives per 10,000 population—or a total of 37.7 health workers per 10,000 population—representing strong capacity in both the number and the mix of skills and competencies.

All MOPH health professionals are posted in tertiary hospitals at the provincial level, secondary hospitals at the district level, and health centers at the subdistrict level. Moreover, VHV networks support the primary health care system at the community level. During the pandemic, health workforce capacities were adequate, which, when coupled with public health and social measures, significantly contained local transmission and minimized the pressure on essential health services.[1]

The Department of Disease Control also developed guidelines recommending that each hospital designate a team of health care workers dedicated specifically to the COVID-19 ward and prohibiting their rotation to other wards. In some hospitals with severely ill COVID-19 patients, medical teams were divided into two groups that swapped every 14 days in case members of one team became infected. These policy adaptations delegated tasks more efficiently between COVID-19 and non-COVID-19 essential health services staff.

To accommodate the rapid increase in demand for services required to implement universal health care in 2002, the Thai government more than doubled the number of qualified nurses and midwives from 84,682 (13.2 per 10,000 population) in 2002 to 191,575 (27.6 per 10,000 population) in 2018 through investments in and capacity building for the health workforce. During the same time period, policies were implemented to almost triple the number of qualified medical doctors, from 18,947 (3.0 per 10,000 population) to 55,890 (8.1 per 10,000 population). And, to address the uneven geographic distribution of health care workers, the government adopted a range of interventions, including increased training capacity; mandatory rural service for graduating doctors, nurses, pharmacists, and dentists; recruitment of health students from rural backgrounds; a training curriculum that included rural health problems; and financial and nonfinancial incentives such as social recognition that addressed geographic inequities.

Village Health Volunteer Network Activation

A national program of more than 1 million VHVs has, for four decades, collected data, maintained health records, and educated the community on how to prevent communicable and noncommunicable diseases (Narkvickien 2020). VHVs are local community members who, after receiving 43 hours of MOPH-funded training from personnel in the local district health office, volunteer to look after around 10–15 households, often with bedridden, disabled, and elderly members. Since they are local to the communities in which they operate—sharing the local dialect, religion, and sociocultural practices of the persons they serve—VHVs generally gain the trust of villagers and collaborate well with the local community, local government, subdistrict health centers, and family medicine teams. VHVs offer the primary health care system an ear on the ground to listen to and understand people's problems and suggestions (Oxford Policy Management and United Nations Thailand 2020).

VHVs are used nationwide to provide health education and deliver medicines for the growing number of individuals with chronic noncommunicable diseases. They support diabetes and hypertension screenings in their communities and aid health workers during home visits to patients (Narkvickien 2020).

This network also plays an important role in infectious disease surveillance and health education efforts. Prior to COVID-19, VHVs were mobilized to support community awareness efforts around dengue prevention and control and, in 2004, during the H5N1 epidemic VHVs monitored abnormal numbers of deaths in domesticated birds and alerted human and animal health authorities to investigate (Rajatanavin et al. 2021).

During the COVID-19 pandemic, the National Health Security Office reallocated Community Health Funds to support VHVs, and local administrations mobilized volunteers to enhance the capacity of the surveillance and rapid response teams for Thailand's early-warning system. VHVs were critical in supporting surveillance, detection, contact tracing, and health monitoring throughout the pandemic as well as in distributing essential supplies, such as face masks, face shields, biohazard bags, and alcohol gel.

Thailand's previous experience with other major outbreaks and its VHV model also supported Communicable Disease Control Units (CDCUs) in responding to COVID-19. Most CDCUs had been trained and responded to outbreaks of influenza and, in some cases, MERS. This training allowed them to be more familiar with the methods and materials required for COVID-19 response. Thailand's long-term investments in primary health care and universal health coverage also strengthened community-based health structures that will extend beyond the COVID-19 pandemic.

Layer 2: Focus on Detection, Containment, and Risk Communication

Agile Funding Mobilization

The two main sources of funding for the public health emergency response for COVID-19 were an emergency loan decree and the central budget. A total of B 45 billion (US$1.3 billion) for an initial emergency loan decree and B 30 billion (US$850 million) for an additional emergency loan decree were made available.

The emergency loan decree, which originated from external and internal loans, was earmarked for the following purposes:

- Payment of risk compensation for public health–related staff;
- Purchase of medical supplies, drugs, and vaccines;
- Disease control and research and development of vaccines;
- Treatment and quarantine; and
- Response plans for COVID-19 (for example, cars for active screening, set up of communication systems).

Diagnostic and Testing Strategies

In the last few years, Thailand's laboratory capacity for processing reverse transcription polymerase chain reaction (RT-PCR) tests has been scaled up significantly due to major budget approvals. During the pandemic, MOPH policy aimed to establish at least one RT-PCR laboratory in each province, which would require a minimum of 77 laboratories nationally. By April 2020, there were 39 certified RT-PCR laboratories in Bangkok with a capacity of 10,000 tests per day and 41 laboratories outside Bangkok with a similar daily capacity. By June 2020, an additional 30 laboratories were up and running, providing coverage in all provinces. This capacity was enhanced by 12 regional MOPH laboratory centers that provided backup testing with a 24-hour turnaround time for provinces that did not offer RT-PCR. And by October 2020, this capacity had increased to 230 laboratories (154 public and 76 private) covering all 77 provinces (Rajatanavin et al. 2021). As of March 2022, there were 513 laboratories nationally (292 public and 221 private), with around 35 percent of laboratories located in the Bangkok metropolitan region (Bangkok, Nakhon Pathom, Nonthaburi, Pathum Thani, Samut Prakan, and Samut Sakhon) and 23 percent of laboratories located in Bangkok. As of March 2022, 327 tests per 1,000 population were being conducted nationwide.

The FETP also played a major role in the detection of COVID-19 cases. During the early phase of the pandemic in 2020, the FETP was tasked with investigating every COVID-19 outbreak across the country. This effort led to the effective control of the first wave of infections, in which a major source of COVID-19 infection was located in Bangkok and came from abroad. Although some outbreaks occurred outside Bangkok, the FETP and its alumni in the area worked collaboratively to contain all major outbreaks.

By late 2020, the source of infection shifted toward migrants entering from Myanmar. The rapidly escalating situation in migrant camps in Samut Sakhon Province led the FETP to prioritize investigating COVID-19 cases for further innovative strategies. As a result of this effort, the FETP implemented a "bubble and seal" strategy, in which mini-quarantine operations were implemented in hot spots in the region of the outbreak. At this stage, FETP alumni proved to be useful liaisons with local teams, as a majority of the cooperation came from local health care professionals in the region.

In 2021, as COVID-19 cases spread throughout Thailand, the FETP shifted from having an operational role to having a more high-level strategic supervisory role, as local strategies proved to be more efficient than case findings. This shift alleviated the FETP workload and enhanced regional surveillance capacities.

Contact Tracing, Isolation, and Quarantine Efforts

Enforced through the Communicable Diseases Act of 2015, contact tracing efforts were conducted primarily by the surveillance and rapid response teams and VHV networks. During the first wave in Thailand in early 2020, the following measures were applied:

- Identification of index cases using case definitions produced and updated regularly by the MOPH,
- Tracing and testing of all high-risk index contacts,
- Treatment of all cases in hospitals, and
- Isolation in quarantine sites for at least 14 days from the onset of symptoms to prevent transmission.

Subsequent waves later in 2020 demonstrated the need to employ active case-finding efforts, particularly for vulnerable groups that were not captured by the formal quarantine system (for example, migrant workers) and for places where clusters of cases were suspected. Furthermore, the government recognized the significant economic impact of the initial nationwide lockdowns in early 2020 and implemented a more targeted strategy in later waves. This approach comprised lockdowns of specific areas and active case finding of all individuals in high-risk areas. While individual contact tracing was time-consuming, active case finding offered a more cost-effective and timely approach, when applied to areas with a high prevalence of infections.

Experiences from the first wave informed subsequent responses during later waves, when essential resources were mobilized, including human resources (for example, case-finding teams and clinicians) and medicines. As a result, although the total number of cases was seven times higher during the second wave (December 2020 to February 2021), the fatality rate was lower (0.11 percent compared to 1.46 percent in the first wave) due to early admission and treatment.

Risk Communication

Numerous stakeholders were involved in efforts to communicate risk during the pandemic. In particular, the Center for COVID-19 Situation Administration led national risk communication efforts through its daily COVID-19 broadcasts based on the concept of "one channel, one message."[2] Beginning at the start of the pandemic, these briefings were broadcast on all media channels, including televised broadcasts, social media, and online platforms. These briefings included:

- Epidemiological updates of the global, regional, and national situation;
- Death counts;
- Number of positive laboratory tests per 1 million population; and
- Preventive measures that citizens were required to adopt.

The Department of Disease Control, through the Emergency Operation Center led by the permanent secretary of the MOPH, contributed to the technical content of risk communications. As a result of his daily public briefing, Dr. Taweesin Wisanuyothin became an icon of the public communication response to COVID-19 (Patcharanaruamol et al. 2020). Through this daily reporting, the general public developed relative confidence and trust in the public health response and interventions. These efforts also improved public awareness of the seriousness of the situation and how citizens could contribute to pandemic containment. These efforts were aligned with risk communication efforts across the MOPH's social media platforms, signage, and other traditional media in which preventive and safety measures were communicated.

Call centers were also established to improve two-way communication between Thai citizens and health care providers. This communication included, among others, various hotlines and a smartphone application for monitoring symptoms of at-risk groups in home quarantine or in isolation. Multilingual messaging in Thai, Burmese, Chinese, Khmer, and Laotian improved individuals' understanding of the virus, its transmission modalities, and how to prevent getting infected and stop local transmission. However, volunteer staffing shortages and large increases in use during the surges in 2021 and 2022 led to unmet demand for these resources (Thai PBS World 2022).

Continuity of Essential Health Services

Several health workforce efforts were enacted to strengthen the capacity of health providers across all levels of the health system, down to communities through the VHV network. These efforts aimed to support the equitable delivery of essential health services despite competing demands due to COVID-19 response.

Tailored community engagement efforts at the local level included community-led door-to-door delivery of antiretroviral drugs and harm-reduction services, including opioid substitution therapy for people with human immunodeficiency virus/acquired immunodeficiency syndrome (HIV/AIDS) and sterile needles and syringes for people with drug addictions. Other promising practices included the establishment of emergency relief funds or reallocation of nonprofit budgets to provide emergency food supplies, housing and rent, transportation, and protective gear for the most affected communities, both supporting basic needs and maintaining essential health services.

The Department of Medical Services under the MOPH established a national New Normal Medical Services initiative to be implemented across all levels of the health system, with the ultimate goal of ensuring that both COVID-19 and non-COVID-19 patients received appropriate treatment and care. The innovations included many pilot efforts to test innovative models supported by digital health solutions. In this way, the "new normal" models aimed to ensure that health systems "build back better" the essential health services that had been negatively affected during COVID-19 and to prepare all levels of the health system for future health emergencies (WHO 2020).

Layer 3: Health Workforce Surge Capacity

Mobilizing the surge capacity of specialist health workforce staff, including intensive care nurses and critical care specialists, was challenging during rapid shifts in the pandemic. However, rapid response efforts ensured that coverage was generally good and provided as needed. For example, in early 2020, while cases were recorded in 68 out of the 77 provinces, the top 10 provinces accounted for almost 9 out of 10 cases (87 percent).

This finding prompted the MOPH to mobilize surplus capacity from other provinces to address the shortage of specialists, especially intensive care nurses, critical care experts, and epidemiologists in certain locations. Some hospitals deployed experienced nurses from nonintensive care units within their own hospital or province to support on-the-job training for the intensive care unit and infection prevention and control.

Lessons Learned

Thailand's experience shows that it is imperative to invest in a multidisciplinary workforce and mobilize patient-centered care at the community level. The broader primary care system at provincial and local levels was a key strength of Thailand's COVID-19 response. Village health volunteers played a crucial role in both reducing the direct impacts of COVID-19 and maintaining the delivery of essential health services. Additionally, the mobilization, deployment, and shifting of human resources allowed for a resilient and adaptive response throughout the pandemic.

Having a robust baseline surveillance system—built on the foundational infrastructure created to address past epidemics—was key to having a dynamic and effective pandemic response. Networks of surveillance teams, including the surveillance and rapid response teams and FETP, allowed the rapid deployment of health care workers to work on detection, isolation, and treatment of active cases. Furthermore, leveraging VHVs and other local actors to support these activities was key to expanding the coverage of surveillance efforts.

Prioritizing the maintenance of essential health services, especially in the prevention, detection, and treatment of noncommunicable diseases, was crucial. Working to bring innovative delivery solutions across different levels of the health system provided an opportunity to maintain service delivery and minimize the indirect negative health outcomes of public health emergencies.

Opportunities

Looking forward, Thailand should improve the availability, access, quality, integration, and openness of health data among key data holders and users. Efforts should be made to improve the overall health data landscape in Thailand. While ensuring data privacy and security, moving away from a disconnected, siloed system to one that is interconnected and open to all will be a key step in Thailand's ability to improve transparency and efficiency and unlock economic value and innovation in the health space.

For the health workforce, Thailand can consider providing additional compensation and other support, such as psychological or mental health support, for the health workforce.

Challenges

Thailand faced a variety of challenges throughout the course of the pandemic. One included misinformation and the resulting health inequity, particularly for different vulnerable groups, such as migrant populations and the urban poor. From a health workforce perspective, Thailand faced challenges in mobilizing the surge capacity of specialist health workers, such as intensive care nurses and critical care specialists.

As with many other countries, Thailand also had trouble maintaining a consistent reporting infrastructure for COVID-19 testing and surveillance, especially in the early days of the pandemic.

Lastly, the digital divide remains a significant challenge in Thailand: only 21 percent of households have access to a computer, which is lower than the worldwide average of 49 percent, and many households access the internet solely through mobile devices. Older people may have less access to electronic devices or the internet, less familiarity and trust with the technologies, or physical and cognitive impairments that present a barrier to their participation in telemedicine.

Notes

1. "Novel Coronavirus," World Health Organization Thailand page, https://www .searo.who.int/entity/asia_pacific_observatory/publications/covid_thailand/en/.
2. Refer to https://www.facebook.com/watch/live/?ref=watch_permalink&v=719105 785926212.

References

Exemplars in Global Health. 2023. *Thailand: COVID-19 Response and Maintenance of Essential Health Services.* Seattle, WA: Exemplars in Global Health. https://www .exemplars.health/emerging-topics/ecr/thailand.

Narkvickien, Montira. 2020 "Thailand's 1 Million Village Health Volunteers—'Unsung Heroes'—Are Helping Guard Communities Nationwide from COVID-19." World Health Organization, Geneva. https://www.who.int/thailand/news/feature-stories /detail/thailands-1-million-village-health-volunteers-unsung-heroes-are-helping -guard-communities-nationwide-from-covid-19.

Nittayasoot, Natthaprang, Rapeepong Suphanchaimat, Chawetsan Namwat, Patcharaporn Dejburum, and Viroj Tangcharoensathien. 2021. "Public Health Policies and Health-Care Workers' Response to the COVID-19 Pandemic, Thailand."

Bulletin of the World Health Organization 99 (4): 312–18. https://doi.org/10.2471/BLT.20.275818.

Oxford Policy Management and United Nations Thailand. 2020. *Social Impact Assessment of COVID-19 in Thailand.* Oxford, UK: Oxford Policy Management Ltd., July 2020. https://www.unicef.org/thailand/media/5071/file/SocialImpactAssessmentof COVID-19inThailand.pdf.

Patcharanaruamol, Walaiporn, Angkana Lekagul, Chutima Akaleephan, Kamolphat Markchang, Mathudara Phaiyarom, Nattadhanai Rajatanavin, Nattanicha Pangkariya, Orana Chandrasiri, Orratai Waleewong, Putthipanya Rueangsom, Ratchaporn Congprasert, Repeepong Suphanchaimat, Sataporn Julchoo, Somtanuek Chotchoungchatchai, Titiporn Tuangrattananon, Thinakorn Noree, Warisa Panichkriangkrai, Watinee Kunpuek, Viroj Tangcharoensathien, Anns Issac, and Nima Asgari-Jirhandeh. 2020. "COVID-19 Health System Response Monitor: Thailand." World Health Organization Regional Office for South-East Asia, New Delhi, updated November 2020. https://apps.who.int/iris/rest/bitstreams /1318248/retrieve.

Rajatanavin, Nattadhanai, Titiporn Tuangratananon, Repeepong Suphanchaimat, and Viroj Tangcharoensathien. 2021. "Responding to the COVID-19 Second Wave in Thailand by Diversifying and Adapting Lessons from the First Wave." *BMJ Global Health* 6 (7): e006178. https://doi.org/10.1136/bmjgh-2021-006178.

Smith, Duncan R. 2021. "Review a Brief History of Coronaviruses in Thailand." *Journal of Virological Methods* 289 (March): 114034. doi:10.1016/j.jviromet.2020.114034.

Thai PBS World. 2022. "Thailand's National Health Hotline in Need of Call Centre Help, Volunteers." Thai Public Broadcasting Service, February 22, 2022. https://www .thaipbsworld.com/thailands-national-health-hotline-in-need-of-call-centre-help -volunteers/.

Thailand, MOPH (Ministry of Public Health) and WHO (World Health Organization). 2020. "Joint Intra-Action Review of the Public Health Response to COVID-19 in Thailand." WHO, Geneva, July 20–24, 2020. https://www.who.int/publications/m /item/joint-intra-action-review-of-the-public-health-response-to-covid-19-in -thailand.

WHO (World Health Organization). 2020. "Thailand Launches 'New Normal' Healthcare System to Build Back Better after COVID-19." WHO, Geneva, August 11, 2020. https://www.who.int/thailand/news/feature-stories/detail/thailand-launches -new-normal-healthcare-system-to-build-back-better-after-covid-19.

8

Three-Layer Health Sector Investment in the Dominican Republic

Magdalena Rathe, Laura Rathe, Ian Paulino, Moytrayee Guha, Arielle Cohen Tanugi-Carresse, Lucia Mullen, Sara Bennett, Jennifer Nuzzo, Jacqueline Maloney, Siobhan Lazenby, and Anne Liu

IN SUMMARY

The government of the Dominican Republic prioritized responding to the COVID-19 pandemic and effectively mobilized the entire country toward a common goal: to protect the population from COVID-19 through mass vaccination, while gradually reopening the economy and recovering growth and employment.

- The Dominican government invested in building trust among the community and health care workers to ensure the rapid uptake of public health interventions, including a widely successful vaccination campaign.

- Community mobilization encouraged strong public-private alliances, providing the Dominican health system with the necessary resources and funding to avoid saturating the health system during surges of the pandemic.

- Following the elections in July 2020, the Dominican Republic strengthened governance and leadership at the highest levels of decision-making across prevention, mitigation, and response systems and aligned across sectors to implement public health interventions and promote social protection for vulnerable populations.

- The pandemic emphasized weaknesses in the Dominican Republic's health system; however, the new government was able to leverage alliances and the public will to fill these gaps.

This research was led by partners at the Fundación Plenitud in collaboration with Brown University School of Public Health and Johns Hopkins Bloomberg School of Public Health and was supported and funded by the Rockefeller Foundation and by the Exemplars in Global Health (EGH) program at Gates Ventures. Fundación Plenitud is an independent nongovernmental organization that provides technical assistance, training, and capacity-building services to countries in Latin America and the Caribbean and elsewhere. EGH has a mission to identify positive global health outliers, analyze what makes countries successful, and disseminate core lessons so they can be adapted in comparable settings. EGH is a global coalition of partners including researchers, academics, experts, funders, country stakeholders, and implementers. A small, core team supporting EGH is based at Gates Ventures, the private office of Bill Gates, and closely collaborates with the Gates Foundation. For the full case study, refer to Exemplars in Global Health (2023).

Country Context

The Dominican Republic shares the Hispaniola Island with Haiti in the Caribbean and is classified as an upper-middle-income country by the World Bank. The Dominican Republic has a population of 10.8 million people, 84.5 percent of whom live in urban areas. That percentage of urbanization has been increasing steadily over the years. The median age in the Dominican Republic is 28 years, with life expectancy of 74.7 years.

The Dominican Republic has had one of the world's fastest-growing economies over the last several decades. This economic growth has helped to reduce poverty and improve equity in income distribution.[1] Despite this rapid economic growth, the country continues to have high levels of maternal, neonatal, and infant mortality, at 95 maternal deaths per 100,000 live births and 19.4 and 23.5 neonatal and infant deaths per 1,000 live births, respectively. These rates are significantly worse than in other Latin America and the Caribbean countries, although the number of hospital beds, doctors and nurses, institutional deliveries, and deliveries with qualified doctors is comparatively better, raising concerns about the quality of services in the Dominican Republic. Additionally, a gap remains in access to services between urban and rural populations.

Health System Structure and Features

The Dominican health system has relatively recently undergone changes in its structure and features. In 2001, the government approved the health system's present organization and financing with Law 87-01, which was intended to address problems of inequity, lack of financial protection, and lack of accountability and quality in the public providers' network.

The law created a universal health insurance scheme, Family Health Insurance, with three financing regimes: (1) a contributory regime financed by payroll taxes, (2) a subsidized regime financed by the government (from general taxation) to protect low-income and unemployed populations, and (3) a contributory-subsidized regime partially financed by the government, which was never implemented due to the difficulties in collecting contributions from the informal sector.

The reform proposed the following vision of a new health system: universal coverage with access to the same basic package of services for the whole population, a compulsory public financing system, government stewardship and supervision, and a network of public and private providers and insurers operating in a context of regulated competition for formal sector employees (Rathe 2018). Figure 8.1 describes the resulting system.

The stewardship of the health system is the responsibility of the Ministry of Public Health (MOPH), which is in charge of governance, regulation, and the provision of collective services, as well as essential public health functions.

Figure 8.1   Health System Financing in the Dominican Republic

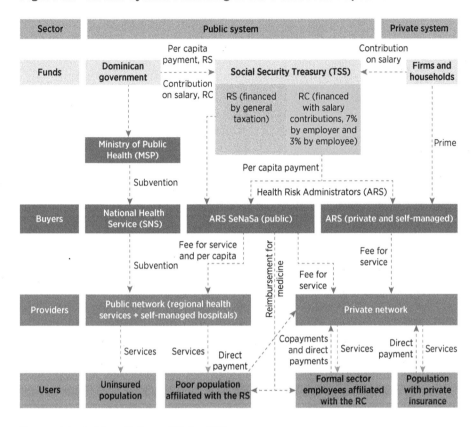

Source: Adapted from Rathe and Moline 2011.

Note: RC = contributory regime; RS = subsidized regime; SeNaSA = national health insurance.

Since 2015, responsibility for providing public services to individuals has been transferred to the National Health Service, which coordinates the network of public providers organized at various levels of care.

Public investments in the Dominican health system have been relatively low, with total health spending as a proportion of gross domestic product (GDP) at around 5 percent.[2] Deficiencies in the first level of care, collective health services, and preparation for health emergencies are especially significant. The lack of investment in public providers has translated into a low quality of service, including old and poor infrastructure, lack of equipment, and scarcity of medical specialists. These shortcomings perpetuate inequity among different social groups, given that public providers are the ones most used by the low-income population.

Insurance in the contributory regime is available through private, public, and mixed companies, which contract a network of mainly private providers organized by levels of care. In the subsidized regime, one public insurer, the

National Health Insurance scheme, contracts mostly public providers, which are part of the National Health Service network. However, if the scheme cannot find quality services in the National Health Service network, it contracts private providers.

Layer 1: Risk Reduction—Promoting Prevention and Community Preparedness

Most of the Dominican Republic's community preparedness and government structures were founded in response to extensive experiences with past epidemics and natural disasters.

Leveraging Past Experiences for Community Preparedness

The Dominican Republic has faced outbreaks of Zika (2016–17) (Peña et al. 2019), chikungunya (2014) (Dominican Republic, MOPH 2014), annual fluctuations in the number of dengue cases, and the avian influenza virus (H5N1) in 2007. In the wake of these crises, the Dominican government developed response plans in three phases: (1) monitoring before an outbreak; (2) community outreach with prevention, prevention strategies, and health system response; and (3) reporting and lessons learned after an outbreak. The Dominican government has created multiple outbreak preparedness and response plans, including one for chikungunya, the first of its kind in the Americas, and one for the influenza epidemic (PAHO 2014). Additionally, it established a national communication plan, with radio and television messages in simple language addressing prevention, posters, and booklets for schools with guidance for the educational community and the public.

The National Council for Prevention, Mitigation, and Response to Disasters, created in 2002, is the governing body on disaster preparedness; it oversees guiding, directing, planning, and coordinating the national system. The law orders the preparation of a contingency plan with specific preestablished procedures for coordination, alerts, mobilization, and response to the occurrence or imminence of a particular event, such as an epidemic or pandemic.

Establishment of Committed Leadership

In February and March 2020, when the pandemic hit the country, the Dominican Republic was undergoing an extensive election process. This situation resulted in a delay of two weeks in the installation of a state of emergency, which contributed to the epidemic spreading to the community very quickly. The government established highly restrictive measures on March 19, which included border closures, closure of all productive activities, except essential ones, closure of schools and public transport, and curfews.

The national elections, which were supposed to be held in May, were delayed until July, with the opposition party winning. The new government, installed in August, vowed to fight the pandemic as its top priority, embarking on a progressive and modulated reopening of economic activity, especially tourism, the backbone of the Dominican economy. The reopening inevitably increased the number of cases in the third wave, but the country did not return to the total closure of the early pandemic. Instead, the new government focused on substantially increasing the number of tests, isolating infected people, and preparing for mass vaccination.

Layer 2: Focus on Detection, Containment, and Mitigation Capabilities

When the Dominican Republic was not able to contain the initial outbreak of COVID-19, the newly elected leadership acted quickly to contain the epidemic and foster community trust. This approach facilitated community mobilization and strong public-private partnerships, allowing the Dominican health system to procure hospital resources, strengthen testing, and roll out a widely effective vaccination campaign.

Building Community Trust

The government invested considerable time in building trust, communicating risk, and mobilizing the country toward the common goal of fighting COVID-19. As a result, Dominican communities were willing to comply with public health recommendations and interventions. For example, health personnel were found to be "willing to face anything, even to give their lives to be there during the pandemic and working on the front lines. There was never an exodus or strikes, as happened in other countries" (key information interview). Therefore, while the Dominican health system still had to deal with increasing demands for health personnel during the pandemic, it was also able to depend on the existing workforce, unlike many other countries.

The government also prioritized social protection measures targeting the social determinants of the pandemic and building trust with vulnerable communities. It used financial transfers to aid vulnerable groups during the pandemic, specifically employees who lost their job to the pandemic and households living in monetary or structural poverty.

The government also focused on insurance coverage by adding to the subsidized regime 2 million people who did not have health insurance, with the intention of guaranteeing financial protection for the entire population. As a result, by June 2022, 98 percent of the Dominican population was insured.

Public-Private Partnerships to Support Testing

Community mobilization was particularly effective in building public-private partnerships, which were key to the Dominican Republic's response. The private laboratory system, which was already strong, was made available to government authorities through public-private partnerships. All testing and treatment were free of charge, both from public and private providers, and were paid for by the government. Monetary incentives were provided to frontline health workers who tested. This collaboration strengthened testing capacity throughout the country and made testing accessible to all citizens.

Public-Private Partnerships to Support Hospital Capacity

Additionally, the Dominican health system used public-private partnerships to maintain the availability of hospital and intensive care unit (ICU) beds for COVID-19 patients (figure 8.2). Occupancy of beds was highest from June to July of 2020, before the new government formed, and, even then, only 52 percent of hospital beds and 77 percent of ICU beds were in use. The government centralized data on patient flows, and each day, according to the demand, the availability of hospital and ICU beds was modified. This effort was possible because of a collaboration between the government and the private sector under the leadership of the MOPH. When the new government took office in August 2020, leadership of the response to the pandemic, particularly regarding the vaccination plan, passed to the Cabinet of Health, led by the vice president of the republic and the MOPH.

Public-Private Partnerships to Support Vaccination

According to President Luis Abinader, the vaccination campaign was the "largest public-private collaboration in Dominican history." The government that was installed in 2020 immediately put mass vaccination on its agenda and was able to acquire enough vaccines through bilateral deals with pharmaceutical companies, mainly AstraZeneca and Pfizer.

Figure 8.2   Total Occupancy of Intensive Care Units in the Dominican Republic, 2020–22

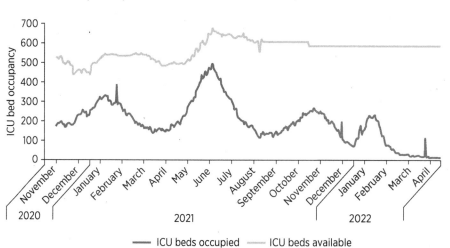

Source: Prepared by Fundación Plenitud from Ministry of Public Health daily bulletins.
Note: ICU = intensive care unit.

The vaccination process began in February 2021 and developed quickly, with 1,400 vaccination centers established in schools, stadiums, shopping centers, and public transport stations. This process was carried out by the Expanded Immunization Program of the MOPH in collaboration with numerous private sector companies. Several private companies contributed resources to buy vaccines, others provided premises for vaccination centers, companies with refrigerators contributed space to ensure the cold chain, and even beer distributors provided refrigerated trucks for transporting vaccines. Priority was also given to reopening the tourist industry, and mass vaccination was undertaken in tourist areas, along with increased access to tests and vaccines for hotel staff and tourists.

Trust in government strengthened the uptake of vaccination. In a survey conducted by Universidad Iberoamericana, 72 percent of the population surveyed expressed interest in getting the vaccine, 18 percent were not sure, and only 10 percent said they had no interest (Pérez Soto and Berríos Viana 2021). Sustained prioritization from the country's leadership, private sector investment, and community willingness were essential to the widely successful rollout of vaccines and to all aspects of the Dominican Republic's response to COVID-19.

Layer 3: Advanced Case Management and Surge Response

Due to strong governance, public-private partnerships, and investments in layers 1 and 2, the Dominican Republic was able to navigate many of the surges of the pandemic while employing emergency strategies.

In April 2020, the Dominican government requested that the Command, Control, Communications, Computers, Cybersecurity, and Intelligence Center (C5i) of the Ministry of Defense, whose purpose is related to crime and national security, be integrated with the health system. The National Health Service had been working since 2019 to develop a technological platform for centralizing data from the public network; with the support of C5i, it was possible to integrate data on public and private hospitals, clinics, laboratories, pharmacies, and insurance, including real-time information on the number of beds available and in use in a hospital and its ICU, the number of ventilators and ambulances, and other data that contribute to creating predictive models that support making evidence-based decisions and predictions on the amount of resources required.

The government was then able to lean on its private sector alliances to procure the necessary resources and avoid hospital overload. The platform was most useful in ensuring that large hospitals, which attracted the most patients, did not reach maximum capacity. With the data on hospital occupancy, the National Health Service sent patients who were not in need of the treatment offered only by large hospitals to less occupied health centers, depending on the complexity and severity of their cases. Therefore, the government's investments in surveillance and effective leadership enabled the health system to respond rapidly and to deploy resources during surges in certain regions of the country.

Lessons Learned

The Dominican Republic is an exemplary model for the impact of committed political leadership on community trust, hospital capacity, resources, and public-private partnerships, especially for a country that had been unprepared for pandemics in the past. The Health Cabinet was able to garner the active participation of many actors of Dominican society and, through public-private alliances, was able to develop the country's ambitious vaccination plan. The capacity of hospitals and ICUs was also sufficient because supply was monitored daily against needs, both in public and in private hospitals.

All of society was allied to face the pandemic and to bring medicines, vaccines, tests, and personal protective equipment to the most remote places. The leadership, the priority assigned to pandemic response and to the vaccination process, the proper communication of risk, the handling of data, the mobilization of the entire society toward a common goal, and the use of public-private alliances were key to the Dominican Republic's achievements.

The Dominican government built resilience into the health system through speed, agility, and adaptability. It made rapid decisions to acquire vaccines and treatments, to change restrictive closing and opening measures, to construct public-private alliances, and to deepen the digital transformation needed to adapt the health system to new challenges. The Dominican Republic was able to work past previous gaps by entering into public-private partnerships and adopting innovative strategies.

In summary,

- The government rectified the absence of an updated strategy to address the shortage of human resources by hiring more than 3,700 new human resources from different health personnel specialties during the pandemic.
- The public and private sectors undertook joint efforts to address the lack of capacity to isolate patients with highly communicable diseases by creating spaces in which to isolate patients, such as using certain hospitals exclusively for the care of COVID-19 patients.
- Public-private partnerships addressed the absence of plans, agreements, and strategies for medical countermeasures in emergencies by acquiring diagnostic tests, new treatments, vaccines, and protective equipment and delivering them to the population free of charge.
- Despite a previously inadequate communication system for public health emergencies, authorities held daily press conferences at the beginning of the pandemic and weekly afterward. They also developed electronic platforms to inform the population daily on the number of cases, deaths, hospital beds, ICU occupancy, and tests acquired and administered; the positivity rate; and orientation on where to get assistance, tests, and vaccination.

- A main achievement of the Dominican response was to include the public and private sectors in the health communication system. The private sector became a great ally in the fight against the pandemic for testing, hospitalization of patients, cold chains, and vaccinations.

Challenges

Many of the challenges that the Dominican Republic faced during the pandemic were related to maintaining essential health services because of prior disinvestment in the health sector and subsequent weaknesses in primary care. Even though reform laws were established to ensure that health care was based on a primary care strategy, this goal has not yet been achieved in 20 years of reform.

There have been continuous challenges due to vested interests in the contributory regime, lack of political will in the subsidized system, and governance issues in the public network (Rathe and Gibert 2020; Rathe and Suero 2017). As a result, the Dominican system is primarily reactive and based on the care of acute cases. Therefore, the COVID-19 epidemic initially spread to the community very quickly, and contact-tracing actions were difficult to implement.

Some services were more affected than others during the pandemic, such as direct observation therapy for tuberculosis and access to treatment for human immunodeficiency virus/acquired immunodeficiency syndrome (HIV/AIDS) patients. Similarly, the lack of public provision made it difficult to reduce infant and maternal mortality rates. The provision of maternal and neonatal services faced major challenges, mainly due to mobility restrictions, the shortage of some essential supplies and personal protective equipment, the reduction of working hours, and the ministerial concentration of efforts and resources to pandemic response. Half of the population still receives low-quality essential health services because the first level of care in the public network has such low capacity.

The Dominican government should consider strengthening the first level of care by changing the way public providers are managed and implementing performance incentives, promoting public-private partnerships to establish a first level of functional care in both the subsidized regime and the contributory regime, and investing more in digital health.

The pandemic initially revealed the shortcomings and weaknesses of the country's health system, especially those flaws that had not been addressed for decades, such as the lack of investment in primary care. At the same time, it provided the opportunity for a responsible and committed political leadership to emerge, capable of facing the pandemic despite the health system's shortcomings. The clarity of the new government's vision made it possible to rally the public will, which allowed all sectors to unite to face it, with decisive and adaptive capacity.

Notes

1. GBD Compare (database), Institute of Health Metrics and Evaluation, https://vizhub.healthdata.org/gbd-compare/.
2. This figure is lower than the published information in the World Health Organization (WHO) Global Health Expenditure Database and World Bank World Development Indicators database. Fundación Plenitud produced new estimates recently using new data for household expenditures. The published figures were prepared before publication of the National Income and Expenditures Survey of 2018 (published in 2020).

References

Dominican Republic, MOPH (Ministry of Public Health). 2014. "Plan de preparación y respuesta frente a brotes de fiebre Chikungunya." MOPH, Santo Domingo. https://repositorio.msp.gob.do/handle/123456789/193.

Exemplars in Global Health. 2023. *Dominican Republic: COVID-19 Response and Maintenance of Essential Health Services.* Seattle, WA: Exemplars in Global Health. https://www.exemplars.health/emerging-topics/ecr/dominican-republic.

PAHO (Pan American Health Organization). 2014. "Estrategia de acceso universal a la salud y cobertura universal de salud." Resolución del Consejo Directivo, en la 66.a Sesión del Comité Regional de la OMS de las Américas. PAHO, Washington, DC.

Peña, Farah, Raquel Pimentel, Shaveta Khosla, Supriya D. Mehta, and Maximo O. Brito. 2019. "Zika Virus Epidemic in Pregnant Women, Dominican Republic, 2016–2017." *Emerging Infectious Diseases* 25 (2): 247–55. https://doi.org/10.3201/eid2502.181054.

Pérez Soto, Armando, and Dayanara Berríos Viana. 2021. *Determinantes sobre la aceptación de la vacuna COVID-19, en el Distrito Nacional, República Dominicana, durante el período de febrero a marzo de 2021.* Santo Domingo: Universidad Iberoamericana. https://repositorio.unibe.edu.do/jspui/handle/123456789/546.

Rathe, Magdalena. 2018. "Dominican Republic: Implementing a Health Protection System That Leaves No One Behind." Universal Health Coverage Study Series 30, World Bank, Washington, DC. https://mapa.do.undp.org/files/publications/Dominican%20Republic.%20Implementing%20a%20Health%20Protection%20System%20that%20Leaves%20No%20One%20Behind.pdf.

Rathe, Magdalena M., and Marc Gibert. 2020. *Atención primaria en salud en América Latina y el Caribe: Experiencias exitosas y lecciones aprendidas.* Santo Domingo: Observatorio de Seguridad Social.

Rathe, Magdalena, and Alejandro Moline. 2011. "Sistema de salud de República Dominicana." *Salud pública Méxicana* [online]. 53 (Suppl. 2): s255–s264.

Rathe, Magdalena, and Pamela Suero. 2017. *Salud, visión de futuro: 20 años después.* Santo Domingo: Instituto Tecnológico de Santo Domingo.

9

Three-Layer Health Sector Investment in Costa Rica

Andrea Prado, Andy Pearson, Claudio Mora, Moytrayee Guha, Arielle Cohen Tanugi-Carresse, Lucia Mullen, Sara Bennett, Jennifer Nuzzo, Jacqueline Maloney, Siobhan Lazenby, and Anne Liu

IN SUMMARY

During the COVID-19 pandemic, Costa Rica's integrated health system allowed one entity, the Costa Rican Social Security Fund (CCSS), to implement changes across the health system to maintain essential health services and respond to urgent health system needs.

- Through a coordinated and centralized response, CCSS and an operational team of hospital directors made real-time and formal decisions about patient care, transfers, and health system needs throughout the many stages of the pandemic, supported by the institution's electronic medical record, EDUS.

- CCSS had access to the government's contingency fund and used the funds to adjust health personnel protocols, hospital capacity and infrastructure, and virtual service modalities to maintain essential health services.

- Costa Rica struggled in several areas: maintaining quality of care for many non-COVID-19 health services, overcoming the limitations of telemedicine and patient absenteeism, servicing all regions equally, and coordinating efforts with the private health sector.

Country Context

Costa Rica is a small upper-middle-income country of 5 million people, located in Central America, between Nicaragua and Panama. Costa Rica has a democratic system of government and a literacy rate of 95 percent (one of the highest in Latin America). It is one of the best-performing Latin American countries in health outcomes, with the second-highest life expectancy in the Western Hemisphere, behind Canada, despite having a lower gross domestic

This research was led by partners at the Instituto Centroamericano de Administracion de Empresas Business School in collaboration with Brown University School of Public Health and Johns Hopkins Bloomberg School of Public Health and was supported and funded by the Rockefeller Foundation and by the Exemplars in Global Health (EGH) program at Gates Ventures. EGH has a mission to identify positive global health outliers, analyze what makes countries successful, and disseminate core lessons so they can be adapted in comparable settings. EGH is a global coalition of partners including researchers, academics, experts, funders, country stakeholders, and implementers. A small, core team supporting EGH is based at Gates Ventures, the private office of Bill Gates, and closely collaborates with the Gates Foundation. For the full case study, refer to Exemplars in Global Health (2023).

product (GDP) per capita and relatively lower health spending than other countries in the region. Costa Rica is home to an aging population, and noncommunicable diseases account for most of the disease burden, with cardiac disease and cancer being the leading causes of mortality.

Health System Structure and Features

Costa Rica operates a national health system that is widely known for its highly integrated public sector. While several institutions provide health care services, the most important in terms of coverage and health expenditures is the Costa Rican Social Security Fund (CCSS). CCSS is an autonomous public institution that dominates the provision of health care in Costa Rica, covers more than 90 percent of the population, and represents around 61 percent of all current health expenditures. CCSS provides general, specialized, and hospital medical services and manages the public network of hospitals and primary care clinics throughout the country. It is financed by the contributions of formal sector workers, employers, and the state to one health insurance fund and one pension fund. As a result, 68.7 percent of Costa Rica's health expenditures are dedicated to social health insurance schemes, and 97.5 percent of those expenditures are for funding CCSS.

The ideology of Costa Rica's integrated system hinges on the One CAJA strategy, which means that the different levels of care and health facilities throughout the country are considered an integrated unit. Specifically, the Costa Rican national health system is integrated both horizontally and vertically.

CCSS is integrated vertically because it provides health care at all levels of care (primary, secondary, and tertiary) through national hospitals, regional hospitals, clinics, and primary care clinics (figure 9.1). It is also integrated horizontally because it also controls several primary care clinics, hospitals, and specialized centers in regions throughout Costa Rica. CCSS oversees 105 primary care clinics and 1,066 basic health care teams (EBAISs, or equipos básicos de atención integral en salud) at the primary care level, 17 clinics and 20 hospitals at the secondary care level, and 3 national hospitals, 6 specialized hospitals, and 6 specialized centers at the tertiary care level (figure 9.2).

Even before the COVID-19 pandemic, the national health system struggled with long waiting lists and financial instability due to a lack of formal workers who contribute to the institution's income and a high central government fiscal deficit. While health care is universal, the system has difficulty providing quality and timely care to its citizens.

A 2020 self-assessment of Costa Rica's health emergency preparedness gave Costa Rica a score of 77 percent (WHO 2020). This is an average score for several health indicators defined by the World Health Organization (WHO) to denote the capacity level for a chosen health system. It places Costa Rica in level 4 or 5, which means that its policies support the implementation of

Figure 9.1   The Costa Rican National Health System

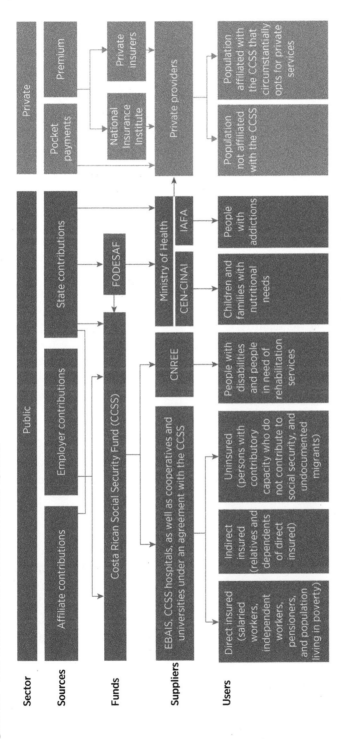

Source: Sáenz et al. 2011.

Note: CEN-CINAI = Education and Nutrition Centers and Children's Nutrition and Food Centers; CNREE = National Center for Rehabilitation and Special Education of Costa Rica; EBAIS = basic health care team (equipo básico de atención integral en salud); FODESAF = Social Development and Family Allowances Fund; IAFA = Institute of Alcoholism and Drug Dependence.

Figure 9.2 The Costa Rican Social Security Fund's Integrated System of Health Care

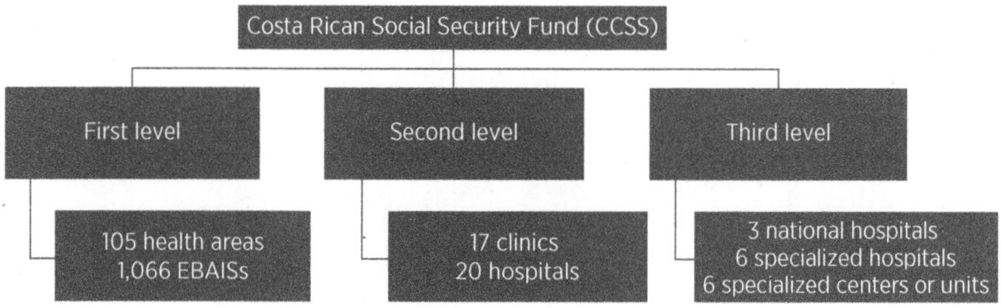

Source: Exemplars in Global Health 2023.
Note: EBAISs = basic health care teams (equipos básicos de atención integral en salud).

international health regulations at multiple levels of the health system and among various sectors (WHO 2020).

The evaluation noted that Costa Rica's health care system is weak in the following areas: planning for emergency preparedness and response mechanisms, effective public health response at points of entry, early-warning function and indicator- and event-based surveillance, capacity for infection prevention and control and chemical and radiation decontamination, and capacity and resources.

Layer 1: Risk Reduction—Promoting Prevention and Community Preparedness

Due to its highly integrated health care system and national health surveillance system, when the COVID-19 pandemic hit, Costa Rica had the potential to adopt a coordinated and consistent pandemic response.

Community Preparedness

The Costa Rican health system was reformed during the 1990s to emphasize integrated care and strengthen primary care. Integrated care means services that provide curative care, prevent disease, provide rehabilitation services, and promote health through information on healthy lifestyles and nutrition. The primary health care model is based on the use of EBAISs; each facility has a team consisting of at least one doctor, a nursing assistant, a technical assistant (or community health worker), a medical clerk, and a pharmacist. Doctors deliver curative and preventive care, nurses are responsible for basic clinical tasks and health counseling, and pharmacists prescribe medication. Technical assistants conduct their activities outside of the clinics, either through home visits or group visits in community settings. They deliver health promotion and disease prevention information, inspect basic housing conditions and sanitation, collect epidemiological data, identify environmental and familial behavioral risk factors, and refer patients to EBAISs or hospitals. Finally, medical clerks are in charge of records and statistics at the facility and are responsible for handling patient intake, collecting and managing patient data, and conducting epidemiological population health surveillance.

CCSS assigns households to an EBAIS based on a strategic geographic division, often referred to as an empanelment or sectorization process. Each facility is meant to serve approximately 5,000 people. All households are geographically empaneled in the EBAIS model, which is why CCSS reached 94 percent of the population by 2018. EBAISs clearly identify their assigned households (location and socioeconomic profile of their members) and perform epidemiological surveillance through home visits. They are integrated into a network structure with the rest of the health system, which includes general and specialized hospitals and clinics. Patients who need specialized medical attention beyond primary care—not available through the EBAIS—are referred to a regional or peripheral hospital that provides secondary care. These hospitals are spread across the country and are geographically accessible.

In terms of community preparedness, the National Emergency Commission has organized committees at the regional and community level throughout the country. These committees develop preparedness strategies for natural disasters (for example, earthquakes and floods) and, when necessary, coordinate efforts with local CCSS representatives to provide support during health emergencies.

Multisectoral Integration and Coordination

Legally, Costa Rica's Health Law (Law 5395) provides the Costa Rican health minister with the authority and resources to enforce an interinstitutional, multidisciplinary approach to promoting health and sanitation. This legal precedent works in conjunction with CCSS's position in the national health system by providing it with the authority to strengthen coordination throughout the system.

For example, CCSS employs an integrated network management strategy to foster continuous collaboration and transparency among health facilities. An Operational Coordination Council meets monthly in which the directors, administrators, managers, and heads of health facilities within the public health sector present the specific needs of each health facility and coordinate resources, patient movements, and priority specialties of care according to the demand for services.

Before the COVID-19 outbreak, the integrated network management strategy permitted CCSS to generate efficiencies, shorten waiting lists, and increase transfer capacity for better, faster, and more efficient care according to the specialties and capabilities of the hospital network. Additionally, CCSS routinely transferred patients among the different levels of care. Numerous health regions were able to shorten their waiting lists through small-scale network coordination, giving CCSS experience in using the network to minimize hospital overload.

Digital Health Innovations

Costa Rica's single digital health record—EDUS—is essential to this coordination, providing fast and easy countrywide access to patient health records and data on health system capacity. In addition, EDUS can produce reports and real-time dashboards on the provision of health care services and other operational information about the health system. In the past, it was used to maintain essential services, exchange patient file information, and provide information to decision-makers. It yields objective data regarding the real-time situation of the entire health system, and this information enables the Operational Coordination Council to make decisions and implement changes throughout the network quickly and accurately.

Additionally, EDUS is critical to primary care, as it enables communication and doctor access to medical records throughout the system. EDUS also has a smartphone app that people can use to access their medical records and appointments. These features facilitate seamless handoffs of patients in a system that regularly conducts patient transfers and gives patients agency in their own medical care.

Contingency Funding

In 2016, the CCSS board of directors established a contingency fund (US$200 million) to provide funding to CCSS in case of disasters, such as earthquakes, floods, or fires that affect health services. The fund received additional investments from the central government and loans from international finance institutions. The contingency fund, only available to the public sector, was expanded to include pandemics and became a fundamental factor in Costa Rica's preparedness and capacity to purchase equipment and hire additional personnel during the pandemic (for example, to adjust infrastructure or the number of intensive care staff, doctors, and nurses).

Layer 2: Focus on Detection, Containment, and Mitigation Capabilities

Costa Rica acted quickly in the early phases of COVID-19, implementing bold interventions and adapting its health system to address the impending pandemic. This quick response was made possible by CCSS's established avenues of coordination and integration.

On March 16, 2020, the president of Costa Rica declared a state of national emergency by signing Executive Decree no. 42227-MP-S, allowing all public institutions, including CCSS, to take temporary extraordinary measures. As a result, CCSS could make decisions that affected the entire health system without having to follow the written protocols or technical documents that are usually necessary for formal decisions. This authorization allowed CCSS to implement changes quickly, to activate existing structures, and to enforce systemwide interventions. Most important, CCSS was able to take full advantage of Costa Rica's channels of coordination and EDUS to implement innovative strategies.

One significant innovation was to create the Centro Especializado de Atención de Pacientes con COVID-19 (CEACO). Anticipating high demand for hospitalization services and intensive care beds, in March 2020 CCSS proposed transforming the Centro Nacional de Rehabilitación (CENARE), a rehabilitation center with 88 beds, into a hospital dedicated exclusively to the care of patients with COVID-19. Hospitals in the network now had a specific place to transfer their COVID-19 patients, especially when they were not equipped to respond themselves.

The creation of CEACO was made possible thanks to a substantial interinstitutional effort with the private sector to coordinate several resources and joint work in the areas of engineering, communications, logistics, and CCSS medical staff, who combined their knowledge to get CEACO up and running in less than 15 days. The team started operations on April 2, 2020, less than a month after the first COVID-19 case was detected in Costa Rica, and received the first patient on the same day. Additionally, CCSS authorized the creation of 784 special service positions for the management and staffing of CEACO. Intended to alleviate some of the burden on overloaded hospitals within the network, CEACO also served as a centralized hub for treating COVID-19 patients.

Surveillance directly from citizens was also crucial in Costa Rica's early COVID-19 response. A COVID-19 menu was included in the EDUS app early in the pandemic, which people could use to report symptoms and obtain information on the disease. To aid contact tracing, the app also included an alert that would anonymously indicate when a person had come into close contact with someone testing positive for COVID-19. While the EDUS was still the primary avenue for surveillance, CCSS and the Ministry of Health quickly implemented call centers to provide remote attention to and daily monitoring of COVID-19 patients and support local follow-up efforts. These call centers, first implemented on March 13, 2020, explained COVID-19 symptoms and received information on possible COVID-19 cases (Costa Rica, Ministry of Health 2020).

In addition to contributing to surveillance and contact tracing, data management was a crucial part of the Costa Rican health system's strategy to deal with the pressure of the pandemic. EDUS, in combination with other data analysis and visualization tools, allowed health system authorities to identify which hospitals or health facilities were experiencing high demand in real time and to resolve the situation among hospitals in the network.

EDUS made it possible to have almost real-time information on the COVID-19 and non-COVID-19 status at the national and local levels through a daily report of available and occupied intensive care beds in every health facility of the system—information that the medical management team could share with hospital directors.

The EDUS also allowed CCSS to implement a mass shift to telemedicine. Following Notice No. 073-S-MTSS, CCSS intensified the use of work-from-home strategies for physicians and other health care workers, increasing the number of people under this modality from 400 before the pandemic to almost 4,800 by the end of 2020, while keeping prioritized services (cardiology, oncology, COVID-19, and emergency) in person. Thanks to EDUS, physicians could electronically review notes from previous medical appointments without having the patient or the medical clerk bring a paper copy, which was very difficult when much of the health workforce was working from home.

EDUS became an essential tool for the shift to virtual service modalities. It protected the health of health care workers while still maintaining care for patients during strict stay-at-home orders. Additionally, public-private partnerships were developed for home delivery of drugs to prevent patients from being left without necessary medicine because they could not visit a health center. As a result, CCSS, with the cooperation of the national post office, universities, and private companies, delivered medicine to patients' homes. While a temporary program, patients with chronic diseases benefited most from the home delivery of medicines during this time.

Layer 3: Advanced Case Management and Surge Response

Due to previously established programs and structures, Costa Rica could respond to surges of the pandemic quickly and effectively. CCSS installed the PRIME team, an emergency response team dedicated to transferring patients with COVID-19.

The directors of the medical centers and the CCSS medical management team took advantage of the fact that the pandemic affected certain regions differently and redistributed COVID-19 patients among the different regions of the country during crisis moments. Just as the transfer of patients shortened waiting lists before the pandemic, during the pandemic, this redistribution allowed hospitals with free beds to take patients and for hospitals under pressure to provide other medical services instead of having to prioritize COVID-19 treatment.

To navigate the burden that COVID-19 put on the health system and essential health services, Costa Rica also implemented a new escalation and deescalation strategy for all health facilities. The plan included a breakdown of eight phases of escalation and deescalation linked to the country's demand for hospital beds, COVID-19 cases, and deaths. The plan allowed CCSS to identify moments of lower hospital saturation, reactivate services that were at a standstill, and mitigate the harmful effects of longer waiting lists. In addition, CCSS used EDUS to monitor the use of health services and provide real-time data for health care facility directors at the regional and community levels to make informed decisions during surges.

On March 12, 2020, the CCSS board of directors authorized the exceptional use of the vacancy substitution scheme, an instrument created in 2017 to ensure that new staff could be hired temporarily to replace health care center personnel who were withdrawn from their original functions.

The CCSS medical management team established official guidelines for implementing this scheme. For instance, they required the management of health centers to prove that there was an actual increase in demand for medical services in their establishment before implementing the scheme; they only allowed hospitals to use replacement personnel for a maximum of two months, and they only allowed managing directors to hire one replacement person per position to be filled (CCSS 2020b). Within these guidelines, CCSS strengthened the health care system by providing pharmacists, nurses, general practitioners, and operational staff where and when they were required during crises. According to the CCSS Human Resources Department, from February 2020 to January 2022, the temporary staff of CCSS increased 11 percent (from 39,785 to 44,173) (CCSS 2020a). Therefore, using the vacancy substitution scheme during 2020 required a budget close to US$12.5 million (Blanco-Chavarría 2020). The urgent transfer and substitution of staff across the health system were then facilitated by the communication and coordination structures of the national health system.

These emergency and surge interventions were made possible by contingency funding allocated to CCSS before the pandemic (figure 9.3). Costa Rica's contingency fund financed most of the resources that CCSS used during the pandemic.

Other significant expenses included the costs of rearranging internal spaces to comply with social distancing standards, establishing space separation barriers and ventilation systems, adapting temporary spaces, as well as installing mobile hospitals and tents to provide care for COVID and non-COVID patients.

However, the COVID-19 response depleted more than 50 percent of the contingency fund. By the end of 2021, the fund balance had dropped from an

Figure 9.3 Contingency Fund Spending on COVID-19 Needs in Costa Rica, 2020

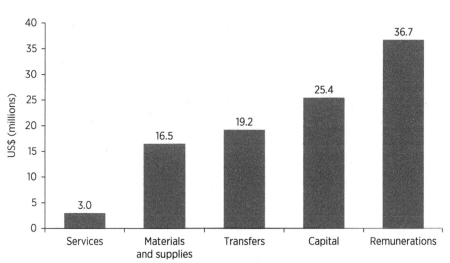

Source: Exemplars in Global Health 2023.

initial US$200 million to only US$38 million, making it difficult to respond to unexpected emergencies in the future. Thus, it is recommended that CCSS assign resources to the fund as soon as it recovers from COVID-19.

Lessons Learned

Costa Rica is an exemplary model for the benefits of an integrated health system during a mass health crisis. Because it controls a broad network of clinics, hospitals, and centers located throughout the national territory, CCSS could respond quickly to maintain essential health services, while responding to regional surges of COVID-19.

In conjunction with an integrated health system, several additional factors contributed to Costa Rica's exemplary response to COVID-19:

- The existence of established resources and structures in the system that were used to working together as a network (for example, EDUS, the integrated network management strategy, and the patient transfer experience);
- The extraordinary flexibility to implement new modalities (for example, the creation of CEACO and the PRIME team, the shift to telemedicine, and the use of call centers and home drug delivery) and to speed up bureaucratic procedures during an emergency (for example, human resource management, technology adoption, and procurement processes);
- Crisis management governance structures for efficient decision-making, data sharing, and coordination of efforts within the health system (for example, EDUS and Costa Rican law); and
- Funding from the contingency fund and support from public-private collaborations, which made urgent resource allocation and surge response possible.

Challenges

Like all countries, Costa Rica also faced great challenges during the pandemic. While CCSS was able to use the vacancy substitution scheme to staff hospitals and clinics, quality of care became a significant issue. The need for qualified personnel in certain disciplines and the difficulty of recruiting health care staff were the result of the lack of specific training in certain areas and lack of experience in caring for patients with COVID-19. Finding the human resources to operate CEACO was challenging (Aguilar-Tassara, Leal-Ruiz, and Acuña-González 2021), and the high demand for extra staff exposed a lack of experience in some direct care positions, such as health therapists and nurses with critical care experience.

Additionally, the mass pivot to virtual health interactions put into question the quality of virtual care, mainly due to the lack of expertise with using these virtual tools, the lack of quality control in the delivery of services, and the problems of accessing technology for low-income patients. Inequity in access to health care increased among vulnerable populations during this time.

Therefore, primary levels of care were most affected by the surges of COVID-19. First, community health workers (technical assistants), who worked mostly at the first level of care, were assigned to contact tracing and testing due to the growing needs of the pandemic. As a result, the routine work of providing the first level of care was deprioritized.

Additionally, there was a large amount of patient absenteeism and fear of accessing care, especially among persons with chronic diseases. Emergency room visits increased for patients with diseases previously treated at the primary level and patients seeking medical attention for critical conditions such as heart attacks.

The increased demand for health personnel in all regions exacerbated historical recruitment problems affecting rural areas. Given differences in the social, economic, and quality of life in various parts of the country, mainly the differences within and outside the metropolitan area, many doctors prefer to live and work in urban areas, leaving rural, remote regions with few or no doctors. This issue became especially evident during the pandemic. Due to the immediacy required to respond to the crisis, motivating more doctors to work in rural areas was difficult.

While public-private partnerships were used successfully for allocating resources and testing, creating substantial collaborations between the private and public health sectors became challenging. For example, between April 2021 and October 2021, authorities from the Ministry of Health, representatives of private hospitals, and CCSS negotiated a system of transfers from the public to the private sector of patients for pathologies not related to COVID-19. However, when the public sector was most heavily saturated, only 11 patients were transferred, even though the private sector had offered up to 100 beds for patient transfers. This disconnect was due to a lack of willingness on the part of hospital directors in the public sector to use the collaboration offered and became a missed opportunity to lessen the pandemic burdens on the public sector.

References

Aguilar-Tassara, Roberto, Casandra Leal-Ruiz, and Rebecca Acuña-González. 2021. "CEACO y la amplicación de la capacidad hospitalaria." In *La caja y la pandemia por COVID-19: Experiencias durante la crisis del 2020*, edited by Carlos A. Zamora-Zamora, 71–76. San José: Editorial Nacional de Salud y Seguridad Social, Caja Costarricense de Seguro Social. https://www.binasss.sa.cr/covid2021.pdf.

Blanco-Chavarría, César. 2020. "Centro especializado en pacientes COVID19 arranca su fase de atención." Caja Costarricense de Seguro Social, San José, April 2, 2020.

Costa Rica, Ministry of Health. 2020. "Se activa la Línea 1322 para atención de consultas sobre COVID-19." Ministerio de Salud, San Jose, March 13, 2020. https://www

.ministeriodesalud.go.cr/index.php/centro-de-prensa/noticias/741-noticias -2020/1567-se-activa-la-linea-1322-para-atencion-de-consultas-sobre-covid-19.

CCSS (Costa Rican Social Security Fund). 2020a. "Módulo de información en recursos humanos." Caja Costarricense de Seguro Social, San José. Accessed March 3, 2023. https://www.exemplars.health/-/media/files/egh/resources/ecr/costa-rica/68 -informacion-estadistica-en-recursos-humanos.pdf.

CCSS (Costa Rican Social Security Fund). 2020b. "Procedimiento para solicitar la susti- tución de personal." Complemento Circular DM-D-3400-2020, Caja Costarricense de Seguro Social, San José, April 8, 2020. https://www.exemplars.health/media /files/egh/resources/ecr/costa-rica/67-asunto-complemento-circular-gmd 34002020.pdf.

Exemplars in Global Health. 2023. *Costa Rica: COVID-19 Response and Maintenance of Essential Health Services.* Seattle, WA: Exemplars in Global Health. https://www .exemplars.health/emerging-topics/ecr/costa-rica.

Sáenz, María del Rocío, Mónica Acosta, Jorine Muiser, and Juan Luis Bermúdez. 2011. "The Health System of Costa Rica [Article in Spanish]." *Salud Pública Mexicana* 53 (Suppl 2): S156–S167. https://pubmed.ncbi.nlm.nih.gov/21877081/.

WHO (World Health Organization). 2020. *International Health Regulations (2005) States Parties Self-Assessment Annual Reporting (SPAR) Tool.* Geneva: WHO. https://extranet .who.int/e-spar/.

10

Three-Layer Health Sector Investment in Uganda

Alice Namale, Steven N. Kabwama, Fred Monje, Rawlance Ndejjo, Susan Kizito, Suzanne N. Kiwanuka, Rhoda K. Wanyenze, Siobhan Lazenby, William Wang, Jacqueline Maloney, Rowan Hussein, and Anne Liu

IN SUMMARY

Uganda acted early and aggressively to limit the spread of COVID-19. Immediately after the World Health Organization declared COVID-19 a public health emergency of international concern at the end of January 2020, Uganda's Ministry of Health activated the Public Health Emergency Operations Center and the National Task Force, shifting from preparedness to response when the first case was recorded on March 21, 2020.[a]

• Because of Uganda's experience with previous outbreaks of epidemic-prone diseases (such as Ebola and Marburg),[b] the country's health care system had developed capacity to respond to infectious diseases. Uganda was able to leverage and adapt existing coordination, laboratory, surveillance, and digital health structures for the COVID-19 context.

• Strong leadership and responsive governance provided support for and ensured adherence to preventive measures. Public health officials in Uganda acted swiftly to implement nonpharmaceutical interventions, such as movement restrictions and mask mandates, and developed and disseminated clear guidance from the national level.

• Innovative strategies were developed to maintain essential health services throughout the pandemic. Ugandan health officials implemented a variety of interventions to mitigate supply- and demand-side obstacles, including shifting tasks to community health workers and leveraging technology for telemedicine and supervision. Service delivery was adapted through the

(continued)

This research was led by partners at the Makerere University School of Public Health and was supported and funded by the Gates Foundation and by the Exemplars in Global Health (EGH) program at Gates Ventures. EGH has a mission to identify positive global health outliers, analyze what makes countries successful, and disseminate core lessons so they can be adapted in comparable settings. EGH is a global coalition of partners including researchers, academics, experts, funders, country stakeholders, and implementers. A small, core team supporting EGH is based at Gates Ventures, the private office of Bill Gates, and closely collaborates with the Gates Foundation. For the full case study, refer to Exemplars in Global Health (2023).

IN SUMMARY *(continued)*

establishment of special clinics and outreach, facilities designated for COVID-19 treatment, community distribution of drugs, and multiple-month dispensing of medicines.

a. "Cumulative COVID-19 Tests," Our World in Data website, https://ourworldindata.org /explorers/coronavirus-data-explorer?zoomToSelection=true&time=2020-03-01..latest &facet=none&pickerSort=asc&pickerMetric=location&Metric=Tests&Interval=Cumulative &Relative+to+Population=false&Color+by+test+positivity=false&country=~UGA.
b. "Ebola and Marburg," United States Centers for Disease Control and Prevention website, https://wwwnc.cdc.gov/travel/diseases/ebola.

Country Context

Uganda has one of the world's youngest populations: in 2020, 46 percent of Ugandans were between the ages of 0 and 14, 52 percent were between the ages of 15 and 64, and just 2 percent were 65 or older.[1] In 2020, Uganda's gross domestic product (GDP) per capita was about US$822,[2] and 41 percent of Ugandans lived on less than US$1.90 per day.[3] Uganda also has the largest refugee population in Africa. Figure 10.1 presents several other demographic indicators for the country.

Figure 10.1 Prepandemic Demographic Indicators for Uganda

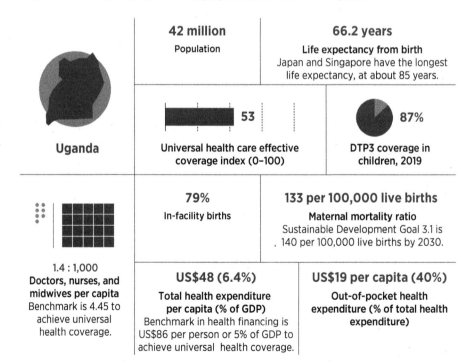

Sources: IHME 2019; IHME Financing Global Health database (https://www.healthdata.org /research-analysis/gbd); World Bank data repository (https:/data.worldbank.org).

Note: DTP3 = diptheria, tetanus toxoid, and pertussis-containing vaccine; GDP = gross domestic product.

Because of Uganda's experience with previous outbreaks of epidemic-prone diseases, the country's health care system had, before COVID-19, developed capacity to respond to infectious diseases. Between 2000 and 2016, Uganda experienced eight public health emergencies of international concern: five outbreaks of Ebola virus disease, most recently in 2018 and 2019, and three outbreaks of Marburg virus disease.

During the most recent Ebola outbreak, diagnostic testing and confirmation at the Uganda Virus Research Institute confirmed only three cases of the disease and did not observe any secondary transmission—a testament to the country's capacity to respond to public health emergencies. The Uganda Virus Research Institute played an integral role in supporting COVID-19 surveillance, boosting testing capacity, and increasing genetic sequencing efforts throughout the pandemic.

Similarly, the country was able to repurpose for COVID-19 the outbreak coordination and laboratory capacity that it had built for other diseases, such as human immunodeficiency virus/acquired immunodeficiency syndrome (HIV/AIDS) and tuberculosis. It also leveraged more than 10,000 health workers and community health workers, locally referred to as village health teams (VHTs), who had been trained in infection prevention and control, epidemic surveillance, and other aspects of outbreak response.

Health System Structure and Features

Uganda has a centralized health system in which officials at the national level make and implement decisions about how to handle health crises that affect the nation. Governance of the country's health system operates on three hierarchical levels: national, regional and district, and community.

At the national level, the Ministry of Health (MOH) is responsible for policy planning, analysis, coordination, and evaluation, while the district and regional referral hospitals oversee and supervise service delivery. Human resource planning, recruitment, and management typically take place at the district level. Community health services, such as health education, commodity distribution, and case management of common infectious diseases, are provided by VHTs whose members (some 180,000 as of 2015) are selected by the communities they serve (Uganda, MOH 2015).

However, Uganda has not invested adequately in the infrastructure necessary to provide care, especially emergency care, to everyone who might need it in a pandemic or other health crisis. In Uganda, total health expenditures in 2020 were 6.4 percent of GDP and US$48 per capita—far below the target of 15 percent of GDP in the African Union's Abuja Declaration and below the World Health Organization (WHO) 2009 recommendation of US$86 per capita (WHO 2010). In 2020, out-of-pocket (private) health spending was 40 percent of the total. In 2018, Uganda had nearly 7,000 health facilities: 45 percent were public government facilities, 40 percent were private for-profit facilities, and 15 percent were private nonprofit facilities (Uganda, MOH 2018). That year, the country had about 200 intensive care beds, most of which (83 percent) were in Kampala City, and about 400 ambulances (Atumanya et al. 2020). That is, Uganda had fewer than 1 ambulance per 100,000 population, and less than half of the country's districts had an ambulance.

Historically, these resource and infrastructure deficiencies have limited the amount and quality of routine or essential health services that many Ugandans receive. According to estimates of effective universal health coverage, which measure a variety of indicators, including reproductive, maternal, newborn, and child health and the treatment of infectious and noncommunicable diseases, Uganda ranks 132 of 204 countries and territories worldwide (GBC 2019 Universal Health Coverage Collaborators 2020). Compared with other countries in Sub-Saharan Africa, Uganda performs well on key indicators of essential health services, such as routine childhood immunization and treatment for lower-respiratory infections. It performs less well on indicators such as antenatal and maternal care and treatment of noncommunicable illnesses such as cancers, stroke, and diabetes.[4]

Layer 1: Risk Reduction—Promoting Prevention and Community Preparedness

Since 2001, Uganda has used the Integrated Disease Surveillance and Response (IDSR) system to monitor and report on high-priority diseases, facilitating the best and most efficient use of scarce resources (Masiira et al. 2019). According to a World Health Organization (WHO 2017) evaluation of Uganda's International Health Regulations (2005) core capacities, Uganda scored 69 percent and had strengthened its capacity in surveillance, laboratory testing, emergency response operations, and risk communication. For example, in 2011, Uganda adopted a free reporting platform using text messaging to replace the older system for transmitting weekly surveillance data, which had used a combination of paper-based reports, paid phone calls, text messages, radio calls, and emails.

At the beginning of the COVID-19 pandemic in the spring of 2020, Ugandan officials used the IDSR and other preexisting tools to monitor the intensity, geographic spread, and severity of disease in the population, to estimate the disease burden, to identify high-risk groups, to assess trends, to mobilize surge capacity and external emergency support, and to inform resource allocation and appropriate mitigation measures.

During the Ebola outbreak in 2019, Uganda's community surveillance program trained more than 10,000 health workers and VHTs on infection prevention and control, epidemic surveillance, and other aspects of outbreak response. These trained health workers supported the country's ability to identify and respond to COVID-19 rapidly. Response structures and protocols were adapted to meet emerging health priorities. For example, rapid response teams, with support from VHTs, verified community reports of suspected cases.

Layer 2: Focus on Detection, Containment, and Mitigation Capabilities

In the early months of the COVID-19 pandemic, Uganda performed better than many other countries: from March 21, 2020, when Uganda reported its first case of COVID-19, until the beginning of August 2020, Uganda recorded just 1,176 cases of COVID-19 (about 25 cases per 1 million population).[5] Experts believe that the country was able to avert widespread community spread during this early period because the government took quick and aggressive actions to limit population mobility, mitigating the transmission of the virus from person to person.

Multisectoral Coordination and Interventions for Risk Reduction

At the end of January 2020, when the WHO declared COVID-19 a public health emergency of international concern, the MOH activated its Public Health Emergency Operations Center and National Task Force to support and coordinate the country's COVID-19 preparedness and response.[6] The prime minister chaired the multisectoral and multidisciplinary National Task Force, which was composed of political and technical leaders from key government sectors, such as health, finance, agriculture, security, gender and labor, local government, trade, and tourism, and was responsible for coordinating Uganda's COVID-19 response.

The National Task Force's incident management team quickly developed a COVID-19 preparedness and response plan that emphasized risk communication as well as community engagement to promote good public health practices in general. The incident management team established a plan to manage six key pillars of direct response, including management of Uganda's surveillance and laboratory systems and logistics for supplies and transport, and to set up rapid response teams in local districts.

As soon as Uganda registered its first case of COVID-19, the National Task Force turned its focus from preparedness to emergency response (Margini et al. 2020). It activated district task forces to coordinate subnational and local COVID-19 response activities like surveillance, contact tracing, and isolation. It established a scientific advisory committee—including public health specialists, physicians, epidemiologists, immunologists, and statisticians from Makerere University's schools of public health, medicine, and statistics, the Medical Research Council, and the Uganda Virus Research Institute—to collate, synthesize, review, and interpret emerging data and translate new and changing information into evidence-based policies and strategies for pandemic response.

In June 2021, during the peak of Uganda's second wave of COVID-19 infections (driven largely by the Delta variant), the National Task Force developed and disseminated a COVID-19 resurgence plan for the next 12 months (Uganda, MOH 2021). The new plan divided the surveillance and laboratory pillar into two pillars: a surveillance and laboratory pillar and a home-based care pillar to keep down costs and reduce congestion in health facilities as case counts increased. The resurgence plan also proposed establishing regional emergency operations centers to support the district task forces' work on disease surveillance and data analysis, but resource constraints hampered their development.

Public-private partnerships with nongovernmental organizations (NGOs), private companies, and foreign governments were also leveraged to enable health workers and facilities to obtain essential goods (Kabwama et al. 2022). For example, one NGO provided 4,300 community health workers with personal protective equipment, Absa Bank Uganda provided 160 medical oxygen cylinders, and the German government provided digital X-ray machines through the TBornotTB project.

Laboratory Capacity and Detection at Scale

Uganda had substantial laboratory infrastructure that had been developed to address health priorities such as HIV/AIDS and tuberculosis, and officials quickly repurposed that infrastructure for COVID-19 testing. However, in Uganda as elsewhere, testing supplies were limited and mostly imported from other countries, especially during the first six months of the pandemic in 2020. Consequently, the country's testing strategy was targeted at high-risk individuals, especially at points of entry and in border districts; symptomatic cases reported through community alerts; and contacts of confirmed cases, including health workers in COVID-19 isolation and treatment units (Uganda, MOH 2020).

At first, Uganda relied solely on polymerase chain reaction (PCR) testing (initially the only test for COVID-19 recommended by the WHO), with an emphasis on reverse transcription (RT) PCR testing in a lab setting. Uganda had used PCR testing in previous epidemics—for HIV testing among infants, for instance. GeneXpert testing (which health providers were already using to diagnose tuberculosis and other diseases) began in July 2020 at border points of entry. The country added rapid diagnostic tests (RDTs) to its official testing strategy in October 2020 and in December 2020 began to pilot RDTs as a screening test for higher-risk people (such as hospitalized patients, symptomatic health workers, and quarantine individuals) in a limited number of facilities.

By June 2021, RDT kits were distributed widely across the country, and during the peak of the second wave of cases, all symptomatic cases that tested positive with an RDT were considered a confirmed case. During the initial pilot phases, RDTs were used for screening, and results were only reported to the national lab database after confirmation with PCR. The official guidance on this policy changed on June 2, 2021, when positive RDT results were required to be uploaded to the MOH electronic Results Dispatch System (eRDS).

This change accompanied a national-level training of trainers and was followed by trainings at regional, district, and local health facilities throughout the month of June 2021. Sixty trainers certified more than 500 end users across the country. While the scale of RDTs facilitated faster turnaround times and enabled clinicians to make rapid decisions, several challenges were reported:

- Information management and real-time reporting were suboptimal. RDTs were distributed to some health facilities that were not linked to the eRDS, making real-time reporting a challenge. The investigation forms were complex, labor intensive, and often submitted with incomplete data.
- To address this issue, the MOH introduced two systems for health care workers to send data from facilities to the central level: a text-based reporting tool called mTrac and an internet-based reporting system called eLIF, which has a direct data pipeline to the eRDS. Both tools have advantages and disadvantages. For example, mTrac is easier to use, but the type of data reported is limited; eLIF is more time-consuming to use and relies on the internet, but it has a direct data pipeline with the eRDS, facilitating near real-time reporting. As of August 2021, 140 facilities across 70 districts were reporting RDT results via eLIF, and 450 facilities across 60 districts were reporting results via mTrac.[7]

Other challenges included adherence to eligibility criteria for RDTs, lower levels of trust in RDTs among patients and health workers (compared to PCR tests), coordination of results with the private sector, and quality concerns.

Data Collection and Information Systems and Surveillance Networks Leveraged for Response

For the first six months of the pandemic, all districts were required to report data daily to the national level on defined COVID-19 indicators. Data from the community were collected by health workers at health facilities, VHTs, and community members and were submitted using phone calls, text messages, or WhatsApp. District surveillance focal persons then compiled data from the various sources and submitted the information to the surveillance team at the national level. COVID-19 situational reports summarizing the daily progress of the various subcommittees at the district level were submitted using a Virtual Emergency Operations Center mailing platform or WhatsApp platform. Both platforms, however, lacked data aggregation and analysis capability for real-time reporting.

Uganda later incorporated digital surveillance platforms, including eIDSR and Open Data Kit for surveillance. The Open Data Kit report contained health worker data, alerts data, calls, and cases, among others. Another report that was submitted daily was the point-of-entry report summarizing the total number of persons screened at the borders, and the institutional quarantine report, which summarized data on the number of persons in quarantine, contacts, and alerts. Uganda further configured the eIDSR system, built in District Health Information Software 2 (DHIS2), to collect COVID-19-related data (DHIS2 2020). Since 2013, Uganda had been working closely with DHIS2 developers to configure and test the tool to support case investigation and lab linkage of notifiable diseases (Behumbiize 2020). The data collected included details about suspected COVID-19 cases, laboratory investigations (including type of test conducted, test results, and confirmed disease), and case management of COVID-19 patients (including daily physical examinations, patients' signs and symptoms, medication given, and test results).

Uganda also established a public, web-based information dashboard on COVID-19 that provides pandemic data in real time to support rapid, evidence-based decision-making for a wide range of stakeholders. The dashboard is updated daily with information on test results, recoveries, active cases, deaths, and cases by district. Officials used these data to monitor high-burden areas, shape each pillar of the pandemic response, and identify the groups and individuals at highest risk.

Public-private partnerships contributed to the response. The nonprofit social enterprise Living Goods recruited, trained, and employed community health workers to provide health services with minimal interruption, while responding to a surge in demand from Uganda's overburdened health system.

A key factor enabling community health workers to respond to this surge was the Smart Health app, a digital health management tool carried by each of Living Goods' more than 7,800 community health workers. The Smart Health app guides community health workers through routine diagnostics and processes, with specific workflows for providing care related to pregnancy, childhood diseases, nutrition, family planning, immunization tracking, and, most recently, COVID-19. Uganda was able to leverage the existing infrastructure and modular platform to adapt the solution rapidly for the COVID-19 context. Priority was given to integrating the app with DHIS2 so that government stakeholders could access real-time data.[8]

Public Health Interventions and Continuity of Essential Services

Prior to Uganda's first COVID-19 case on March 21, 2020, President Yoweri Museveni closed the country's airports and territorial borders. Shortly thereafter, officials suspended public transportation and declared a nationwide curfew, prohibiting all movement between 7 p.m. and 6:30 a.m. (Kyeyune 2020).[9] The government also suspended all public gatherings—including worship services, concerts, rallies, and cultural gatherings—and closed public places, such as bars and restaurants. On April 1, 2020, officials instituted a nationwide lockdown, banning all forms of public and private transportation and closing all businesses except for a few essential services. All educational institutions were closed indefinitely.

Prior to the COVID-19 pandemic, Uganda had a strong system for communicating public health risk (WHO 2017). In 2020 and 2021, officials were able to draw on this prior experience to develop wide-ranging communication strategies that informed the public about COVID-related service delivery and risk management. For example, the MOH used traditional platforms such as newspapers, radio, television, and billboards, a designated website for COVID-19 updates,[10] and Twitter,[11] Facebook, and other social media platforms to increase community awareness of testing and prevention measures and to publicize adjustments to the delivery of essential health services, including critical services, such as family planning, during the pandemic.[12]

As a result of these measures, mobility in Uganda was severely limited during the first months of the pandemic. This situation likely limited COVID-19 transmission, but it also limited commercial activity, depressed incomes, slowed economic growth, and introduced supply- and demand-side barriers to delivering essential health services.

To address these challenges, the MOH organized its COVID-19 response via committees organized around eight pillars, one of which was the continuity of essential health services. In April 2020, the ministry published guidelines for maintaining essential health services and established a national committee on the topic. This guidance included a list of priority essential health services to be maintained, including the prevention, management, and control of communicable and noncommunicable diseases and maternal, child, and adolescent health.

Ugandan officials also established district task force subcommittees on maintaining essential health services in the context of COVID-19, with weekly meetings chaired by the resident district commissioner. Decisions were made at hospital and district levels about how to allocate health workers effectively between frontline COVID-19 services and routine medical services.

To maintain essential services, Uganda used patient networks to distribute supplies. For diseases and conditions such as HIV/AIDS with established patient networks, where patients know one another from support and treatment groups, service providers gave medicines to selected patients, who then distributed them to others within their community. In April 2020, the MOH recommended continuing community-based health service delivery and access to medications and supplies for chronic conditions through multiple-month dispensing and community distribution. For example, medicines for chronic conditions such as HIV/AIDS were dispensed for three or more months to decongest health facilities, minimize transmission of COVID-19, and protect people with underlying conditions.

In the event of stock-outs of essential supplies—such as personal protective equipment, antiretroviral drugs, and laboratory diagnostic tools—national distribution mechanisms allowed the government to place emergency orders and transfer goods from one health facility to another. By July 2021, Uganda had a centralized system of monitoring, warehousing, and distributing commodities to all public health facilities. To avoid stock-outs and ensure the availability of drugs and medicines for essential services, the MOH Pharmacy Division reviewed supply and procurement plans for infection prevention and control materials and used the electronic logistics management system to process orders for Ebola and COVID-19 commodities. To ensure and maintain the availability of family planning methods, it also reviewed family planning procurement plans and asked the national medical stores to supply facilities accordingly.

MOH guidelines recommended shifting tasks such as temperature and symptom screening and referral for case management of childhood illnesses to VHTs whenever possible. To this end, officials provided protective gear to VHTs, which helped to maintain community-based services, such as indoor residential spraying for mosquito control and integrated community case management of childhood illnesses. In health facilities, health care providers leveraged the availability of nonmedical staff such as guards to do nontechnical jobs, including temperature screening for COVID-19.

Uganda adapted service delivery models to maintain essential health services. For example, MOH officials designated special clinics for essential health services during the pandemic (such as clinics for maternal and child health services, HIV/AIDS services, and immunization services), provided patients with multiple months of medication (HIV/AIDS and heart-related medicine), rearranged service delivery schedules to ensure continuity, and designated certain regional facilities for COVID-19 treatment.

The MOH directed district local governments to provide transportation and psychosocial support to infected and otherwise affected staff; it also undertook targeted risk communication for health care workers about the key actions required to stay safe and healthy.

Maintaining essential health services required leveraging resources from international partners, particularly the United Nations Children's Fund and WHO, and from the seven other COVID-19 response pillars. Because the funding was directed specifically to essential health services and not to public health in general, it was not diverted to COVID-19 care. Health facilities therefore continued to receive quarterly funding on time and in full, which minimized the disruption to most essential health services.

In June 2021, Ugandan health officials published a COVID-19 resurgence response plan that focused in part on continuing to provide access to essential health services. The plan included activities such as national and subnational coordination, availability of commodities, data reporting and monitoring, health workforce capacity strengthening, and occupational safety of health workers with respect to COVID-19 risk. The plan allocated US$31 million to the continuity of essential health services between June 2021 and June 2022.

Layer 3: Advanced Case Management and Surge Response

Uganda's health system includes national referral hospitals, regional referral hospitals, district hospitals, health centers, and community health workers. The regional referral hospitals became COVID-19 treatment units so that health service delivery at other levels of the health system could continue. Officials also designated special clinics for essential health services, such as young child clinics for maternal and child health.

Clear guidelines and protocols helped to give health care workers confidence about working safely during the COVID-19 pandemic. For example, Mulago Women's Referral Hospital set up a virtual hospital for training and sensitizing staff, and the MOH developed guidelines for managing health care workers who contracted COVID-19 while on duty. In adherence to COVID-19 restrictions, health worker support and supervision were provided via e-platforms or by telephone. To strengthen the capacity of health workers providing family planning services, training partners transitioned from in-person to online training starting in September 2020. Some in-person trainings continued, with social distancing protocols in place.

In March 2020, Uganda's parliament approved a supplementary budget amounting to US$30.7 million (U Sh 114 billion) to handle the COVID-19 pandemic response for the first three months (Nambatya 2020). The resources were not specific to maintaining essential health services and were used to support all aspects of the response, including paying contact tracers, procuring test kits, and strengthening the capacity of intensive care units. Maintaining essential health services and minimizing disruptions required resources from partners and other pillars.

Lessons Learned

Like most countries, Uganda faced substantial challenges related to risk reduction, detection, containment, mitigation, advanced case management, and surge response. Challenges ranged from inadequate laboratory capacity and long turnaround times to limited genomic surveillance and disruptions to routine services caused by supply- and demand-side obstacles.

Uganda leaned on best practices and structures that had been developed to address previous epidemics. It had strong leadership and coordination to control the spread of COVID-19 and maintain access to essential health services.

Uganda increased equitable access to COVID-19 testing by decentralizing testing systems and encouraging private sector partnerships, established an essential health services continuity committee to monitor and address disruptions in service delivery, and addressed drug delivery challenges by using the community to distribute medicines and allowing drugs to be dispensed in larger quantities.

Lessons learned for future pandemic preparedness include the utility of leveraging private sector engagement for testing, surveillance, and overall pandemic response; developing national capacity for manufacturing and distributing supplies, such as personal protective equipment, RDTs, and reagents; and strengthening regional and international cooperation to ensure a robust supply chain of commodities, such as vaccines and testing equipment.

Uganda also responded to the COVID-19 pandemic with interventions that could be sustained for health system strengthening, such as investing in human resources and infrastructure to address disparities in care delivery and investing in health information systems with a focus on improving data quality and surveillance.

Notes

1. Uganda population statistics page on the World Bank website, https://data .worldbank.org/indicator/SP.POP.1564.TO.ZS?locations=UG.
2. Uganda GDP statistics page on the World Bank website, https://data.worldbank .org/indicator/NY.GDP.PCAP.CD?locations=UG.
3. Uganda statistics page on the Opportunity International website, https://opportunity .org/our-impact/where-we-work/uganda-facts-about-poverty.
4. World Bank Data Repository, accessed December 6, 2022, https:/data.worldbank .org.
5. "Essential Health Services: Uganda," Exemplars in Global Health website, https:// www.exemplars.health/emerging-topics/epidemic-preparedness-and-response /essential-health-services/uganda.
6. "Overview: Testing and Surveillance," Exemplars in Global Health website, https:// www.exemplars.health/emerging-topics/epidemic-preparedness-and-response /testing-and-surveillance/uganda.
7. "Overview: Testing and Surveillance," Exemplars in Global Health website, https:// www.exemplars.health/emerging-topics/epidemic-preparedness-and-response /testing-and-surveillance/uganda.
8. "Smart Health in Uganda: Community Health Workers Use App to Provide Critical Health Services during COVID-19 Pandemic," Exemplars in Global Health website, https://www.exemplars.health/emerging-topics/epidemic-preparedness-and -response/digital-health-tools/smart-health-in-uganda.
9. "Tears in Kampala over Coronavirus," *Daily Monitor,* March 26, 2020, https://www .monitor.co.ug/uganda/news/national/canes-tears-in-kampala-over-coronavirus -1882614?view=htmlamp.
10. Uganda, MOH COVID-19 information portal, https://covid19.gou.go.ug/.
11. Uganda, MOH Official Twitter account, https://twitter.com/MinofHealthUG?ref _src=twsrc%5Egoogle%7Ctwcamp%5Eserp%7Ctwgr%5Eauthor.
12. "Use of Telehealth Services to Support the Continuity of Family Planning Information, Access, and Utilization during the COVID-19 Pandemic in Uganda— Survey," *UGNEWS24,* April 20, 2021, https://ugnews24.info/kampala-sports-news /use-of-telehealth-services-to-support-the-continuity-of-family-planning -information-access-and-utilization-during-the-covid-19-pandemic-in-uganda -survey/.

References

Atumanya, Patience, Cornelius Sendagire, Agnes Wabule, John Mukisa, Lameck Ssemogerere, Arthur Kwizera, and Peter K. Agaba. 2020. "Assessment of the Current Capacity of Intensive Care Units in Uganda: A Descriptive Study." *Journal of Critical Care* 55 (February): 95–99. doi:10.1016/j.jcrc.2019.10.019.

Behumbiize, Prosper. 2020. "Electronic COVID-19 Point of Entry Screening and Travel Pass DHIS2 Implementation at Ugandan Borders." *dhis2community* (blog), April 2020. https://community.dhis2.org/t/electronic-covid-19-point-of-entry-screening -and-travel-pass-dhis2-implementation-at-ugandan-borders/39083.

DHIS2 (District Health Information Software 2). 2020. "Digital Data Packages for COVID-19 Surveillance and Reponse." Health Data Collaborative WebEx Event, University of Oslo, April 29–30, 2020. https://www.healthdatacollaborative.org /fileadmin/uploads/hdc/Documents/2020/DHIS2_for_COVID19_HDC _Webinar_Apr_2020_vF.PDF.

Exemplars in Global Health. 2023. *Uganda: COVID-19 Response and Maintenance of Essential Health Services."* Seattle, WA: Exemplars in Global Health. https://www.exemplars.health/emerging-topics/ecr/uganda.

GBC (Global Burden of Disease) 2019 Universal Health Coverage Collaborators. 2020. "Measuring Universal Health Coverage Based on an Index of Effective Coverage of Health Services in 204 Countries and Territories, 1990–2019: A Systematic Analysis for the Global Burden of Disease Study 2019." *Lancet* 396 (10258): 1250–84. https://doi.org/10.1016/S0140-6736(20)30750-9.

IHME (Institute for Health Metrics and Evaluation). 2019. *Global Burden of Disease Study 2019.* Seattle, WA: IHME.

Kabwama, Steven N., Suzanne N. Kiwanuka, Mala Ali Mapatano, Olufunmilayo I. Fawole, Ibrahima Seck, Alice Namale, Rawlance Ndejjo, Susan Kizito, Fred Monje, Marc Bosonkiw, Landry Egbende, Según Bello, Eniola A. Mamgboye, Magbagbeola D. Dairo, Ayo S. Adebowale, Mobalaji M. Salawu, Rotimi F. Afolabi, Issakha Diallo, Mamadou M. M. Leye, Youssou Ndiaye, Mane Fall, Oumar Bassoum, Tobias Alfvén, William Sambisa, and Rhoda K. Wanyenze. 2022. "Private Sector Engagement in the COVID-19 Response: Experiences and Lessons from the Democratic Republic of Congo, Nigeria, Senegal, and Uganda." *Global Health* 18: Art. 60. https://doi.org/10.1186/s12992-022-00853-1.

Kyeyune, Hamza. 2020. "Uganda Declares Curfew to Curb Spread of COVID-19." *Anadolu Agency,* March 31, 2020. https://www.aa.com.tr/en/africa/uganda-declares-curfew-to-curb-spread-of-covid-19/1785775.

Margini, Federica, Anooj Pattnaik, Tapley Jordanwood, Angellah Nakyanzi, and Sarah Byakika. 2020. *Uganda's Emergency Response to the COVID-19 Pandemic: A Case Study.* Washington, DC: ThinkWell and MOH. https://thinkwell.global/publications/?type=28&category=0&country=0.

Masiira, Ben, Lydia Nakiire, Christine Kihembo, Edson Katushabe, Nasan Natseri, Immaculate Nabukenya, Innocent Komakech, Issa Makumbi, Okot Charles, Francis Adatu, Miriam Nanyunja, Solomon Fisseha Woldetsadik, Ibrahima Socé Fall, Patrick Tusiime, Alemu Wondimagegnehu, and Peter Nsubuga. 2019. "Evaluation of Integrated Disease Surveillance and Response (IDSR) Core and Support Functions after the Revitalisation of IDSR in Uganda from 2012 to 2016." *BMC Public Health* 19 (1): 46. https://doi.org/10.1186/s12889-018-6336-2.

Nambatya, Prosscovia. 2020. "COVID-19 Supplementary Budget: Pandemic Response or Cash Bonanza?" *Chr. Michelsen Institute* (blog), accessed December 1, 2022. https://www.cmi.no/publications/7279-ugandas-covid-19-supplementary-budget-pandemic-response-or-cash-bonanza.

Uganda, MOH (Ministry of Health). 2015. *National Village Health Teams (VHT) Assessment in Uganda.* Kampala: MOH and Pathfinder International, March 2015.

Uganda, MOH (Ministry of Health). 2018. *National Health Facility Master List 2018: A Complete List of All Health Facilities in Uganda.* Kampala: Division of Health Information, MOH, November 2018. https://www.health.go.ug/cause/national-health-facility-master-list-2018.

Uganda, MOH (Ministry of Health). 2020. "Corona Virus Disease—2019 (COVID-19): Preparedness and Response Plan: March 2020–June 2021." Ministry of Health, Kampala. https://covid19.gou.go.ug/uploads/document_repository/authors/ministry_of_health/document/COVID19_PreparednessResponse_Plan_Signed_Vers_July2020.pdf.

Uganda, MOH (Ministry of Health). 2021. "National Corona Virus Disease—2019 (COVID-19): Resurgence Plan: June 2021–June 2022." MOH, Kampala. https://www.health.go.ug/cause/national-corona-virus-disease-2019-resurgence-plan/.

WHO (World Health Organization). 2010. "The Abuja Declaration: Ten Years On." WHO, Geneva. https://iris.who.int/bitstream/handle/10665/341162/WHO-HSS-HSF-2010.01-eng.pdf?sequence=1.

WHO (World Health Organization). 2017. "Joint External Evaluation of the IHR Core Capacities of the Republic of Uganda." WHO, Geneva. Accessed November 23, 2022. https://extranet.who.int/sph/sites/default/files/document-library/document /JEE%20Report%20Uganda%202017.pdf.

World Bank. 2020. "Sub-Saharan Africa: Uganda." Poverty and Equity Brief, World Bank, Washington, DC. https://databank.worldbank.org/data/download/poverty /33EF03BB-9722-4AE2-ABC7-AA2972D68AFE/Global_POVEQ_UGA.pdf.